ARCHITECTS OF DEATH

THE FAMILY WHO ENGINEERED
THE HOLOCAUST

ARCHITECTS

OF

DEATH

KAREN BARTLETT

Biteback Publishing

First published in Great Britain in 2018 by
Biteback Publishing Ltd
Westminster Tower
3 Albert Embankment
London SE1 7SP
Copyright © Karen Bartlett 2018

ISBN 978-1-78590-042-6

10 9 8 7 6 5 4 3 2 1

A CIP catalogue record for this book is available from the British Library.

Set in Adobe Caslon Pro and Futura

Printed and bound in Great Britain by
CPI Group (UK) Ltd, Croydon CR0 4YY

MIX
Paper from
responsible sources
FSC   FSC® C020471
www.fsc.org

For Max

CONTENTS

CAST OF CHARACTERS

TOPF FAMILY

JOHANNES TOPF (1816–1891): founded J. A. Topf and Sons in Erfurt on 1 July 1868.

JULIUS TOPF (1859–1914): son of Johannes Topf. Ran Topf and Sons jointly with his brother Ludwig Sr, until he relinquished his share due to ill health.

LUDWIG TOPF SR (1863–1914): son of Johannes Topf. Ran Topf and Sons until his death in 1914.

ELSE TOPF (1882–1940): wife of Ludwig Topf Sr, mother of Ludwig Jr and Ernst Wolfgang.

JOHANNA (HANNA) TOPF (1902–UNKNOWN): the eldest child of Ludwig Sr and Else. Sister of Ludwig and Ernst Wolfgang.

VIKTOR KARL LUDWIG TOPF (1903–1945): son of Ludwig Topf Sr. Brother of Ernst Wolfgang. Director of Topf and Sons from 1933 until 1945.

ERNST WOLFGANG TOPF (1904–1979): son of Ludwig Topf Sr. Brother of Ludwig Jnr. Director of Topf and Sons from 1933 until 1945.

HARTMUT TOPF (B. 1934): grandson of Julius Topf, great-grandson of Topf and Sons founder Johannes Topf. Puppet diplomat and journalist.

TOPF AND SONS EMPLOYEES

KURT PRÜFER (1891–1952): joined Topf and Sons in 1911. Head of the oven construction and cremation department.

FRITZ SANDER (1876–1946): employed at Topf and Sons since 1910. Authorised company representative, and co-head of the Furnace Construction division, D I. Reviewed all of Kurt Prüfer's work.

KARL SCHULTZE (1900–UNKNOWN): head of Department B, Ventilation Systems, at Topf and Sons.

MAX MACHEMEHL (1891–UNKNOWN): manager of the commercial department at Topf and Sons and SS security representative.

HEINRICH MESSING (1902–UNKNOWN): a Topf and Sons fitter from Department B (responsible for ventilation technology), who was deployed to Birkenau for five months in 1943.

WILHELM KOCH (1876–UNKNOWN): a Topf and Sons furnace builder who worked on the installation of the ovens in Auschwitz Crematorium II.

MARTIN HOLICK (1874–UNKNOWN): a Topf and Sons furnace builder who worked on the installation of the ovens in Auschwitz Crematorium II.

WILLY WIEMOKLI (1908–UNKNOWN): bookkeeper at Topf and Sons from 1939 onwards. Wiemokli's father was Jewish, and both were imprisoned by the Nazis.

GUSTAV BRAUN (1889–1958): Operations Director at Topf and Sons from 1935–1945.

UDO BRAUN (B. 1936): son of Gustav Braun and head of VEB Erfurter Mälzerei- und Speicherbau (EMS), formerly J. A. Topf and Sons.

THE PUPPETEER

AUSCHWITZ, 22 MARCH 2017

It is not Hartmut Topf's first visit to Auschwitz, and, at the age of eighty-three, it may or may not be his last. Wearing his flat cap and the earphones for the German-language audio tour, Hartmut straggles a way behind the rest of his group, quietly taking in the scene of the main camp. It is raining heavily. After three hours of walking through the grounds of the neighbouring camp, Birkenau, his clothes are soaking. With wild grey hair sticking out over his ears, a beard and a long raincoat buttoned to the neck, he looks something like an electrified Sherlock Holmes. His blue eyes flick from scene to scene; a barrack, the laundry room, the famous gate with the sign that says *Arbeit Macht Frei*. Hartmut appears to be listening intently to something – although it turns out that the audio guide has not yet begun. Instead he is thinking, as he must be, about what it means to be a Topf at this place. A place he is umbilically linked to, through a connection he has been trying to be make sense of for almost his entire life. It would be easy for him to say he feels regretful, guilty. Sad. Instead, he holds back. Pauses for a long second, and frames his words carefully. 'The crimes that happened here… are very sad,' he says eventually.

Hartmut is a strange sort of guest of honour at Auschwitz. It is the opening day for an exhibition exploring the work of the family company he was born into, Topf and Sons, a name immortalised globally when post-war newsreels showed images of Topf and Sons stamped in iron on the crematorium ovens that fuelled the Holocaust. Once a venerable German family firm, well known for making machinery for brewing and malting; it was a company that descendants like Hartmut, whose great-grandfather J. A. Topf had founded the company, could feel proud of. During the 1930s, however, Topf and Sons developed a new line of business building ovens and ventilation systems for the growing trend of human cremation – which promoted an altogether more modern, regulated and hygienic way of death. Although this work remained a tiny part of the business, and only ever accounted for 3 per cent of profits, its grim achievements and legacy would consume the company, and ensure that Topf and Sons would live in infamy.

By the end of the 1930s, a series of business decisions, family feuds and bitter personal rivalries between employees would tie Topf and Sons ever more closely into the ugliest work of the Nazi regime by producing the ventilation systems for the gas chambers and the ovens that disposed of the bodies of millions of their victims. The men behind these crimes, company directors Ludwig and Ernst Wolfgang Topf, along with their managers, engineers, oven fitters and ventilation experts, were not ignorant paper pushers or frightened collaborators

– instead they willingly engaged with the Nazis, reaping the benefits, taking every advantage they could, and pushing their designs for mass murder and body disposal further and further until they could truly be described as the engineers of the Holocaust. They were men who, by the end of the Second World War, were dreaming dreams of extinction so outlandish that even the SS were unable to accept their plans.

In Berlin, their cousin Hartmut Topf was still a teenage boy when, sitting in a cinema, he saw the post-war newsreel that showed the Topf and Sons name inscribed above the oven in a concentration camp. Almost seventy years later, he remains a man in shock: how did it come to be that a conservative family firm in the pleasant Thuringian city of Erfurt could be responsible for such heinous crimes?

'When I got home, I asked my mother about what I'd seen in the newsreel, but she knew nothing about it,' Hartmut says. 'By then my father was a prisoner of the Soviet army. It seemed that no one could give me any answers, and no one wanted any questions.'

Hartmut's younger sister Karin looks blank when he asks her for her reaction to the family's place in history. 'We've never talked about it,' she admits, sitting in their family home in Falkensee, a suburb just south of Berlin. This is the house that their father built, and where Hartmut and his sisters Elke and Karin grew up and lived out the war years. Karin makes clear though that although she respects and supports Hartmut's efforts over the years to reveal the truth about Topf and Sons, in a quest for atonement, she remembers no similar moment of astonishment upon discovering the dark side of the family name. 'I've never thought about it,' she says, after giving the question puzzled consideration.

Back at the Topf and Sons' exhibition at Auschwitz, a small crowd gathers as the German First Minister for the State of Thuringia arrives. Among the group are some of the founders of the Topf and Sons' memorial that now houses a permanent exhibit at the site of the original factory. Annegret Schüle, the director of the memorial and author of the German history of the company, is there, as are two local journalists from Erfurt – and the leader of Thuringia's small Jewish community. Although Hartmut is the only member of the family present, he melts inconspicuously into the background, coming forward only when he is called. Yet he is undoubtedly part of a tireless effort over nearly three decades to bring the truth about Topf and Sons to light.

Born into a family of engineers, Hartmut struck out on a separate path, finding that his passion lay with theatre and journalism instead. After trying and failing to become an actor, he pursued a lifelong interest in puppet theatre.

'The beauty of puppet theatre is that you can soar, you can fly, you can crash, you can die. You can do all the things that you cannot do as a human on stage. And, of course, there is the mask,' Hartmut says. 'The puppeteer who can do anything and ask anything without being seen. Without revealing himself.'

As a small boy, Hartmut remembers his father acting out puppet shows through the open dining room window of their house, while the children watched from the garden. His real fascination with puppets, however, came from his friend Hans Laessig, who lived down the street. 'He made beautiful wooden puppets, and I put them all along the shelf on the wall in my bedroom,'[1] Hartmut says. But Hans came from a partly Jewish family – and one day he vanished. As a boy,

Hartmut understood the silent complicity of asking no questions, but as an adult he would seek to find out what had happened to his friend Hans, just as he would unravel the truth about Topf and Sons. In doing so, he would discover that his family firm had played an integral and crucial role in the murder of millions.

CHAPTER ONE

BORN AND BRED
AT J. A. TOPF

Two years after Germany launched the vast territorial land-grab across Europe that had spurred the start of the Second World War, the citizens of Erfurt, a small city near Weimar in central Germany, still convinced themselves that they were winning. France was conquered. Swathes of eastern Europe lay 'reunited' under Nazi control. Britain had been beaten back to its own shores. Local articles in the *Thüringer Allgemeine* still confidently reported cultural snippets and details of mundane daily life – wives of German soldiers holidaying in Italy, who were enjoying spending time on sunny beaches with their children; allotments that needed to be prepared for winter; the mayor of Erfurt warning its citizens to maintain the good name of the town by keeping the streets clean.

Nonetheless, even the most complacent and dedicated Nazis were beginning to feel a twinge of unease. In early December, Hitler announced that Germany would also be waging war on the United States, following the Japanese attack on Pearl Harbor. In the dead of winter in Russia, German forces gathered for a perilous and unprecedented march towards Moscow. The *Thüringer Allgemeine* began to use photo-reporting from the Eastern Front, dedicating endless front-page articles to news about the fighting. 'Heroic' and 'victorious' as it all appeared to be – the scale of the war was now vast. Stories about success in the Crimea, the sinking of British ships, enormous Soviet losses were churned out daily, followed by maps of Asia, illustrating the sweeping Japanese advance. No ordinary citizen can escape the reality that, just as it had done since taking power in 1933, the Nazi regime continued to raise the stakes, increment by increment, restlessly and insatiably moving towards a final goal.

For the Jews of Europe, the horror of that goal was becoming clearer: from 1933 to 1939 German Jews had been systematically stripped of every human and civil right, banned from working in almost any profession, owning property, going to school, marrying a non-Jew, walking the streets in safety and were forced to carry a passport or identity card stamped with a large letter 'J'. Jewish families had watched in horror during the Kristallnacht (Night of Broken Glass) of 9 October 1938, when more than 7,000 Jewish businesses, homes and synagogues were looted and burned down. Their terror spread across Europe while the onslaught of Nazi occupation led to the establishment of massive Jewish ghettos in Poland and the rest of eastern Europe alongside plans to 'resettle' European Jews in the lands of the east.

Hitler's aim to murder the Jews of Europe had never been particularly well hidden. In 1945, former journalist Major Josef Hell claimed that, as early as 1922, Hitler had told him:

> Once I am really in power, my first and foremost task will be the annihilation of the Jews. As soon as I have the power to do so, I will have gallows built in rows – at the Marienplatz in Munich for example – as many as traffic allows. Then the Jews will be hanged indiscriminately, and they will remain hanging until they stink; they will hang there as long as the principles of hygiene permit. As soon as they have been untied, the next batch will be strung up, and so on down the line, until the last Jew in Munich has been exterminated.[2]

Since the summer of 1941, the Nazis had been mulling over how to implement Hitler's 'final solution of the Jewish question' and in August of that year they discovered a horrible possibility. When testing a delousing agent, Zyklon B gas, on Soviet prisoners of war at a prison camp in Silesia known as Auschwitz, they discovered that the noxious substance had the ability to kill all those who breathed in its fumes. In the winter of 1941, the chief of the German police and SS, Heinrich Himmler, summoned Auschwitz Kommandant Rudolf Höss to Berlin to answer what the Nazis considered to be the vital question of how best to achieve annihilation. On 20 January 1942, while newspapers focused on collecting woollen fabrics for the war effort and celebrating the successes of German engineering and the Autobahn, Himmler hosted the infamous Wannsee Conference. 'Whatever Jews we can reach are to be eliminated,' Himmler tells Höss, 'without exception.'[3]

The resolution the Nazis reach will require a cold-blooded alchemy of technical ingenuity and moral bankruptcy, and will be brought into being not in the cold swampy flatlands of Poland, but, in part, in a comfortable office in one of Germany's most pleasant cities. An office with drawing boards and a view of the Ettersberg mountain – where middle-aged men wearing stiff white collars dream up horrors, each more demented than the last.

These are the offices of Topf and Sons, a proud local company noted for expertise in producing agricultural equipment for brewing and malting. Topf and Sons has been working with the Nazis since 17 May 1939, when engineer Kurt Prüfer produces a drawing for a mobile, oil-heated Topf cremation oven, securing the company's first commission with the SS. The mobile ovens will be used to incinerate the growing number of bodies at concentration camps, including the nearby camp at Buchenwald. Although the initial order is for only three mobile ovens, the company has crossed its first and most important moral line in producing them. For the ovens are based on Kurt Prüfer's design for a mobile waste incinerator intended only for animal use and which does not meet the strict technical requirements necessary for human cremation chambers. According to German regulations, when incinerating a human body it should never come into direct contact with flames, it must instead be cremated in super-heated air. By late 1941, Topf and Sons have produced mobile and static single and double-muffle ovens for four Nazi concentration camps, and have designed a new series of triple-muffle ovens to meet the demands of the SS at Auschwitz, where Nazi administrators calculate that Soviet prisoners will die at a rate of 1,000 per day.

(The muffle is the incineration chamber, a double-muffle oven would have a source of fire for each chamber, but Prüfer's design for a triple-muffle oven broke convention by using only two sources of fire for the external chambers, and allowing the flames to burn the body in the central chamber by passing through gaps in the walls.)

It is work that the company appears to be proud of: instead of recoiling from the immediately apparent nature of these horrors, company director Ernst Wolfgang Topf writes to the SS at Auschwitz on 4 November 1941 to explain that the new design will 'improve efficiency', even taking into account the higher fuel consumption of 'frozen' corpses. 'Rest assured,' Ernst Wolfgang writes, 'we shall supply an appropriate and well-functioning system, and we commend ourselves to you with a Heil Hitler.' So proud are they of their work that Kurt Prüfer takes the opportunity a month later, on 6 December, to write to Ernst Wolfgang and Ludwig Topf demanding more money for his design: 'It was I who worked out how to create the three- and eight-muffle cremation ovens, mostly in my free time,' he boasts, 'These ovens are truly ground-breaking, and may I assume that you will grant me a bonus for the work I have done.'[4]

This staggeringly inhumane debate seems a far cry from the origins of J. A. Topf and Sons, founded in Erfurt sixty years earlier, in 1878, by master brewer Johann Andreas Topf. Yet the company was marked from the beginning with some of the same characteristics of technical innovation, unsteady business fortunes, and a strain of mental instability in its founders.

Johann Andreas (J. A.) Topf was born in Erfurt in 1816, the eldest son of farmer Johann Sebastian Topf and his wife Maria Magdalena, who was part of the town's Schlegel brewing family.

Alongside glassblowing, brewing was one of Germany's few growth industries at the time. Nevertheless, to live in Erfurt, or in fact almost anywhere in Germany, was to live in a small world. Erfurt was a 'working town' that had become wealthy in the fourteenth and fifteenth centuries due to the trade in woad, a yellow-flowered plant used in blue dye. In comparison to its close rivals, Erfurt had neither the cultural and literary delights of Weimar, which still gloried in its golden age of being home to Goethe and Schiller, nor the university tradition of Jena. The term 'working town' was relative, however, and a visitor would have encountered small handicraft businesses, crooked streets and livelihoods controlled by strict guilds all conducting local commerce. Germany itself (still a loose assortment of states just beginning to map out some of the bureaucratic processes it would become known for) was considered by fellow Europeans to be a slumbering, 'quaint, half-timbered land' of poets and dreamers, and 'a country whose industrial goods were still regarded, even in the 1870s, as cheap and nasty'.[5]

J. A. Topf lived with his parents and five siblings at 34–35 Krämpferstrasse, where the family continued to run their farm. When he was fourteen he left school and undertook military service. He then began training as a brewer with his uncle, Johann Caspar Schlegel and, after serving his apprenticeship, J. A. Topf struck out on his own – moving to Stolberg in Saxony to set up his own brewery. By the age of thirty-six he was ready to marry, and chose the daughter of a local master baker, who was nine years his junior, Johanne Caroline Auguste Reidemeister. Together they moved back to the Topf family home in Erfurt and had five sons, four of whom lived to adulthood. Gustav was born in 1853, Albert in 1857, Max Julius Ernst in 1859 and Wilhelm Louis, known as Ludwig, in 1863.

Back in Erfurt J. A. Topf began brewing beer on the family farm, but he proved to be a poor businessman. Topf's first attempt to establish a brewery on the property met with disaster when his business partner turned out to be a crook, according to Topf's son Julius, and the family lost both their property and all of their funds, including Johanne Topf's dowry. Remembering the 'great hardship in the house',[6] Julius Topf said the family's poverty had made a lasting impression on the four sons, especially by comparison to some of their rich relations. The situation was so dire that even the baker refused to give the Topfs credit to buy bread.

After the loss of their home, the family moved to another address while J. A. Topf tried his hand at cultivating vegetable seeds and earning money as a self-employed firing technician. Although his business skills were always limited, Topf had discovered that his real talent lay in invention and innovation. In 1867, he began advertising his boiler and oven optimisation services and two years later persuaded the well-known Erfurt food manufacturer, Casar Teichmann, that they could produce a high-quality beer together using Topf's brewing methods. The beer, which was called Nestor, was indeed so successful that Teichmann acquired the old Topf family property in Krämpferstrasse and established his own brewery there, with J. A. Topf in place as master brewer. Once again, however, the partnership foundered when Teichmann asked Topf to work for half his previous salary due to his increasing age. Julius Topf would later claim that Teichmann had not appreciated his father's 'mightily forward-striving spirit', and the two parted company – with Topf choosing to try again to capitalise on his own technical expertise.

At the age of sixty-two it was a bold move, and one his children did not agree with. Despite their opposition, by July 1878 J. A. Topf had moved the family again, to 10b Johannesflur, and restarted the business using his patent for the firing system used in the brewing process. In the brewing process malt was ground and then cooked in the brew pan along with water and hops. The Topf-controlled firing system was innovative and more efficient, as it led to less burning on the base of the brew pans and used less coal. Future generations of the family would consider 1878 the official founding of Topf and Sons, but despite winning a few contracts in the Thuringia region, the company was still struggling.

In 1884 J. A. Topf's second youngest son, Julius, joined the business. Julius, who would become Hartmut Topf's grandfather, had given up training for the civil service and also a prospective career as a fruit farmer and gardener to become a furnace technician. A year later, his youngest brother, Ludwig, joined him in the firm and in 1885 they refounded J. A. Topf and Sons as specialists in heating systems and brewery and malting installations, employing a draughtsman and moving the business out of the family home and into rented office space.

Julius felt he had relieved his parents of a burden by taking over the business, particularly as his father was now mentally unstable. Julius said the 'hard times' and worries his father had endured had sapped his spirit, later writing to his wife that while his father was no longer '*au fait*' enough to work, when left to his own thoughts he 'quickly turns almost crazy' and that he suffered from an 'enormous vanity' bordering on megalomania.

When he died in 1891, J. A. Topf left behind little in the way of business success, but he had founded a company and his technological innovations would outlive him. During his troubled lifetime, Germany had undergone the most profound transformation. Moving from a country which had, at the time of his birth, resembled a Grimms brothers' fairy tale (a place of dark woods, wolves and bereavement, where people were often poor and hungry and suffered random cruelties) to become a fully-fledged nation. Although it was a unification led throughout the 1860s by the Prussian statesman Otto von Bismarck, it was driven in part by the underlying forces of social and economic dynamism emerging from a new, confident and wealthy class of businessmen, bankers and manufacturers. Men who were similar to, but more successful than, J. A. Topf.

These were the years of Germany's explosive industrialisation and the development of a bourgeois middle class, in love with the idea of technology and progress. In Prussia, coal production increased fourfold between 1849 and 1875, raw iron output increased fourteen-fold and steel output increased 54-fold. Firms which would become synonymous with German technology and manufacturing, including Hoechst, Bayer and BASF, were founded and flourished – while the workforce employed by industrialist Alfred Krupp rose from sixty men in 1836 to 16,000 in 1873.

Essayist Otto Gildemeister wrote in 1873: 'It is not exaggeration to say that when it comes to trade and communications and industry, the gulf that separates 1877 and 1773 is greater than the gulf separating 1773 and the Phoenicians.'[7]

Historian David Blackbourn claims that while this *is* an exaggeration, it is one that sums up the spirit of the time. In the towns and provinces across Germany, small businessmen were buoyed by a 'mushroom-like growth' of factories, gasworks, waterworks and railways. A particular area of prosperity related to food production and milling and brewing – fortuitously for Topf and Sons, as this was their line of business.

While J. A. Topf had not been able to seize these advantages himself, the years between 1885, when the Topf brothers refounded the business, and the turn of the twentieth century would lay the foundations for its future commercial success. Two other brothers, Albert and Gustav, joined the firm, strengthening its prestige in the case of Gustav who, as a chemist and biologist, set up an on-site laboratory to test innovative machinery. The company would also enter into a series of successful business partnerships that would enable it to expand and prosper. The first of these saw Erfurt's oldest metal processing firm, J. A. John and Company, take over the processing, invoicing and supply for all Topf products. Within the course of a few years, commercial success meant that Topf and Sons expanded, adding malt kilns to their range, and moving premises four times before finally building their own works and administration building outside the town near the railway station.

From 1889 onwards, this site in Daberstedter Feld (now called Sorbenweg) was the seat of the company – and it was where Topf would continue to operate from until the end of the Second World War. At first the administration building held an office on the ground floor, and accommodation for the Topf family above. The site also contained production facilities, a goods shed and a place for workers to wash and change. The Topf brothers had chosen well; Erfurt had been defortified since the founding of the German Reich in 1873, opening up new areas of land and increasing industrial development. During these decades, the population of Erfurt doubled and the town was given city status in 1906.

The deaths of Albert and Gustav Topf, in 1893 and 1896 respectively, meant that Julius and Ludwig Topf would co-run the company for the next eight years. Within three years the company had started producing its own equipment, and formed a new manufacturing partnership with master mill builder Reinhold Matthias, which it would later take over in its entirety, and Beyer and Co., a machine factory that concentrated on steam driven machines. Topf and Sons also bought into, and later took over, a relative's company, Topf and Stahl, which sold malting and ventilation equipment. Internally J. A. Topf and Sons was now divided into a malting division and a boiler equipment division, and employed fifty fitters. This period of rapid expansion, consolidation and success was symbolised by the decision in 1899 to register a trademark in which the letters of the name Topf formed a pot (Topf means pot in German). In time, of course, this trademark would become infamous.

After several successful years, Julius Topf decided to step down from his role in the business on 1 January 1904. Citing 'ill-health' he dedicated his remaining time to his love for fruit tree cultivation, and his work on the city council and as a freemason. By now he had had nine children with his wife Babette, including his son Albert, who would become Hartmut Topf's father. The family had now moved from the Topf site to their own home at 4 Nonnerain, where they would play only a peripheral role in the history of the company.

As of 1904, Topf and Sons was now under the sole control of Julius's brother Ludwig Topf Sr – and eventually his heirs. Julius's decision to step down from the business coincided with the birth of Ludwig Sr's first son, who was christened Viktor but always known by his third given name, Ludwig. In 1901, the then 38-year-old Ludwig Sr married a woman nineteen years his junior, Pauline Else Getrud Kuhnlenz, known as Else. They celebrated their wedding with a company party and a newsletter that showed the couple surrounded by flaming hearts on one side and pictures of the Topf and Sons works on the other. Their first child, Johanna, was born the following year in 1902, followed by Viktor Karl Ludwig in 1903 and then Ernst Wolfgang in 1904.

As the wedding/works party demonstrated, the lives of the Topf family were now bound up with the success and prestige of the company, and the new generation of Topf children began their lives in the accommodation quarters of the Topf administration building. Ernst Wolfgang would later say that he had been born and bred at 'J. A. and Topf's machinery factory'. By now, however, Ludwig Sr had become one of the seven wealthiest businessmen in Erfurt, earning a salary of 10,000 Reichsmark per annum (more than ten times what a working-class carpenter or miner would have made at the time) as well as a share of the company profits. By 1909, the family had moved out of the administration building into a rented apartment in the city centre, but Ludwig Sr was determined that his children would not be spoilt by wealth, and insisted that they visit workers' homes and hospitals – dispatching the young Ludwig to spend his summer holidays with a worker's family where he even had to share a bed with a boy the same age.

Ludwig Sr's one extravagance was to establish a 'summer residence' – on an area of parkland only a ten-minute walk from the factory. Topf built a house on the land between Hirnzigenweg, Rubensstrasse and Wilhelm-Busch-Strasse, and then created a string of allotments around the edge of the park to be used by Topf and Sons' workers. The allotments were in keeping with a movement of the time where workers were encouraged to cultivate small plots of land, grow their own vegetables and relax. It also shows a strong bond between the Topf family and their workers that extended far beyond the work of the factory floor. Ludwig Sr set up a staff pension fund, introduced Christmas bonuses and built a non-profit housing cooperative. At the firm's twenty-fifth anniversary celebration in 1903, he announced that he considered himself, and his brothers, to be 'the company's first workers' and, in response, Topf furnace builders presented Ludwig Sr with a silver goblet with depictions of the Topf family and their workers. At the presentation one worker recited a poem he had written, proclaiming that he hoped both the tankard and Topf and Sons would survive for 1,000 years.

For the next decade Ludwig Sr fully lived the life of a prosperous early twentieth-century businessman: he was both a board member of the Thuringian Industrialists Society and vice-president of the Erfurt chamber of commerce. His company, Topf and Sons was able to take advantage of a stable political climate and a boom in German beer brewing, and grew to become a mid-sized business of 517 employees by 1914. Topf and Sons was now the global leader in producing malting systems, selling high-quality patented products through an international sales network that stretched to fifty countries, and with technical offices across Germany and in Poland, Austria and Belgium.

This golden era for Topf and Sons reflected a spirit of natural optimism, urban vigour and nationhood that had emerged more widely in Germany. An 'optimism about mechanical civilisation, pride in German culture, the importance of mobilising civic energies and belief in social and moral improvement'[8] went hand in hand with a second industrial revolution focused on chemicals, electronics, precision instruments and optics. Germany was now a world leader in technology, philosophy, law, medicine, biology, chemistry and physics. It was a revolution driven by a growing class of salaried workers who went to work in modern offices every day, like those in the administration building at Topf and Sons, and who spent their wages on better food and drink.

Then, on 15 February 1914, Ludwig Sr committed suicide. It was a shocking end to a seemingly successful life. In one generation, he had taken his company from shaky beginnings to an established international business, and had cemented his own role as an Erfurt civic leader. Local newspapers proclaimed that he was the epitome of the 'city's industrial magnates', yet at the age of fifty-one he had taken his own life while suffering from 'nervous exhaustion' at a sanatorium in the Harz Mountains. Like his father before him, it appeared that the strain of running Topf and Sons had proved too much for him, and he had long talked about selling off one of the company's two divisions. Although the company remained on a sound commercial footing, Ludwig Sr left behind a wife and three young children, who were fractured by his death and the sudden change in their family life.

Both his sons would mythologise his memory, while trying, and often failing, to live up to his legacy.

In the aftermath of his death, control of the company passed to Ludwig's widow Else Topf with the expectation that it would then eventually be handed on to the Topf sons. The unfolding of tortured family relationships between Else Topf and her children, and the rise of other powerful forces within the company, would make this far from certain, however.

Unwittingly, Ludwig had chosen to commit suicide only a few months before the outbreak of First World War – an event which would fundamentally transform the nature of both his country and his company. During the war itself, Topf and Sons expanded its areas of production to include war vehicles and grenades. After the war, the Treaty of Versailles demanded that Germany pay huge reparations to France and Europe via its coal supplies (some local German currency at the time showed enormous coal trains snaking across Germany, heading for Paris) – forcing German industry to turn from coal to lignite. The ever innovative Topf and Sons responded to this by developing lignite furnaces, expanding their chimney construction business, and then, from 1925, producing ventilation systems.

The year of Ludwig's suicide would become a significant one for Topf and Sons for another reason, too – it was also the year that the company began producing furnaces for crematoria. Rising urban populations in the nineteenth century and concerns about hygiene and lack of space in graveyards had given rise to a new European movement in favour of human cremation.

Despite religious objections and a ban by the Catholic Church that remained until 1963, a social movement, 'the cremationists', sprang up in Germany to advocate a more modern and technologically advanced way of disposing of human remains. Although cremation had long been practiced in other parts of the world, it was an idea that required a huge shift in European culture, essentially away from Christianity and the belief in life after death and resurrection.

The debate about the nature of cremation, and the rules it must adhere to, still shape the practice today. For example, before cremation can take place the body must be examined by two people to ensure that the person is dead, and that they have not been killed by unnatural means. Furthermore, the European Cremation Congress of Dresden in 1876 ruled that cremation should be carried out quickly and be completely odourless in furnaces used exclusively by humans. A person should be cremated alone, and their ashes collected together. Two years later, German crematoria had taken this reverence for the human body a stage further, opening a crematorium in Gotha that used super-heated air – meaning that the body never came into contact with the fire. The Siemens-Schneider regenerative furnace was pre-heated with coke for four hours to reach a temperature of 1000°C. After that it was forbidden to add any further fuel, and the cremation itself took place solely in the hot air and gasses that surrounded the body.

The years of the Weimar Republic, and its emphasis on secular modernism, saw an enormous increase in cremation rather than burial – with the number rising from 630 cremations in five crematoria in 1900 to more than 50,000 in 103 different crematoria in 1930. Such prospects for a profitable industry meant that not all companies agreed with the stringent requirements for human cremation. Notably, Heinrich Kori from Berlin opposed the 'sacred cow' of human cremation in favour of his already commercially successful methods for animal incineration. He opposed the Prussian Cremation Act of 1911 and argued in favour of replacing cremation by hot air in favour of burning bodies using direct burning gasses. When Kori and Topf went head to head in competition to supply the crematorium at Arnstadt in 1924, Kori's 'furnaces for wastes of all kinds' lost out to Topf because of Kori's disregard for the human reverence regulations.

Topf and Sons complied with the spirit, as well as the letter of the law, meaning that by the mid-1920s they were national and international leaders in supplying technologically advanced cremation solutions. Not only did they support the regulations surrounding 'reverence', they created ingenious solutions to make human cremation even more dignified. Under the supervision of engineer Kurt Prüfer, who ran the furnace construction department at Topf and Sons, the company developed what was known as a 'muffle' – a slider between the coke generator and oven chamber that meant the oven could be sealed before the coffin was in place. The company introduced the first gas-heated oven in 1927, followed by the first electric oven in 1933.

Prüfer was not only responsible for innovative designs, he was also the figurehead of the company's innovation in this area, promoting the work of Topf and Sons to the wider industry and crematoria movement. He kept abreast of debates about cremation, and was a member of the Erfurt People's Cremation Society. In 1931 he wrote to *Flame* magazine, published by the Berlin cremation society, explaining why Topf avoided the methods used by Hamburg designers Volkmann and Ludwig in which a gas pipe was directly placed near parts of a human body that were more difficult to incinerate, blowing compressed air directly over the body. Within the company, he clearly distinguished between his work for human cremation ovens, calling them 'cremation systems' and other animal and waste incinerators, which he termed 'elimination ovens'. These distinctions would later prove crucial in evaluating the role Topf and Sons played in the Holocaust.

When Ludwig Sr's sons, Ludwig and Ernst Wolfgang, took control of Topf and Sons in the early 1930s they inherited a company that was established as an international leader in the malting industry, with a small but technologically advanced sideline in cremation technology. Their inheritance, however, came about only as a result of a bitter court battle they waged against their own mother and the other Topf and Sons company directors.

After the death of their father in 1914, Ludwig and Ernst Wolfgang endured a peripatetic and patchy upbringing. Their mother gave up the family home, and sent both sons away to boarding school in the Thuringian town of Gumperda. Although the brothers were close, the differences between them became apparent even at an early age. By the time the boys took their *Reifeprufung*, the equivalent of a high school diploma or leaving certificate, it seems Ludwig was already falling behind. Although he was a year older than his brother Ernst Wolfgang, the boys took their examination together, indicating that Ludwig had already taken a break from education. Indeed, it was Ludwig Topf who became the first of his siblings to fall out with his mother, when, upon leaving schoool, she refused to give him any more financial support.

In the following twelve years, Ludwig unsuccessfully embarked upon, and then discarded, a bewildering array of studies and possible careers. After leaving school he first set out to study mechanical engineering in Hannover, paying his way by working as a coal trimmer, tutor and bank assistant. Soon, however, he collapsed, suffering from gall bladder problems and the psychological strain of his estrangement from his mother. Leaving Hannover in bad health, Ludwig then attempted to continue his education elsewhere – trying out a range of courses in economics, business, sociology, law and journalism at universities in Berlin, Leipzig and Rostock. By the time he eventually joined Topf and Sons, Ludwig was supposedly studying for a PhD in malt production – but the truth was that in his many years of study Ludwig Topf never achieved a single qualification in any subject, nor did he successfully pursue an alternative career.

While Ludwig acted out the role of family playboy, who 'looked and behaved like a film star',[9] the burden of plodding productivity fell to his younger brother, Ernst Wolfgang, who was described as having the 'pedantic, grudge-bearing' countenance of an office worker. After taking his *Abitur*, Ernst Wolfgang undertook and completed training to become a merchant with Oskar Winter Ironwear Wholesalers in Hannover, and then added to his commercial understanding by completing six months of work experience, first at a bank in Erfurt and then at a malting company in Arnstadt. With solid experience under his belt, Ernst Wolfgang joined Ludwig in Leipzig, and graduated from commercial college with a business diploma in 1929.

Superficially, the two brothers could not have been more different, but their fraternal bond was strong. At every stage of their early education and career they invariably chose to move to the same city, and would sometimes share the same lodgings. Once they were ensconced as the directors of Topf and Sons, they lived separately – with Ernst Wolfgang moving into a rented apartment while Ludwig chose the more glamorous setting of a house in the Topf family park. At work, however, they fell back into their earlier pattern – choosing to share an office with desks that faced each other (perhaps also because neither entirely trusted the other.)

Ernst Wolfgang Topf was the first of the brothers to take up an official role with the company, joining the business at the end of 1929. His appointment came only after the death of Felix Paul – the last remaining director from Ludwig Topf Sr's time in control. After the war, Ernst Wolfgang would claim that the strong dislike which existed between Felix Paul and the Topf brothers was caused by Paul's anti-Semitism and the Topf brothers' friendships with Jewish families; however, this was part of a larger narrative concocted by Ernst Wolfgang Topf to try and persuade the Soviet authorities that he was not guilty of Nazi war crimes. It is true, though, that Felix Paul disapproved of both brothers and did not speak to them or acknowledge them for years. Paul went out of his way to make sure that Topf and Sons did not come under the brothers' control.

With Paul out of the way, however, Ernst Wolfgang Topf caved in under pressure from his mother to join the company – with Ludwig following in late 1931. Now aged twenty-eight, Ludwig Topf swapped his status of perpetual student for that of wealthy playboy industrialist, but he chose not to work in the area in which he was supposedly pursuing a PhD – malt production. Instead he focused on furnace construction, specifically, crematoria furnaces, working with Kurt Prüfer to associate the name of Topf and Sons with advanced cremation technology and dignity after death.

As the familial heirs of Ludwig Topf Sr it appeared that both brothers had finally taken up senior roles in the business, but they would have to overcome another significant hurdle to make sure that the spoils were theirs.

By the early 1930s, Germany was deep in recession. The German economy had enjoyed what seemed to be a brief period of stability in the mid-1920s after overcoming the economic crisis and hyperinflation of 1923. Paper money had been rendered worthless, employer–employee relations had broken down, France occupied large parts of Germany's industrial heartland, and crime and unemployment rose dramatically. The agreement by the Weimar government to settle the question of reparations (effectively admitting that Germany had lost the First World War) ushered in a new era of foreign, notably American, investment – along with state intervention in public building projects and a social welfare state. Rising living standards went hand in hand with political support for parties that occupied the centre ground. However, the number of people now financially dependent on the government for welfare payments and war pensions meant that the Weimar Republic was, in fact, desperately overstretched and unable to cope with the advent of the Great Depression.

In March 1929, Germany was plunged into deflationary crisis with prices and output falling by one-fifth. When the government proved reluctant to implement economic measures out of fear of causing a 'second great inflation', the economic situation worsened with wages falling and unemployment rising until by the summer of 1932, 45 per cent of German trade union members were considered to be out of work.

Faced with such bleak circumstances, Topf and Sons, like many other businesses in Germany, found short-term remedies in cutting salaries and laying off staff, but it still struggled to pay its bills. As early as December 1930, Else Topf instituted the first pay-cut, slashing directors' salaries by 17.5 per cent. Those earning more than 500 RM a month had their earnings reduced by 10 per cent. Only the lowest strata of workers, who earned less than 300 Reichsmarks a month, were left untouched. For the next three years salaries would be cut further while productivity dropped by a quarter – down from 4 million Reichsmarks in 1930 to only 1 million Reichsmarks in 1933.

Ernst Wolfgang had only joined the business at the end of 1929, but by April 1932 he and his mother, Else, had become estranged, with Else choosing to side with the company directors when they moved to dismiss both brothers from Topf and Sons by the end of that year. Although their departure took place during the worst of the economic turmoil, the reasons were less financial, than political. In the election of July 1932 the Nazis won 230 seats, making them the largest party in the Reichstag, which began a complicated series of negotiations that culminated in Hitler being named German Chancellor on 30 January 1933.

Ernst Wolfgang Topf would later point out that with trade debts of 98,000 RM there was no reason to stop paying creditors – instead Ernst Wolfgang and Ludwig had been ousted in a plot engineered by the Nazis and senior members of the company, under the leadership of authorised company officer and senior engineer Dr Edmund Spindler, to take control of the business themselves and set up a new company – Topf Furnace Construction, which they would control.

At first the plot appeared to be successful. Spindler and his associates told both the Chamber of Industry and the Bankruptcy Court that the losses incurred by the brothers at the company were unsustainable and that the company was unable to meet its debts. At the same time, Dr Edmund Spindler, a senior engineer and authorised officer of Topf and Sons (and a Nazi) spoke at a company meeting to denounce both brothers for 'associating with Jews' and inform the workers that the Topfs had lost their right to run the company.

Banned from the company premises, without resources, and estranged from their own mother who had, astonishingly, sided against them, Ernst Wolfgang and Ludwig decided to fight back and reclaim what they believed was rightfully theirs. Their battle to win back the company in 1933 would take on enormous importance in their own minds and they would be prepared to do anything to ensure that they took back their inheritance.

In the case of the Topf brothers the reality of 'doing anything' meant only one thing – becoming members of the Nazi Party. A leading Thuringia Nazi, Friedrich Triebel, informed the brothers that, given their relatively young ages, there was nothing to prevent them from 'retraining' as party members and regaining control of the firm. Even Jewish friends and business acquaintances agreed that this seemed to be the only solution, and so without having shown any prior political interest, both Ernst Wolfgang and Ludwig became National Socialist Party members in April 1933. Kurt Prüfer and other senior Topf officials followed suit.

Now the Topf brothers were granted a hearing at the Board of Creditors and their dismissal from Topf was overturned; reinstated, the brothers then sacked the acting Topf board of directors. By July 1933, the battle for Topf and Sons was over. Ernst Wolfgang Topf was listed as commercial director with Ludwig Topf named technical director. The brothers were finally in control of their father's company, but their deal with the Nazis would prove costly. Ultimately, they would pay by sacrificing every shred of moral decency and humanity they possessed.

CHAPTER TWO

A DEAL WITH THE DEVIL

Honour your work! It confers dignity
And with confidence in your own strength
Life's burdens become light
When you work cheerfully and with firm purpose
The company's management
Along with the band of workers
Will gladly proclaim
That our loyalty was always true
It has been even more beautiful in Germany's regions
Since the coming of the Third Reich
It is splendid to behold
The way Hitler has united us
Status and castes have gone
Unity reigns everywhere
Poverty and distress have been overcome
After a painful fall, came Germany's rise
POEM TO COMMEMORATE SIXTY YEARS OF TOPF AND
SONS PUBLISHED IN A COMPANY BOOKLET 1938[10]

By 1938, Ernst Wolfgang and Ludwig Topf felt they had much to celebrate – and celebrate they did. An elaborate ceremony was held to
mark the sixtieth anniversary of the re-founding of Topf and Sons
with a party in the Topf family park on 28 August, a commemorative
booklet full of cartoons, witty epithets and poems was published, and
an ambitious plan to rebuild the company's administration building
launched (the plan was to erect a company sign with the logo and
the words 'Topf and Sons 1878' to fit on a new, more impressive, and
steeply pitched roof). The Topf brothers had been in full control of the
family firm for five years and they were starting to enjoy the prosperous upturn in their fortunes.

For the moment, the dominating presence of their mother continued to restrain any impulse the brothers had towards luxury. Else
maintained control over the company as a majority shareholder, even
after the appointment of her sons as directors in 1933. In the most
crucial matters, Else's decisions were all important: she held a veto
over large investments, property purchases or sales and investment in
other companies; she stipulated that all profits should be ploughed
back into company development for ten years. Knowing, perhaps, her
sons' true characters, she also kept their salaries at a moderate sum of
700 RM a month. Only her death in 1941 would finally set them free,
and one of the Topf brothers' first acts, as their mother had feared,
was to award themselves a massive pay rise and start spending their
company dividends.

However, even before their mother's death, the Topf boys had started to enjoy the good life. Although Ludwig used the opening of the
new administration building to remind staff to be as careful with their

coffee cups and cigarette ends as they were in their own home, by the time that the brothers were using the sixtieth anniversary of Topf and Sons to celebrate their father's wisdom as a thrifty businessman, they had acquired no fewer than fourteen luxury cars, including an Adler-Diploma Horch V-8 and a limousine with a rolling roof, all of which sat gleaming in the parking lot.

While Ernst Wolfgang lived with his wife and two children in a rented apartment, Ludwig endeavoured to live up to his reputation as the family playboy by building a modernist villa for himself in the Topf family park, and resisted any pressure to marry and settle down. In 1936, he took the opportunity of writing a will to exhort his more staid married siblings to 'rise above the messiness of life' as he claimed to do, 'stay healthy, and don't get worked up about things, and do drink and smoke mightily'.

Ludwig claimed the Topf family villa (which he also decorated with the company logo) was a suitable 'expression of the prosperity of the company proprietors to the very numerous visitors and customers from abroad'. In the spirit of expressing his prosperity to the fullest, he installed two bathtubs, one black and one white, for use respectively by the brunettes and blondes he entertained. Outside the front door he built a swimming pool, enjoyed mainly by his cousin Agnes, who would come over in the morning for a dip before starting work at the famous kindergarten she had founded in a neighbouring street.

After the shocking suicide of their father, and the lost and lonely years of their youth, it must have seemed to the Topf brothers that the good times had finally arrived. There was no doubt that the company was doing well or that the decision by Ernst Wolfgang and Ludwig to join the Nazi Party was a fortuitous one, at least economically. Topf and Sons owed its financial success to the fact that the Third Reich was investing heavily in military preparations. With decades of expertise, Topf and Sons was the ideal supplier for the four-year militarisation plan announced by the German Reich in 1936, and the company had in fact begun producing large storage tanks for grain as early as 1934. The purpose of these tanks was to provide food for an army and civilian population in the event of war, and supplying them would come to dominate production at Topf and Sons. Storage tank production, now housed in its separate department in the company, would become the largest source of income for the company during the second half of the 1930s and drove the increase in the company's turnover from 1 million RM in 1933 to 7 million RM in 1940. In July of that year, Topf and Sons received 6.3 million RM for producing forty-six military storage tanks and twenty-seven for other purposes. Storage construction work was not only the backbone of the company's financial success, but also played another key role, too – it allowed Topf and Sons to petition the Reich to classify a large proportion of company employees as 'Uk' workers (those in occupations deemed indispensable for military or civilian life, and thus exempt from army service).

Like many German companies, Topf and Sons was clearly profiting enormously from its collaboration with the Third Reich in war preparations (a staggeringly inept economic strategy, supported by Hitler, which meant that the country was mortgaging its future assets and racking up unsustainable levels of debt) but there remained little sign that either Ernst Wolfgang and Ludwig were any more ideologically in tune with the Nazis than they had been when they conveniently joined the party in 1933.

Neither brother displayed any signs of anti-Semitism and the Topf family had a long history of business dealings with Jewish families who had been allowed to resettle in Erfurt since the early nineteenth century, and were now intertwined with business and cultural life.

Examples of prominent Jewish businesses included the hugely popular Römishcer Kaiser department store, which was launched by Siegfried Pinthus and Arthur Solms Arndtheim and, at its height in the late 1920s and early 1930s, employed 450 people, before it was forcibly 'Aryanised' and appropriated in a compulsory sale to non-Jewish owners in 1936 (or 'fell under new management' as the newspaper advertisements stated). The Römischer Kaiser brought a touch of glamour to Erfurt that included a large lounge to host fashion shows, a lending library with 5,000 volumes and a company crèche.

Both Topf brothers had grown up in close proximity to Jewish families after their father moved them to 29 Neuwerkstrasse in 1909. Two of the three other families living at this address were Jewish: the Hess family and the Nussbaum family. The history and fate of the Nussbaums remains unknown, but the Hess family were important shoe manufacturers in the town (the other important shoe company was Eduard Lingel AG which popularised 'German' shoes and boots during the Third Reich era). Although Adolf Hess was seventeen years younger than Ludwig Topf Sr, their wives and children were of a similar age – and both men shared the fact that they were prominent town citizens who had assumed responsibility for their companies at an early age. Like the Topfs, Adolf Hess had architectural aspirations and commissioned local architect Max Brockert to build a large neo-classical villa for his family that has now been turned into a youth hostel. Adolf managed his business with his cousin Alfred Hess, who was also a local political for the German Democratic Party during the Weimar Republic and a major collector of modern art. The Hess family escaped from Germany before the Holocaust.

In business, Ludwig Sr came into frequent contact with trading company Henry Pels & Co., which produced the machine tools used by Topf's then business partner J. A. John. The Pels company had been founded by Jewish businessman Henry Pels, who was a leading metal manufacturer in Erfurt, although the family lived in Berlin. Pels and his wife both died in the early 1930s, leaving their daughter, Johanna, the sole heir. In 1937, Henry Pels & Co. was sold for far less than it was worth as part of the Nazis' forced sale of Jewish businesses; it became part of the Aryanised 'German Weapons and Ammunitions Factories AG'. Johanna Pels and her husband both died in 1941 after being deported from Berlin to Lodz. Their two children escaped from Germany and survived.

Ludwig Sr was also closely involved with the Benary family in Erfurt, serving for seventeen years on the Erfurt Chamber of Commerce with Friedrich Benary, the son of Ernst Benary, founder of Erfurt's major florist and seed cultivation business. Although Ernst Benary was Jewish, Friedrich converted to Christianity. This meant that, despite the business being labelled 'mixed-blood grade two' and included on a list of 'non-Aryan' firms drawn up by the Nazis, it remained in family ownership. Friedrich Benary attended Ludwig's funeral in 1914, and praised him in the death notice as 'a man distinguished by rich commercial knowledge and experience who worked for the public good'.

What these specific examples show is that the Topf family were interlinked with Jewish families in a web of business and personal relationships quite typical for middle-class German life at the time. Those same relationships would continue to touch on the lives of the two younger Topf brothers as they went about establishing themselves in the Erfurt business world. Ernst Wolfgang undertook his first work-experience placement in 1925 at the Adolph Sturcke Bank, where one of the co-owners, Max Sturcke, was married to a member of the Benary family. His second work-experience stint was with H&S Windesheim Malting plant, and he remained friends with the notary Hans Windesheim, one of the sons of the family until Windesheim emigrated to the US in the 1930s. It was the Windesheims who, Ernst Wolfgang later claimed, suggested that the Topf brothers join the Nazi Party as a means of regaining control of their company.

'A family with the qualities of humanity was especially chosen to protect its persecuted Jewish fellow-citizens and colleagues to the very best of its ability, and that we demonstrably did, to the point of self-sacrifice, right up to the end of the war.'[11]

Given that it spared no effort in technologically advancing the Holocaust, it is hard to imagine a more breathtaking lie than Ernst Wolfgang's claim that Topf and Sons was, in fact, a friend to the Jews.

Neither Topf brother could have been under any illusions about the fate of Erfurt's Jews. In the early 1930s, people shopping in Jewish stores emerged to find that they had been secretly photographed and were publicly shamed. From 1936 onwards, Jewish businesses were appropriated and sold for knock-down prices. Jewish doctors were struck off; Jewish teachers banned from their profession. Businessmen like Carl Ludwig Spier, a director of the Lingel shoe factory, was forced from his job, before dying at the end of the war on a death march to Buchenwald. In 1938, the Great Synagogue was burned to the ground. After 'Aryanisation', the imposing front of the Römischer Kaiser department store now sported flags emblazoned with large Swastikas. On 9 May 1942, the first mass transit from Thuringia took 101 Jews from Erfurt to the ghettos and concentration camps – where no one from the transport survived. Among the victims was four-year-old Gunther Beer, the youngest Erfurt resident to be deported.

In his own mind, however, Ernst Wolfgang no doubt believed that he was a 'friend to the Jews' due to the fact that his company was offering a safe haven to some opponents of the regime – even though Topf and Sons was also conspiring with the Nazis in their plan to wipe-out the Jewish race.

Ernst Wolfgang would later claim that the company had kept four 'half-Jews' as part of their workforce, protecting them from persecution, although only two archive records for 'half-Jewish' employees exist – Willy Wiemokli and Hans Fels. Employing a 'half-Jew' (someone with one Jewish parent) was not illegal in the Third Reich, and posed no official risk to Topf and Sons. Nonetheless, it was hardly encouraged, and the Topf brothers demonstrated that they were prepared to personally intervene on their employees' behalf.

At the end of the Second World War, Willy Wiemokli gave a sworn statement in support of Ernst Wolfgang Topf to the occupying authorities, stating that Topf had 'done everything he could' to have

Wiemokli released when he was arrested by the Gestapo in 1942, and had then intervened again when Wiemokli was sent to a forced labour camp in 1944. 'Then, too, Herr Ernst Wolfgang Topf did everything in his power to prevent it happening, using all of his personal contacts on my behalf.'

Wiemokli was born in Halle in 1908 to a protestant mother and a Jewish father. Although he had been baptised a Protestant, he was arrested for the first time on the night of 9 November 1938, Kristallnacht, and sent to Buchenwald concentration camp with his father. Following his release from Buchenwald, Wiemokli discovered that he had lost his job as a trader in Erfurt and could no longer support his father. Soon after, however, he found a new job with Topf and Sons, and an ally in Ernst Wolfgang Topf, who had attended high school with him.

After the war, Willy Wiemokli submitted this resumé of his life and career to the socialist government:

Willy Wiemokli

Erfurt

Gustav Adolfstr. 2a

RÉSUMÉ

I was born on 5 December 1908 in Halle/Saale to David Wiemokli, commercial employee and Anna Wiemokli, née Kaufmann. I attended secondary school in Erfurt and, in 1925, started a traineeship with the Römischer Kaiser department store. After I finished my training, I worked in the commercial departments of several different firms.

In 1938 my father and I were put in the Buchenwald concentration camp, since my father was Jewish and I was half-Jewish.

After I'd been released from Buchenwald, my employer, Herr Hans Türck dismissed me on the grounds of my imprisonment. My father had been without work or a means of supporting himself since 1933. In 1939, however, I managed to get a job at the Topf and Sons machine factory. Between 1939 and 1944, I was arrested by the Gestapo three times on suspicion of having failed to comply with the Race Laws.

However, nothing could be proven against me. At work, too, I suffered a great deal of nastiness from my colleagues.

In 1943, my father was imprisoned in the Auschwitz concentration camp, where he must have died shortly after his arrival. My father's prisoner number was: 119684. My mother had died of a stroke in 1942, a result of all the stress.

In 1944, the Gestapo put me in a forced labour camp near Suhl, where, along with numerous other half-Jews from Erfurt, I was made to do extremely hard labour in a stone quarry. After the Allied troops liberated the camp, I returned to Erfurt.

Immediately after my return I returned to my previous company. I was one of the staff elected to the works council, and later I was appointed sequestrator of the Topf and Sons Machine Factory in Erfurt. Following the lifting of the sequestration, I worked there as departmental manager and am now head bookkeeper.

I swear on oath that the above details are true.

Erfurt, 13 October 1949[12]

Not only did Ernst Wolfgang Topf protect Wiemokli from the Gestapo, he also protected him from other opponents within Topf and Sons, going as far as to sack four members of the accounts department who had denounced him. Wiemokli's particular nemesis was Wilhelm Behnke, a colleague in the same department and an ardent Nazi, who reported Wiemokli to the Gestapo for breaking the Race Laws and having a relationship with a non-Jewish woman at work. 'Herr Topf protected me in every respect and in some cases even sacked people who tried to act against me,' Wiemokli noted. Wiemokli was arrested and released three times on suspicion of breaking the Race Laws between 1939 and 1944 (he was, in fact, in a secret relationship with Erika Glass for the entire duration, and married her in September 1945). On each occasion Ernst Wolfgang came to his aid, even, according to Topf's secretary Ingeborg Prior, intervening to stop Wiemokli being called up for forced labour.

After the war, Ernst Wolfgang would claim that he had himself been denounced to the Gestapo for his actions in defence of Wiemokli, a claim impossible to verify as Gestapo files were destroyed after the war. Yet, while some of Ernst Wolfgang's actions were self-serving (he may have wanted to sack Behnke and the others for his own reasons), there is no doubt that he defended Wiemokli to the best of his ability, and also tried to help another half-Jewish employee, Hans Fels, who was a commercial apprentice. Fels later recalled that Ernst Wolfgang had intervened with all possible offices to stop his call-up for forced labour in the autumn of 1944.

Wiemokli's gratitude seems even more mystifying when we learn that not only did he experience the horrors of Buchenwald himself – but that his father died at Auschwitz, and therefore almost certainly ended up being incinerated in a Topf oven.

Topf and Sons not only provided protection for a small number of employees vulnerable to persecution under the Race Laws, it also sheltered a number of political opponents of the Nazi regime, including communists.

One example was Georg Reinl, who was prepared to join Willy Wiemokli in making a post-war statement in defence of Ernst Wolfgang, claiming that Topf had employed him, protected him from the Gestapo and had been complicit in his determination never to manufacture so much as a screw or a rivet for 'Hitler's war'. Reinl was an engineer from the Sudetenland whose democratic views and 'political unreliability' had already led to him being imprisoned several times by the Nazis and sacked by defence companies Messerschmitt and Junkers. Yet, despite his lengthy record of dissent, Topf and Sons respected his wish not to take part in any military work, such as making aircraft parts, and employed him in the malting and grain storage construction division to work on grain conveyors – a protected 'Uk' position that meant that he was exempt from call-up to the army. Reinl stated that on several occasions Ernst Wolfgang had 'protected [him] from the Gestapo, and from serious reprimands from the political shop steward,' and also allowed Reinl to take an 'illegal holiday' to visit his father who was imprisoned by the Gestapo in the Sudetenland.

As well as acting as a haven for a small number of those persecuted by the Nazis, Topf and Sons was also a hotbed of communist resistance – with a strong network of highly organised communist workers, many of whom had been imprisoned and then released from concentration camps. One worker and KPD (German Communist Party) member, Bernhard Bredehorn, claimed the reason for this was that Topf and Sons undertook no armaments work so metal workers from concentration camps could be sent there without fear that they would steal or sabotage arms work. Another reason, later offered up by one of Bredehorn's comrades, was that the Gestapo sent political prisoners to Topf and Sons because the hard work they endured at the company tired them out and kept them under control.

Whatever the reason, the communist workers would later claim that, once there, they immediately banded together and operated as an active political resistance throughout the war. Bernhard Bredehorn was an Erfurt native and former employee of the town's shoe industry who had spent a year and a half incarcerated in various concentration camps before retraining as a welder and joining Topf and Sons. In the 1950s, Bredehorn described how he had worked with well-known communist resistance figures during his time at Topf and Sons. Among these were Hermann Jahn, who became the first mayor of Erfurt when the city was part of East Germany, as well as Magnus Poser, who died in Buchenwald in 1944, and Theodor Neubauer, who was executed by the Nazis in 1945.

'Throughout the entire Nazi regime I always maintained contact with known Erfurt comrades and stayed in constant touch with them … Since the top priority was the organisation of steadfast political cadres, I was given the task of building up the organisation in the company again.'[13] Bredehorn goes on to describe how this 'illegal factory cell' at Topf and Sons distributed pamphlets to forced workers and prisoners of war in the company and smuggled Soviet forced labourers into the homes of communist sympathisers so that they could listen to banned radio broadcasts from the Soviet Union.

There was also some suggestion that communist leader Hermann

Jahn was also employed at Topf and Sons during this time, working directly with Heinrich Messing who was the ventilation mechanic for the gas chambers at Auschwitz.

These statements, however, must also be examined in the context of workers trying to impress their new post-war socialist masters with their own resistance credentials. Historian, Ronald Hirte from Buchenwald Memorial believes that communists were sent to Topf and Sons as the SS considered the company completely reliable, and knew that the resistance there posed very little threat.

> There was a communist resistance at Topf and Sons, but there was also communist resistance even within Buchenwald camp itself. No action was taken against it because it was known that it posed no real threat. In the case of Topf and Sons there is little evidence about what real actions the resistance there ever undertook.

Speaking after the war, when Erfurt was in the Soviet occupation zone and then part of the German Democratic Republic (East Germany), none of the communist workers from Topf and Sons referred to a personal relationship with either of the Topf brothers (they remained the 'enemies' in the class struggle), but company records show that all of the communist employees of Topf and Sons, with the exception of two, were kept on the list of 'Uk' protected workers.

This was a deliberate attempt to protect them, Ernst Wolfgang Topf would claim in 1946 as part of his own defence and efforts to keep control of the company.

As self-serving as this explanation is (not to mention horrifyingly hypocritical given the wider context of the work undertaken at Topf and Sons), there is some truth in the fact that Nazi opponents, or victims of persecution, were singled out for protection within the company, and that Ernst Wolfgang himself publicly spoke out against Nazi propaganda at several company meetings.

In a company training course on 27 January 1942, long-term member of staff and Nazi supporter Eduard Pudenz began outlining why unity and support for the Nazis was essential among workers to prevent 'England the Jew' from 'exterminating all Germans'. Yet, in response, Ernst Wolfgang replied that

> We are duty bound to see the individual in every person ... Everyone wants to be treated decently. We are a company and not a barracks. Some people have seen that as a weakness in us. Others, however, have recognised that in a somewhat more relaxed working community the individual people within it bond together into a whole – provided that any unsuitable ones, of whom there are always a few, are swiftly removed. In 1942 more than ever, now that the Front is calling again, we must relinquish any individual who personally invoked Adolf Hitler but positions himself outside our community.

That sense of the Topf community mattered more than anything else to Ernst Wolfgang. In the commemorative company brochure of 1938, the Topf brothers devote the first few pages to praising the 'far-sighted genius' of their father, the achievements of the 'corporate community of J. A. Topf and Sons' and the endeavours of employer and employee in the sixty years of 'shared work in the service of a shared goal'. Only on the last page do they include the words of the German nineteenth-century folk song, reworked in tribute to Hitler.

Yet, however much Ernst Wolfgang and his brother Ludwig liked to sup from the Nazi cup with a long spoon, their work for the Third Reich was the black heart of their business.

Not only was Topf and Sons creating and building the technology of the Holocaust, the company would also become actively involved in armaments work and employ hundreds of forced labourers – who were essentially slaves.

At Topf and Sons, forced labour would at one point account for 40 per cent of the workforce and total more than 600 people. Although these workers were supposed to replace Topf and Sons employees who had been called up for military service, their lives differed greatly from those of ordinary Germans. They were confined to a guarded barracks on the southern edge of Topf and Sons land, known as the 'prison camp', where they lived in one of six huts each housing fifty-two labourers in a shared sleeping area, living area and washroom. Once installed at Topf and Sons they would have longer working hours than German employees (fifty-six hours per week rather than forty-two) and were paid 25–50 per cent less. Almost all of their wages were actually retained by the company for 'board and other services' so that these workers would receive virtually nothing. The first forced labourers at Topf and Sons were thirty French prisoners of war, followed by Ukrainians, forced workers from lands to the east known as *Ostarbeiters*, as well as Soviet prisoners and people from Belgium, the Netherlands, Croatia, Poland and Czechoslovakia. Although some were women, most workers were men and consisted of a mixture of captured soldiers and civilians.

Like forced labourers in most other locations, there were widespread reports of abuse and mistreatment – with one camp leader at Topf and Sons, Wilhelm Buchroder, being dismissed in 1944 for assaulting workers, who retaliated by refusing to work for him. Most of these workers were assigned directly to war work for the Third Reich, including the special production unit at Topf and Sons which produced grenades, or repairing or building new aircraft parts for the Luftwaffe.

In directing its output towards the war effort, and profiting from forced labour, Topf and Sons was doing nothing out of the ordinary. It would come to light that many German companies did the same, and on a far larger scale. The economy of the Third Reich had been propped up by this practice since 1937, and by August 1944 there were 7.5 million foreign workers in Germany, most of them forced labourers. Steel giant Krupp employed 75,000 forced labourers; Audi (then known as Group Auto Union) used more than 20,000 concentration camp workers; carmaker BMW has admitted to using more than 50,000 forced labourers producing arms and U-boat batteries; and the chemical and pharmaceutical companies BASF, Bayer and Hoescht had a total of 80,000 forced labourers on their books. Records of Erfurt's Jewish families show that local companies were also using forced labour – including one called Thuba that made bathroom boilers, and another that manufactured aeroplane parts.

What made Topf and Sons unusual, however, was not their use of forced labour, abhorrent as that was, but the initiative the company would take in developing the technology to drive the Holocaust. It was this work that would demonstrate a combination of technical innovation and a horrifying lack of human empathy. Yet, such disinterest and disregard for human life should not be confused with a lack of emotion. Far from it. Topf and Sons regarded their work as nothing less than a 'project of passion' – and it would inflame the pride, loyalty, jealousy and ambition of several men, including company directors Ernst Wolfgang and Ludwig Topf; engineers Kurt Prüfer, Fritz Sander, Karl Schultz and Paul Erdmann; and operations director Gustav Braun.

Out of this handful of men, it is Kurt Prüfer and Ludwig Topf who demand the most immediate attention.

Prüfer would come to distinguish himself as the true 'pioneer of annihilation'. Without his singular focus, technical skills and drive to better himself, it is doubtful that Topf and Sons would have developed the expertise to become market leaders in crematoria or that the company would have forged such a mutually beneficial partnership with the SS.

Prüfer was born in Erfurt in April 1891, the youngest child in a big working-class Protestant family of thirteen children, who relied on their father, an engine driver, to support them. After spending eight years at school, Prüfer started work, undertaking a three-year bricklaying apprenticeship which he completed successfully, passing with a grade of 'very good'. He went on to study at the School of Arts and Crafts in Erfurt for two terms, before taking a course in building construction at the Royal Building Trades School.

With this training behind him, Prüfer was now well equipped to earn a good living working in the construction industry. During this time his father had opened a restaurant near Topf and Sons and Prüfer would often overhear conversations about the company that piqued his interest. The workers who came to the restaurant on 12 Nonnerain to eat and drink talked about an exciting, expanding, international company – a machinery factory and furnace builders that seemed in spirit with the scientific and technical revolution of the times. The promise of living a more ambitious life obviously appealed to a young Kurt Prüfer (who spoke English and some French) and he made his first, handwritten application to join Topf and Sons on 12 December 1909 at the age of eighteen:

> The undersigned takes the liberty of enquiring whether it would be possible to join your firm as an engineer in April 1910, and permits himself to include his CV below.
>
> I, Kurt Prüfer, son of the locomotive driver Hermann Prüfer, was born on 21 April 1891, and from the ages of six to fourteen attended citizen school, from which I graduated from the highest class. After my confirmation I did three years' practical training with the master carpenter Herr Otto Berghof. I then did two semesters at the state School of Arts and Crafts, and I am currently in my fourth semester at the Royal Building Trades School, Erfurt, where I shall remain until the end of the semester.
>
> In the hope that my request will meet with your valuable consideration, I remain, yours faithfully,
>
> Kurt Prüfer[14]

He was swiftly rejected by Ludwig Topf Sr, but this did not deter him from applying again only four months later. In his second application he stated that although he had now completed a fourth term in a building construction course and was working for Erfurt architect Gustav

Leithold, 'a post in your honoured institute ... would correspond more to my wishes'. Again Prüfer was rejected. He worked another year as a foreman and engineer in the construction industry for the A. Dehne building company before making a third application to Topf and Sons in the summer of 1911. This time he was successful and, after a four-week probation period, he was given a full-time job at Topf and Sons on 16 June 1911. Prüfer's determination to join Topf and Sons seems all the more remarkable given that his starting salary of ninety marks a month was significantly lower than what he had been earning before, and he had less responsibility – working not as a foreman but on construction drawings and structural calculations.

Prüfer was employed at Topf and Sons for more than a year, until October 1912 when he was called up to do military service. Enlisted into the 71st Erfurt Regiment, he remained in the army until the end of the First World War. The 71st Erfurt Regiment first saw battle on the Eastern Front in the first Battle of the Maurasian Lakes, but was then transferred to the Western Front in October 1915 and fought at Verdun, the Somme, Arras and Passchendaele.

Historian Annegret Schüle speculates on the impact of these experiences on Prüfer's character: 'The significance of Prüfer's wartime experiences for his later actions should not be underestimated. As a soldier on the Western Front he learned that human life is worthless and he was confronted with mass death. The fact that he himself survived can only have intensified his ambition and pride.'[15]

In truth, though millions of other men were also scarred by the horror and mass casualties of First World War, very few went on to inflict suffering on others in their later lives with such cold calculation.

On 21 December 1918 Kurt Prüfer was discharged from the army and returned to Erfurt to work for the city council as a structural engineer where, for five months, he helped with the clearance of war damage. Prüfer then went back to the Building Trades School and spent another two terms studying civil engineering. He passed his exam on 15 March 1920 and then reverted to his original pre-war ambitions – he returned to work at Topf and Sons.

More than ten years had passed since Prüfer sought to join the company as a teenager. He was now a 29-year-old qualified engineer working in Division D, Furnace Construction. To round out his life, Prüfer also got married at this time, to his wife Frieda, who was a year older than him, but the couple would never have children.

Working in furnace construction, an offshoot of the company's main activities and such a small part of Topf and Sons' income, seems like an odd choice for an ambitious man – but Prüfer had foresight. In 1920, the furnace construction division worked mainly on building industrial furnaces, but Prüfer saw and understood the rising movement for human cremation and anticipated a growing area of business. Annegret Schüle prescribes his interest in cremation as a 'way of working through his encounter with mass death at the Front and of finding a way of dealing with death, within ordered, technical parameters'.[16] It was just as likely, however, to have been a shrewd career move by a man always looking for the next step ahead.

Like most German workers, Prüfer's fortunes fluctuated in the early 1920s and the years of the Weimar Republic. His salary rose dramatically in line with the rampant inflation of the times, but in 1924 he wrote about being dismissed from his job. By mid-1924, however, the situation had stabilised and Prüfer began to receive pay rises that mirrored the growing importance of his work. On 1 March 1924, his wage rose to 290 Goldmarks (the German currency that preceded the Reichsmark) then to 345 on 1 April, before reaching 380 on 1 November. Six months later, he began to receive a commission of 1 per cent gross profit for sales of cremation furnaces and fixtures.

Yet, despite his pay rises, and his seeming determination to work for Topf and Sons against all odds, Prüfer would always feel that he was being treated unfairly at the company and that his 'loyalty' went unrecognised. His personnel file contains none of the warm notes written by the Topf brothers to other employees upon hearing of the birth of babies or death of relatives – and Prüfer himself sends Ludwig Topf only a brief, curtly written Christmas card, which he posts on Christmas Eve, too late to reach his boss on time.

This sense of grievance would be inflamed over the years by a series of tense working relationships – none more strained than that between Prüfer and his soon-to-be manager, Fritz Sander.

Sander was fifteen years older than Prüfer, and came from a more middle-class family, with a father who was an office worker in Leipzig. Like Prüfer, however, Fritz Sander had studied for only an intermediate technical qualification, and had not attended university, nor had he fought in the First World War. But if Prüfer believed that the two men should have been equals, the reality was that Sander was Prüfer's boss as the most senior man in the furnace construction division, and in charge of overseeing all of Prüfer's designs. Sander was also bestowed with a rank and series of responsibilities that demonstrated he was held in a regard by the Topf family never extended to Kurt Prüfer.

After ten years with the company, Sander was promoted to senior engineer. In 1928 he was given joint powers of attorney, meaning that he could represent the company legally with two other company officers. In 1939 this was extended, and Sander was given power of attorney alongside only one other company representative. Despite the crucial role he would play in mediating between the company and the SS, Kurt Prüfer was never awarded this privilege – and the slight rankled. (The Topf brothers note in Prüfer's file that he must never be given the right to oversee business dealings alone, as he is not to be trusted.)

The animosity between the two men was visceral – and ran both ways. Sander often commented on Prüfer's absence record, changing 'due to illness' to 'supposedly due to illness' – or specifically 'supposedly due to gall bladder trouble' on various occasions. His suspicions were perhaps well founded, as Prüfer's absence record totalled more than twenty-four days in 1944 – and he petitioned the company on many other petty matters, including the right to leave work ten minutes early to catch his train:

Erfurt, 2 October 1943

To the company directors

RE. WORKING HOURS

Dear Herr and Herr Topf

The new working hours mean I often have to catch the 17:30 train which, to make matters worse, regularly runs fifteen minutes late. You may not be aware that, due to my wife's illness, I also have to take care of all the food shopping. I am therefore requesting permission to leave ten minutes before the official close of business, so that I can catch the train at 17:12 (which, incidentally, runs on time).

Since my official start time is still 7.30 a.m. but the train gets me here at 7 a.m., I would still be working my full hours.

Hoping you will grant my request.

Kurt Prüfer[17]

Prüfer also filed an insurance claim for a new suit after snagging his jacket on a filing cabinet (the claim was rejected). Sander's distaste for his colleague, and his attitudes, was reflected in a disparaging poem about Prüfer that was published in the 1938 commemorative booklet, which referenced Prüfer's lack of enthusiasm for his work.

Realising that he had little room for advancement in a company that neither liked nor respected him, Prüfer ruthlessly pursued what he considered to be the most effective way forward: developing a successful cremation oven production unit from which he initially took a commission, and cementing a strong personal bond with the SS which he could use as leverage with regards to his employers.

His professional partner in crime would be the dilettante Ludwig Topf, self-styled cremation expert and supposed author of a 1934 Topf advertising brochure, lauding the 'modern process of cremation' used by Topf – and calling the Topf technique 'the purest expression of perfection in cremation technology'.

Together Ludwig Topf and Kurt Prüfer had worked hard to associate Topf and Sons with technologically advanced cremation that fully supported human dignity in death, and had put the company in pole position when the Cremation Act of May 1934 made cremation legal throughout Germany. Now they would also be fully prepared to take advantage of economic opportunities that arose from the mass murders committed by their new political masters.

Ludwig believed that his faith in Topf and Sons was in fact very similar to faith in National Socialism. 'Just as with the war in which we currently find ourselves,' he expounded, 'we must not count the cost but must simply believe, and when we believe then we achieve. The political example of our Führer proves this. He started with just a very small number of men. People back then could have said he was crazy, but he did it.'

CHAPTER THREE

A BEAUTIFUL NAME

Hartmut Topf did not know his father's cousins, Ludwig or Ernst Wolfgang. As a child he never enjoyed the opulence of the family park, and never saw the famous company letters spelled out on the steep roof of the administration building. All that Hartmut knew was that he was from a famous family, a family that had built a business that could make him proud of the Topf name.

> I knew that we were the Topf family, and that Topf was known all over the world for their big factories and chimneys and ovens. I knew I had this beautiful name, and that I belonged to some sort of a dynasty. I still have the contract, written in original handwriting, from when my grandfather decided to leave the business – and the brothers promised each other mutual help.

Hartmut's father, Albert, was the son of Julius Topf, who had dissolved his partnership with Ludwig Sr to concentrate on market gardening.

We all knew that that my great-grandfather founded J. A. Topf and Sons, and that his two sons, my grandfather Julius and his brother Ludwig Sr, took over the company. My grandfather left the company in 1904 and died of sepsis in 1914. Ludwig Sr committed suicide in the same year. I never knew them.

Hartmut's one remaining link to his grandfather Julius is a copy of Julius's curriculum vitae. In a later version, typed up by Hartmut's Uncle Heinz during the Third Reich, all references to being a Freemason have been removed. 'He omitted all signs and secret hints of Masonry, because under the Nazis it was forbidden.' Despite the dangers, however, Hartmut's father, Albert, would always keep the last vestiges of Julius's history as a Mason. 'My father, Albert, lost his own father when he was fourteen,' Hartmut says. 'He was always longing for a father.'

As the youngest of the nine siblings, Albert Topf was the baby of the family. Hartmut says: 'Everybody loved him because he was the youngest. His older sisters all took care of him wherever they could. My father was sort of a pet child for the whole family, and he was helpful to everybody.' Albert grew up and lived in Erfurt until he was twenty-eight. After completing a compulsory year of military service, he graduated from the engineering school at Ilmenau and then worked in a factory before moving to Berlin. By this stage Julius's widow and children were no longer on speaking terms with Else Topf or her two sons, Ludwig and Ernst Wolfgang so, despite Albert's inclination towards science and engineering, there was no possibility of a career at the family firm. Instead Albert took a job with electrical giant Siemens and moved to a wooden hut in Siemensstadt a town close to the factory near Spandau, on the outskirts of Berlin. Returning to Erfurt to see his family, he would meet and then marry a local girl, Irmgard, who was working at his sister Agnes's kindergarten – just across the street from the Topf family park.

Part of Albert's work involved developing 16 mm film and film cameras for Siemens and he often took home movies of his new wife and young family. One silent reel shows Irmgard sitting in the back garden of the kindergarten singing with her colleagues; another shows their new baby Hartmut being spoon-fed dinner by his grandmother. 'I was born and baptised in Siemensstadt,' says Hartmut. 'Berlin was a booming industrial town and Siemens had a huge factory. I spent the first year of my life in that wooden cabin, and my father would add on to it every year, making it very comfortable and well fitted out.' Although Siemensstadt was his father's world, Hartmut would occasionally visit the homes of some of the men Albert worked with, and come away with the odd present, like a toy train.

Hartmut's most vivid memories of his childhood begin, however, when the family bought a parcel of land in the then almost rural suburb of Falkensee, where they built their own home. Albert's brother Karl, an architect who had also built the Erfurt kindergarten, helped design a large modern house with two rooms downstairs, three rooms upstairs and a central heating system: 'There was a bathroom with an oven that you could heat with coal or wood and once a week on the weekend everybody got a warm bath,' Hartmut remembers. It was a major step up for the family who had received no notable upturn in their finances – Albert Topf cycled the two miles to the station every day for his train ride to Siemens where he worked at the same engineering job.

At Falkensee, Hartmut, his parents and his two sisters, Elke and Karin, settled into a happy family life.

'I saw our house being built as a small child,' Hartmut says. 'I remember some of the craftspeople working there, like the bricklayers. I grew up in that house and in that garden. We had a piano, a very important thing in those early years.'

Hartmut's father could be taciturn and quiet: 'He was sometimes a bit blunt and he could be very short with you. He had a strange sense of humour. He was not a big speaker.' At home Albert would work away on a big table, making progress on his latest film project, or his glass photography negatives.

We did have some books in the house, like an encyclopaedia and books about the Masons and the Nazis, but really my father was a very good craftsman.

He was interested in the development of film and photography from an engineering point of view, not an artistic point of view. My Uncle Heinz in Erfurt was a stamp collector and he tried to interest me in that – but my father always made it clear that he thought stamp collecting was a waste of time, even though he often had to buy the latest stamps and seals and send them back to Erfurt.

Yet, for a German family of the time, Hartmut remembers his parents were also unusually open people – leaving their desk open with their chequebook and bank statements for Hartmut to look at.

Despite living in Berlin, the family made frequent trips back to Erfurt where they saw Hartmut's grandmother Topf for the remaining few years of her life, as well as his mother's parents who were originally from poor village families, but who had come to town to be tailors. Hartmut remembers his father adopting the role of little diplomat and peacemaker among his brother and sisters.

> One of his sisters lived in the countryside where she had bought a strange house that looked a bit like a castle but was actually a folly built by a coffee importer. She lived with another woman, a painter. I think they were lesbians and sometimes they had terrible fights and my father would have to go down to help them get back together. My father was judge and jury in all the family quarrels.

This tendency of subservience to his siblings would play out most notably in Albert Topf's relationship with his older brother, Hans.

Hans had been active in a German youth movement called *Wandervogel*, which translates as 'wandering bird'. The aim of the group was to encourage young men and women to shake off the shackles of society and get back to nature and freedom. Unlike the boy scouts, the society had no uniform but encouraged hiking, playing folk songs and avoiding smoking or drinking. 'I still have the songbook of this movement – the *Zupfgeigenhansel*,' Hartmut says. 'It was deeply rooted in German tradition, fairy tales and music, and they played the guitar and sang a fantastic collection of German songs.' Hartmut's father, Albert, also joined the *Wandervogel*, practising craftwork and making lamps and toys from plywood. 'That was my father's philosophical background. They were a bit nationalist but not too much.' The *Wandervogel* certainly stressed the spirit of adventure and Germany's 'Teutonic roots', but also had many Jewish members. It was outlawed by the Nazis in 1933, along with other youth groups that were not part of the Hitler Youth – and *Wandervogel* members became both prominent supporters and opponents of the Third Reich. In the case of the Topf brothers, both became Nazi Party members, with Albert following the ideological lead of Hans.

> My Uncle Hans was an engineer, a respected person – and a smoker. My parents did not smoke and my mother would always say: 'Hans is smoking again!' At Christmas he sang traditional Christmas songs, and my father, who thought religion was humbug, would mock him a bit behind his back. But Hans was the oldest brother and he liked to show off that he was a Nazi, and better than my father. He had children from his first marriage to the Reemtsma family, who were an established tobacco family, and then he'd married again to my Aunt Berta and had a step-daughter called Hanni who taught me piano.

Vividly, Hartmut recalls that Hans liked to show off his Nazi uniform.

> My father didn't have a uniform. Hans had a party uniform that he would wear at important events – he was silly like that – and he sometimes would tell me: 'You don't say "Guten Tag, Uncle Hans," you say "Heil Hitler, Uncle Hans!"' He showed off a bit about being a Nazi.

Hartmut believes that Hans encouraged his brother to become a Nazi, and although the records show that both men were 'cell leaders' (leaders of several blocks), Hartmut recalls that his father only ever reached the lowest rank of block leader.

Perhaps Hans encouraged my father to join the Nazi Party, because in Siemensstadt my father put a warning on his letterbox not to push in any newspapers or letters that would disturb the nesting birds. But in a letter that he wrote to my mother in Erfurt, my father complained that the Nazis were 'so nasty' they ignored his warning – and didn't even care about the birds. That was my father's reaction to the Nazis – they were nasty – yet later he became a member of the party. I don't know exactly when he joined the party, but he did.

After building the house in Falkensee, Albert and Hans Topf were closer in both proximity and ideology – living only a few houses apart and connected through a special telephone line. During the air raids in the war, one family would ring the other and make sure everything was alright.

Uncle Hans had built his house earlier. It was a wooden house, and so the neighbours called us the 'wooden Topf' and the 'stone Topf', based on the type of house we lived in. In between us there was our Uncle Kurt, a friend of my father, who lived in his little house with his wife and son. So we were the children in the neighbourhood, and every family had a certain call or whistle in the evening when the children were supposed to come home. The Trumans simply shouted: 'Doris! Gerda!', when they wanted their girls to come home. An engineer whistled for his children, and they knew to listen out for that. My family had a tune that was whistled when it was time for us to come home. We were always playing outside and I remember my father would approach on his bicycle and ring his bell for us, which had two tones, bing-bong, bing-bong, bing-bong. That sound remains a vivid memory for me.

Hartmut's parents encouraged him to enjoy a carefree childhood; playing games and learning the piano with Hanni – but he was also a young boy growing up in the Third Reich and his adolescence would be shaped by the formative years he spent near wartime Berlin.

Before the war we heard that Hitler was coming through our neighbourhood, and my father went to a furniture shop to buy a folding table that you could sit on top of so that we could all climb on and see the Führer. I was quite excited because normally the Führer did not come to a place like Falkensee – and we got a glimpse of this big, mysterious, figure.

Once the war had started, like any young boy, Hartmut immersed himself in the adventures of battles and German heroes:

We collected postcards of all the military heroes who had earned distinctions for their service in the air force or in submarines – and we saw the bombers flying in big formations, and then we saw the strikes. At night the pilots made light marks for where to bomb, red or green, and then the other planes came and bombed. In Falkensee itself there were only a few bombs: one that destroyed two houses and left a big crater in the street, and another one that hit the house of a neighbour. It blew her arm off, which was left behind in the kitchen.

In the streets, Hartmut collected bomb splinters and traded them with his friends at school: 'We'd say: "I've got a big one; this is a bronze one; this is only steel", and so on.'

At Christmas time, Hartmut noticed that their traditional glass and ceramic ornaments were replaced each year by something of poorer quality, either pieces of decorated metal or even badges with war slogans on them.

While no one spoke openly about the dark side of life under the Nazis, ominous signs were there. Hartmut remembers that:

There was a man called Uncle Max. He was actually the uncle of a neighbour and he was a member of a police guard of a military airport. He had this fancy uniform, not the regular uniform – he looked like a forester, actually – and he called himself a Luftwaffe inspector. But really he was just the night guard of an airport. One day a boy from the neighbourhood told me a funny story, but told me not to repeat the joke, as Uncle Max had told him it would land you in a concentration camp. Then this boy explained to me the little that he knew from Uncle Max about what a concentration camp was.

The boy told Hartmut:

It's a prison camp for our enemies. These enemies could be brutal robbers, murderers, or communists. The boy didn't really have more details, but he knew that at least there was a distinction by the colour of their triangle, and they all had numbers like prisoners. That's all he told me – but then I had an image that there are camps for those enemies that we don't want to have with us.

When Hartmut's mother once questioned what was happening to the

Jews, Uncle Hans told her: 'Don't ask questions like that. You might end up in a concentration camp.' Hartmut says:

> I heard that people disappeared, but we did not live in a neighbourhood with communists or Jewish people. In his party function, my father had to collect for winter relief, and there were some people he did not like because they didn't want to give. That was their tiny bit of resistance; we don't want to give. They were well-off people but simply didn't give their two or three marks. My father was angry about that.

Although Hartmut describes his father as a rather naïve Nazi, haplessly collecting fur coats and skis to send to the German troops on the front line at Stalingrad, Albert was committed enough to send ten-year-old Hartmut for a trial at a Nazi boarding school near the town of Ballenstedt on the edge of the Harz mountains. Wearing his Hitler Youth shirt, Hartmut was ushered into a room with another boy who immediately told him that he was hungry.

> I think that was a test. It felt like they wanted to find out whether I would share what I had. I had some sandwiches and I shared them with this boy and I passed the test. Then I was taken to the dormitory with twenty beds, and for two weeks we had classes and exercises and very hard things to do, things that would really test your courage. There were many things I did not like and which I did not do well in.

Hartmut cemented his disappointing record as a young Nazi on the last night when the boys were roused from their beds with the threat of an air raid.

We got dressed and had to queue up in a big square where some officers in uniform started speaking to us. 'Boys,' they told us. 'American parachutists have landed and they are stealing our firewood, but we'll get them!' We had no guns, only stones and sticks and we started running through the forest. The moon was shining, the wind was blowing. It was a very magical night and there were a lot of explosives going off. We would run this way and that and then behind us a big bang would go off.

Eventually Hartmut got separated from the group, and made his way back to the dormitory alone.

One of the young officers, about fourteen or fifteen years old, came in with a list and he told us that one boy had died in his arms by the creek – and he wanted to know how many we had captured or even killed or beaten. I spoke up and I said it was all organised by them, and that they had used explosives. As boys we had already learned how to open unexploded bombs and grenades. It was very risky to play with those, but I was from the city and knew all about it. The other boys at the school were country boys, and this was their big adventure. Now their heroic fight had been ruined by this big mouth from Berlin who had told them it was all fake. Everyone was very angry with me.

The next morning was Hartmut's tenth birthday and when he went down to breakfast he found his place at the long table decorated with apples and treats. He was told, however, that he had failed the entrance requirements to become a pupil and his father had arrived to take him home.

They felt that I was too weak for them, and I was lucky to be weak.

Because these schools were breeding institutes for the next generation of leaders and those leaders had to be, as the Nazis put it, 'quick as wind, as hard as Krupp's steel and as enduring as leather'. Those were the phrases they coined for their future leaders. I failed the test.

Later Hartmut's father told him that when he arrived at the school to collect him, he had passed the sick bay that was full of those supposed 'American parachutists' – who were really older boys in the school who had been badly beaten by Hartmut's young classmates.

German fears about American parachutists and invasion were far from baseless, though. Despite newspapers continuing to speak of German successes and claim victory as the only possible conclusion, defeat at Stalingrad had turned the tide against the Nazis. The war was going badly for Germany and Albert Topf and his brother Hans knew it.

I remember my father was very nervous, pacing up and down. When the news came in about Stalingrad, he literally had a heart attack. They could feel that it was to be the beginning of the end, and I listened to conversations about the Eastern Front moving closer and closer towards us in Berlin. A few weeks before the end of the war I heard the adults in the family talking and they were saying – should we commit suicide or not? I heard this and even as a child I was very much aware of the possibility that a person could kill themselves. I knew that, and I think the will to survive and not to commit suicide is a testimony to freedom of decision. I think the definition of freedom to me is that I accept my life, and that was something I learned as a child.

More than seventy years later, the conversation remains vivid: 'I remember it so clearly,' Hartmut says. 'My Uncle Hans was so preoccupied he burned the skin on my hand with his cigarette.' Yet, despite their role as active members of the Nazi Party, Hartmut says his family's discussion about suicide came about due to fear of the Russians, not because of guilt over any wrongdoing.

> My father and Uncle Hans were afraid of revenge from the other side, nothing else. They didn't feel guilty. They wanted to escape punishment and revenge from the Allies, mainly from the Russians. The Russians were still big monsters in our imagination, and when they came of course there were a lot of assaults and rapes. But the propaganda made them seem even worse – man-eaters who would come and burn everything and kill everybody. As far as I remember, there was no discussion about guilt. They had not denounced anybody; they had not punished anybody. They had not stolen anything from anyone, not consciously. Of course, the Nazis had stolen from the Jews on a big scale, the state had stolen. But my father and uncle did not take part.

On Hitler's birthday, 20 April 1945, Hartmut watched his father sling a small Italian gun over his back and set off on his bicycle to fight as part of the *Volkssturm*, men forming the last defence of Berlin. Albert Topf and Hans headed towards a part of the suburb where there was heavy bombardment and, at first, Hartmut would go out to meet them with supplies of food until his mother told him it was too dangerous to continue. After a few days word reached them that the Russian army was coming.

Hartmut was playing outside, wearing his cap which he'd adorned with an aluminium badge from the SS. One of his neighbours told him: 'Take that badge off; they'll kill you.'

There they were. The Russians. Many of them were drunk and they were already celebrating a great victory. We were astonished that they were so different from the German soldiers. They would not even stand up to salute an officer – they'd say 'hello, yeah…' They had a rough style. They came with little horses and very small trucks, and some of them would occasionally give something to the children like a piece of bread. They were simple fellows, and they saw home comforts they had never seen in their lives. Most of them had never used a toilet before.

As the Russians came closer the children ran in off the streets and families locked their doors. Hartmut's father had not returned from the fighting, and when the Russians went house to house in Falkensee, it was Hartmut's responsibility as the man of the family to let them in.

I opened the old door to the basement and they came in; men, men, men, and they also said 'uri, uri', that was their word for watches. They had five wristwatches or ten spread out on their arms. They were so proud to have them all. We only had a very old-fashioned clock somewhere, no wristwatches at all. So they went through all the rooms, 'look, look, are there any soldiers?' Nothing. They opened the cupboards, and then they left. They didn't steal. My main feeling was not fear, but excitement – they were not so dangerous.

On the last day of fighting a car pulled up and Uncle Hans fell out, bleeding profusely after having been shot through the neck, but there was still no sign of Hartmut's father. 'Some neighbours who returned said that he had never been able to fire a shot, he was probably dead.' Instead Albert Topf had been captured, but had managed to talk his way out of being sent to Russia to work as an engineer. Some weeks later he returned to the family home, but he was soon summoned for further questioning by the Russians.

'He went there one evening without any force,' Hartmut says. 'I met him in the street when he was on his way there and he sent me back home. That was the last time I ever saw him. He did not come back.'

The next day Hartmut took some bread and a razor, but the guard told him that the men had been rounded up and taken away in lorries.

'Much later we got this secret smuggled note from my father saying: "I'm in Sachsenhausen, try to send me a pencil and a sweater."' Sachsenhausen was a former Nazi concentration camp north of Berlin in Oranienburg, which had been repurposed as a Soviet prison camp for holding German prisoners. Renamed Special Camp No. 7, the Soviet camp at Sachsenhausen housed as many as 16,000 prisoners in 1946 and the Sachsenhausen memorial records the following information about conditions there:

Hunger and cold prevailed in the Special Camp. The inadequate sanitary conditions and insufficient nourishment led to disease epidemics. Usually the barracks were overcrowded; the prisoners had to sleep on the bare-wood frames until 1947, when the Soviet camp administration distributed blankets and bags of straw. The only clothing which the prisoners had during their imprisonment was what they were wearing at the time of their arrest. The possession of personal items, particularly books and writing material, was strictly forbidden. Violations of these rigid camp regulations, which were for the most part unknown to most of the prisoners, resulted in harsh punishment imposed by the Soviet guard personnel or the German prisoners who held special functions.

Unlike camps within the Soviet Union, however, Special Camp No. 7 was not a work camp, and prisoners endured a life of enforced idleness.

'I went with my mother and we stood outside and tried to get a glimpse of him, but we could see nothing,' Hartmut says. Years passed with no news, until a former German officer knocked on Irmgard Topf's door and told her that her husband had died, at least two years earlier, on 27 March 1947. 'Death certificates would always attribute the cause of death to pneumonia, a lung infection or a heart attack, but prisoners were really dying of starvation. I was sorry when I heard the news.'

On a grey day in April 2017, Hartmut Topf revisits the place where his father died. The remains of the Soviet camp are further back from the main camp, which is now a memorial for the victims of the Nazis. Hartmut acknowledges it is difficult to know how to appropriately remember the German Nazi prisoners who died in Soviet camps which had previously been Nazi concentration camps. 'Not all victims are equal,' Hartmut says, 'but all suffering is equal.' He bypasses a large monolithic monument constructed in the Soviet era, and chooses instead to visit a small museum erected to house the story and artefacts of German prisoners at the Soviet camp. He seems to struggle to explain his feelings for the man who was, in many ways, a very traditional German father:

> If you ask me were we close, I can't say. He taught me to do things, like how to skin one of the rabbits we fattened up in the back garden and ate on special occasions. And, of course, my father was the person who introduced me to puppet theatre. He put a blanket into a doorframe, and we had funny shadow puppet shows with classical texts and music from a guitar. My father would be filming with his camera and we would be watching through the window. It was magical. People are wrong when they say that puppet theatre is an imitation of life. It's not an imitation of life, it's a different life.

Both Albert and Hans Topf died in Sachsenhausen, but years later Hartmut discovered that Uncle Hans had withheld from them the biggest secret of all.

> Hans's wife, Tante Berta, and her daughter, Hanni, emigrated to Brazil in 1948 and we would get small parcels from them with coffee, chocolate and soap. My mother was mystified by the address on the envelopes, because they were from a Jewish family. One day she blurted out – 'But we don't know any Jewish families!' and Uncle Kurt, our neighbour in Falkensee, shrugged and said that Tante Berta was not quite 'so Aryan' after all. So Uncle Hans must have known this, but he showed off: 'I'm a Nazi.'

As the remaining male heir of one branch of a 'beautiful' family, Hartmut was astonished and horrified to sit in a darkened Falkensee cinema and see the Topf name branded above the ovens of the Nazi concentration camps in post-war newsreels. 'I had many questions that I would have liked to ask my father: why was he a Nazi? Did he know what was happening?' Hartmut says. However, with his father and Uncle Hans gone there was no one left to ask – and it would take decades for him to unravel the truth about his family legacy.

CHAPTER FOUR

BUCHENWALD

'Between us and Weimar lies Buchenwald.
There's no way we can get around that.'[18]

Deep within the grounds of Buchenwald concentration camp lie the remains of an oak tree. This broadened, flattened stump is no ordinary tree; it symbolises the last vestiges of the beautiful old oak where connoisseurs of German literature believe Goethe once met with Frau von Stein, sat on the banks of the Ettersberg hill and carved inscriptions. The Ettersberg dominates the otherwise flat Thuringian farmland and looks down on one sunny side to Weimar, and on the other colder side to Erfurt. This divide speaks much about the common distinction held about the two cities, and is reflected in the fact that the camp was built so that the prisoners faced down to Erfurt, while the SS officers were housed across the ridge, gazing down every morning across the green forests into Weimar, the mythical city of Goethe, Schiller and Liszt.

Ettersberg concentration camp, as it was originally known as, was rather urgently renamed when the Nazi cultural organisation complained about any link between this golden age of German history and the outcasts and enemies of the Third Reich. Although it was officially known as KL Buchenwald/Post Weimar from then on, the farmers of Thuringia called it by another name: The Lighthouse.

Every night the searchlights of Buchenwald would illuminate the top of the Ettersberg and flood the surrounding landscape with their glare – so that no one could ignore the presence of this place. By morning another group of local residents would turn their faces from their drawing boards and look up at the Ettersberg through their office windows. These would be the furnace engineers of Topf and Sons who, sitting in their third-floor offices in the administration building, not only knew of the presence of Buchenwald, but also understood its true meaning. Kurt Prüfer's desk gave perhaps the clearest view of all.

Working in front of this window, on 17 May 1939, a whole four months before the outbreak of the Second World War, Kurt Prüfer produced his first drawing for a 'mobile oil-heated cremation oven' with muffle. To distinguish this from his work in civil crematoria Prüfer carefully labelled it an 'incineration chamber' not a 'cremation chamber'. This conveniently spirited away, in two words, the normal requirements for 'human reverence', which required bodies to be cremated in super-heated air. From this point on they could be disposed of in the same way as animal carcasses or garbage.

By October, Topf and Sons were ready to demonstrate their invention; they set up their mobile incineration chamber just outside the gates of Buchenwald so that they could trial it. Prisoner Max Mayr later reported that 'a mobile incineration oven was tried out in front of the camp gate'.[19] Other prisoners told him it was supplied by Topf and Sons. Another prisoner, architect Franz Ehrlich, who was forced to work in the SS construction management unit after his release on October 24 1939, made a note that at the time of

test buildings for a mobile crematorium by the Erfurt company Topf and Sons, all leading engineers and technicians of the company were involved. Crematorium taken over by representatives of the Chancellery of the Führer in the presence of company representatives. The Topf and Sons representatives are aware that these drivable crematoria are intended for the liquidation of whole municipalities in Poland. They performed the capacity calculations.

From their establishment in 1933, the death rate in concentration camps was always much higher than in ordinary life, or even in normal prisons – and the work of the directors and engineers of Topf and Sons would be to immerse themselves in finding technical solutions to this horror.

Although local residents would later say: 'We didn't know,' when shown evidence of the years or torture and mass murder that occurred at the camp, the life of Weimar, Erfurt and hundreds of local businesses was inexorably intertwined with the camp from the very beginning.

Since the nineteenth century, Weimar had been a hotbed of anti-Semitism. It was 'the centre for gravity for the most Germanic Germany and for the most German of Germans',[20] serving as home to Elisabeth Forster-Nietzsche's cerebral anti-Semitism, and a group of semi-intellectuals including Ernst Wachler, Friedrich Lienhard and newspaper art critic Mathilde Freiin von Freytag-Loringhoven who focused on the idea of the German *volk* as defined by a racist perspective.

It was also home to Adolf Bartels, a torridly prolific writer based in Weimar, and a vicious anti-Semite. It was Bartels who introduced the idea that Jews were biologically inferior, as well as suggesting the re-settlement of the eastern European Slavs with racially pure Germans.

This ideology overlapped with another group of thinkers in Weimar – exemplified by Johannes Schlaf, who adopted a theory of biological inequalities through which people could redeem themselves by eugenic self-selection, the most ideal genotype being Nordic man. Schlaf had welcomed First World War believing it a good chance for cleansing Europe of decadent French and English culture and letting German customs and culture triumph throughout Europe. For these men Weimar was a 'healing antidote to the intellectual urbanity and attendant perversions of the capital'.[21]

As Michael Kater writes in his book on the town, 'Weimar became a hunting ground for anti-urbanists, eugenicists, befuddled German history memorialists all buttressed by anti-Semitism of various shades.'[22]

Weimar of course also had a very different legacy during this time – being the home to both the Bauhaus movement, which attracted possibly the biggest collection of artistic geniuses of the twentieth century, including Paul Klee, Wassily Kandinsky, Lyonel Feininger and sculptor Gerhard Marcks – and giving its name, through hosting the country's first national assembly in 1919, to the Weimar Republic, Germany's ill-fated attempt at social democracy which ended with Nazi rule.

Yet such strong countervailing trends did not stop Weimar

becoming an early base of the Nazi movement, and the town proved so sympathetic to Hitler he visited more than thirty-five times before he became Chancellor, enjoying, in particular, the Hotel Elephant in the main market square. In 1926, the Nazis felt the town was a safe haven for their first party rally (a role subsequently taken up by Nuremberg). Hitler was unaware that Rosa Schmidt, the wife of the owner of the downmarket Hotel Hohenzollern, which served as the organisational headquarters for the rally, and the site of his first speech in Weimar in 1925, was in fact Jewish. The Nazis would catch up with Frau Schmidt eventually; she died in Auschwitz in 1944.

Thuringia and Weimar always had a higher percentage of Nazi Party members than the Reich as a whole (14.3 per cent versus 11.7 per cent nationally) – as well as a higher number of Nazis represented in individual professions, like medicine. In 1930, Wilhelm Frick became the first Nazi minister in Germany, taking up the post of Minister for Internal Affairs and Education for Thuringia. By 1932, Thuringia had a Nazi First Minister, Fritz Sauckel, and in the elections of that year more than half of Weimar's citizens voted for Hitler, in comparison to 37.3 per cent nationally (a figure that was 10 per cent lower again in most of the big cities).

Weimar had no synagogue and the town's Jewish population, which had never been large, had dwindled to forty-three families by 1933. Five years later and only one Jewish business remained, a doll shop run by a widow called Hedwig Hetteman. On Kristallnacht the shop was destroyed, the front display window smashed and the dolls, which the children of Weimar had loved, were thrown out on to the road. After being driven from their homes into 'Jew Houses', Hedwig Hetteman joined Weimar's last remaining Jews on one of the three transports between April and September 1942 to the death camps of the east. She died in the 'liquidation camp' at Majdanek in Poland (where all victims were sent immediately to their deaths).

'Weimar is a centre of Hitlerdom,' wrote Thomas Mann who visited the town in 1932, and was unnerved by the strange mixture of Nazis and Goethe. 'Everywhere you could see Hitler's picture etc. in the National Socialist newspapers on exhibit. The town was dominated by the type of young person who walks through the streets vaguely determined, offering the Roman salute, one to the other.'[23]

The region's deep links to the Nazi Party were symbolised by the founding of the very first concentration camp in Germany near the Thuringian village of Nohra in early March 1933, which lay a few miles west of Weimar on the road to Erfurt. As the concentration camp system became more organised and established, a larger, permanent concentration camp at Dachau, near Munich, was opened on 22 March 1933. This was followed by a large network of up to 150 smaller camps within Germany, which were then consolidated by Reich Leader Heinrich Himmler. The camp at Sachsenhausen, outside Berlin, was opened in July 1936 – and Buchenwald followed in July 1937.

From the first, Buchenwald aimed to be a proto-type concentration camp and in early 1945 it was still the largest concentration camp in existence. The formal history of the camp states that 'all of the system's functional expansions found concrete realisation here. Buchenwald was the camp for the isolation of "community enemies" and for the repression of resistance in Germany and the occupied countries. Furthermore, with its total of 136 sub-camps, it was part of the SS's vast forced labour emporium.'[24] In other words, it would combine the political and economic interests of the SS in one vast complex.

The SS had ambitious plans for concentration camps and Weimar had ambitious plans to be at the heart of Nazi Germany. Buchenwald, constructed in a spot of great meaning in Germany history, and, until then, a popular local destination for day trips, represented the apex of such designs.

Buchenwald inmate, and later historian of the camp, Eugen Kogon wrote:

The choice of the site was symbolic in a higher sense: Weimar, the national centre of German culture, formerly the city of German classical writers who had given German emotion and intellect their highest expression, and Buchenwald, a raw piece of land on which the new German emotion was to flower. Together a sentimentally cultivated museum culture and the unscrupulous, brutal will for power thus created the typical new connection Weimar-Buchenwald.[25]

Plans to build the camp were initiated in May 1936 by Inspector of the Concentration Camps and Chief of the SS Totenkopf Squadrons, Theodor Eicke, and the Reich leader of Thuringia Fritz Sauckel. The chief of the Thuringian police department for the Ministry of the Interior Hellmuth Gommlich, a longstanding Nazi and anti-Semite, was charged with finding the site for the camp and its establishment. After considering several alternatives, Gommlich and Eicke decided on a wooded limestone ridge on the north slope of the Ettersberg – a decision much welcomed by the local farmers, according to a letter from Gommlich to Eicke: 'At a joint meeting the local farmers' association submitted a declaration to me to the effect that the establishment of a camp at the site I have proposed meets with their fullest approval. The association urgently requests the realisation of the plan as quickly as possible.'[26]

The SS constructed the first barracks on the north side of the camp before the inmates arrived, and on 15 July 1937 the first lorries pulled up with 149 inmates from Sachsenhausen, followed in subsequent weeks by transports from newly closed concentration camps at Sachsenburg near Chemnitz, and Lichtenburg.

Helmut Thiermann described his transport from Sachsenburg on 27 July:

The lorries were covered with tarps and it was only through the noise on the roads and the ventilation flaps in the tarps that we could guess more than witness the course of the journey ... when we drove into a densely wooded area [on the far side of Weimar] we knew that we had reached our destination.

Thiermann goes on to describe his first night at Buchenwald:

On the first night we shared the barracks with the SS and the next day we moved to the actual camp, Block 7. Following our arrival we received red cloth triangles and two long canvas strips with numbers which we had to sew to our jackets and trousers in precisely designated places. I received number 318. From now on we were mere numbers and name-less beings. We completed the construction of a partially built barrack, Block 7, and moved into this block the same day.'[27] The red triangle denoted that Thiermann was a political prisoner.

During the 1930s, concentration camps accommodated the victims of the Nazis' progressively more extreme racial and social persecution. The Nazi vision of a society in which 'natural simplicity of the German people' would unite with 'energy strength and assertiveness'[28] first focused on disabled people – leading to their forced sterilisation 'for the prevention of genetically ill offspring' in 1933, and their eventual murder under the Nazi euthanasia programme during the war.

In addition, the Nazis tightened their grip on 'asocials', a category of 'national vermin' that included convicted criminals and homosexuals. In 1935, increasingly the police began using 'preventive police detention' as a way of 'cleansing' society. Aimed initially at criminals and gay men, in February 1937, Himmler ordered the rounding up of 2,000 of those who 'endanger society through their asocial behaviour'. Many of the victims of these mass arrests found themselves transported to the gates of Buchenwald. By December of that year 7,746 people were held as prisoners in Nazi concentration camps.

Five miles of wooded road separate Buchenwald from Weimar, but 'blood road', as it was known by the inmates who built it and often died doing so, created a symbiotic connection between the life of town and camp.

'There existed many everyday connections between Weimar and the camp, from the beginning to the end.' Michael Kater notes, 'Many of these were part of a tight administrative, commercial and human-relations network. There was no escape from this.'[29]

Buchenwald became an incorporated part of the town of Weimar on 1 April 1938, six months after the town council had filed an application to bring the two together, expecting it to be a union of great financial benefit. From this point on Buchenwald had a Weimar telephone code, and soon its own suburban post office. Weimar supplied both a water supply, and firefighters responsible for the camp until 1942, as well as convening a special Nazi court in the town when two inmates murdered an SS guard and were subsequently recaptured and executed. A municipal bus service connected the two locations, six times a day for a thirty-minute ride that cost 40 pfennig.

SS officers were a common presence on the streets of Weimar; attending the opera, giving free music recitals in town squares, entering their German Shepherds in dog shows and playing in SS football teams against neighbouring sides. Children of SS officers often attended local schools, and one theatre even offered a special SS subscription rate. In August 1939, the SS organised a huge summer festival in Weimar, on land near the camp, where they laid on sausage stands, coloured balloons, games booths and much singing and dancing. 'Everywhere something was frying and steaming,' wrote one happy local participant. 'Two huge oxen were grilled on spits.'[30]

The presence and movements of the SS regiments up at the camp were frequently reported in the local newspapers and ordinary town people often saw the inmates of Buchenwald for themselves; marching past in labour detachments, or employed in local businesses like wholesalers, or in construction teams on prominent sites, including the Hotel Elephant. When the SS feared that potential bombing raids could destroy historic Weimar sites – like Goethe or Schiller's houses, former craftsmen now incarcerated in the camp were forced to make replicate furniture to be displayed in the houses until the end of the war while the real furniture was safely stored elsewhere.

More than sixty Weimar firms used labour from Buchenwald

between 1942 and 1945, and for the duration of its existence more than forty Weimar firms profited from serving and supplying the camp. Nazi Party chapter leader, town councillor and SS officer Thilo Bornschein provided almost all the foodstuffs to the camp, and became rich enough to afford *Bauhaus-Muche's Haus am Horn*. His turnover in 1941 alone was half a million Reichsmarks. Hans Kroger, who had taken over the Aryanised Herman Tietz mixed goods department store for the equivalent of less than a penny, operated a near monopoly on textiles, while local butcher Karl Daniel provided sausages (known as rubber sausages due to their appalling quality) and brewery Deinhardt shipped beer to the SS. The historic apothecary in the quaint main town square supplied SS physicians with the drugs they frequently used to kill people.

In total, many local people either serviced the camp, or met its inmates on the road, on a building site, or even in town itself working on a forced labour project. A snapshot photo, taken in 1939, shows a gang of inmates marching down a street in the neighbouring village of Gaberndorf, while a man and a small boy lean against an open door watching curiously, but impassively.

For some local residents, interaction with the camp was even more sinister. Take, for example, the doctors, nurses and administrators in the Weimar municipal hospital that treated both SS officers from the camp, and some camp inmates, up until the summer of 1938. It was in these hospitals that some camp prisoners were brought to be forcibly sterilised. Those physicians were certainly aware of the terrible circumstances in Buchenwald. So, too, was the Weimar office of public health and its employees, who were responsible for setting rations for camp food and for overseeing the response to the typhus epidemic of 1939 that arose due to appalling hygiene conditions.

Until the outbreak of war there were three main categories of prisoners. Criminals had a green triangle on their uniforms, while political prisoners, mostly communists, had a red triangle. The uniforms of Jewish prisoners bore a yellow star. Buchenwald also had several hundred Jehovah's Witnesses, who had a purple star on their uniforms, and forty-three gay men who had a pink star. The number of inmates rose significantly during the war, but looking at a timeline of arrivals in the late 1930s the following main points stand out: by spring 1938 the camp held 2,500 men. In June that number was bolstered by 500, when the first Jewish prisoners arrived. Then, in September 1939, a further 2,300 political prisoners arrived from Dachau. But by far the greatest influx of prisoners occurred in November and December 1938, after Kristallnacht. More than 10,000 Jewish prisoners were rounded up and committed to Buchenwald, but most were released again after pledging to leave Germany.

During these years Buchenwald was officially designated a Category II camp, for prisoners who could be 'reformed', but only with difficulty. (By comparison Mauthausen was the only Category I camp, for prisoners deemed impossible to reform, Dachau was a Category III camp where it was supposedly easier to gain release.)

Yet for those imprisoned within its 3 km of electrified fencing, this must have seemed the most arbitrary of designations. Life for inmates at Buchenwald was designed to be as intolerable and inhumane as possible. Later in the history of the camp, the SS would recognise the economic benefits it could reap from such a large slave-labour population – but in the beginning the emphasis was less on 'efficiency' and far more on punishment and probable death, usually at the hands of sadists and psychopaths. Before the outbreak of war, Buchenwald had the highest mortality rate of any concentration camp.

The regime of Buchenwald's first commander, Karl-Otto Koch, and his equally detested wife, Ilse, was characterised by capricious cruelty, corruption and graft. Prisoner William Gellinick recalls hearing Ilse Koch saying to her husband: 'My little pigeon, I think it is time for that old man to grovel a bit,' before the prisoner was made to roll up and down a hill, sustaining injuries which led to his death. The Kochs had two children during their time in charge of Buchenwald, and Karl Koch was photographed with his small son petting a deer in the grounds of the Buchenwald Zoo, which was located just outside the perimeter fence, overlooking the crematorium. The caption in the Koch family photo album read: 'At the zoo with Daddy'.

Visibly resisting any rules led to certain death, and the SS specialised in introducing conflicting ones that made it impossible to survive. For example, a guard would throw an inmate's cap in the direction of the barbed wire fence and order him to fetch it. If he did so he was shot for trying to escape, if he refused he was shot for disobeying orders.

Those who survived the long hours of roll call, standing outside every morning and evening in snow and rain, could then be crushed to death by falling boulders in the quarry or hit by runaway loading cars. In one such 'occupational accident', Jewish inmate Horst Loewenberg was chased to his death by a lorry driven by the SS.

Prisoners were routinely tortured. They were hung from trees in the woods and whipped, or locked up in the infamous arrest cells run by notorious sadist Martin Sommer – who liked to personally strangle his victims and kept an electrified skull on his desk. Those who did not die from overwork or torture could starve on the tiny rations of food (prisoners were allowed no more than 550 grams of bread with a small piece of sausage, some thin soup and ¼ litre of drinking water per day, but were often served half of this portion), or be killed in one of the camp's notorious medical experiments where they were injected with typhus, yellow fever or diphtheria, or horrifically burned with phosphorus. Many died due to lack of sanitation (the camp had toilets, but no running water for years); disease was rife and prisoners were left to fester without treatment.

It was this hellish combination of punishment, torture, non-existent sanitation and complete lack of regard for human life that brought Topf and Sons into contact with Buchenwald – and into bed with the SS.

Between 1937 and 1940, bodies from Buchenwald were transported down the hill for cremation in the main Weimar crematorium, and, from the first, the SS had subverted and broken German law. The law stated that family members had to consent to cremation in writing beforehand, but this agreement was set aside in the case of the inmates of Buchenwald as early as 27 September 1937, when Weimar's Chief Burgomaster wrote:

I hereby consent to the petition by the concentration camp commander to carry out the cremation of the corpses for a lump sum fee of 20 RM. I request that the camp command headquarters be informed of this and be instructed that the certificate required according to Article 3, Item 2 of the Reich law governing cremation be submitted at the time of the transport of the corpse. For the sake of simplicity I am enclosing a number of forms...[31]

The form, which was supposed to be submitted by a family member, could now be filled in and signed by the SS in Buchenwald.

Yet, even setting aside the inconvenience of cremation law, the SS could not completely overcome some of the logistical problems of disguising the murder of mass numbers of people, and the disposal of their bodies.

The transportation of the bodies often drew unwanted attention to camp conditions, when , on at least one occasion, the crude boxes housing the bodies fell off the lorry that was transporting them, splitting and causing bodies to roll into the road. 'Corpses lay on the pavement for everybody to see; the bodies looked "mutilated"', remembered one undertaker's helper.[32]

In addition, the scale of the task was noticeable, taxing town facilities to the limit. In the three years between 1937 and 1940, the bodies of 2,000 inmates were cremated in local crematoria and, as conditions in the camp worsened, the death toll continued to rise.

Buchenwald prisoner Erich Haase wrote:

In the Polish camp, in the winter of 1939/40 alone, 40–70 comrades were dying every day. Either from dysentery or from camp fever, or from being beaten to death or being murdered in other terrible ways, with the result that so many bodies were being taken to surrounding towns for cremation that the crematoria in Weimar, Jena and Leipzig simply couldn't cope with them all.[33]

In comparison, a small town at the time would average only twenty-five cremations per month, with the number for large towns reaching only 100.

The rising death toll did not surprise the SS – they had caused it. In October 1939, filthy hygiene led to an outbreak of dysentery in the 'special Polish camp' in Buchenwald that held 3,000 people including Jews and non-Jewish Poles, and Jews from Vienna. The SS did nothing to eradicate or prevent prisoners from contracting the disease, and instead left 800 people to starve or die from infection.

Prisoner Walter Poller was a medical recorder in the quarantined camp; he made the following report:

> The living with the dead, the healthy with the dying, old men with children, the terrified and the fatalistic. Unbelievable blight, indescribable filth, people rotting while they still lived, mad people writhing in spasms, people in comas ... an apocalypse such as no brain could ever invent and no pen describe.[34]

Rather than treat the sick, or improve conditions, the SS planned to deal with the situation by moving cremation to inside the camp itself. As Kurt Prüfer's May 1939 design for a mobile incineration oven demonstrated, they had already approached Topf and Sons about this task. Now their relationship could begin in earnest.

The SS had restructured their organisation and control of concentration camps under the leadership of SS Gruppenführer Oswald Pohl, who was now in charge of two newly created offices in Berlin: the Office for Administration and Economy and the Office for Households and Buildings. One of Oswald Pohl's first tasks was to organise the disposal of the bodies in concentration camps, and in October 1939 the name Pohl appears for the first time in Topf and Sons' records.

Kurt Prüfer maintained meticulous handwritten records of all his sales during the period that he was paid commission, and these records are available to look at in the Thuringia State Archives in Weimar.

In October 1939 Prüfer records an unusually large amount of money, 15,948 RM against order number 39 D 1018/19 for customer 'G. Pohl Trade Group Berlin'. The order does not state the product, but it was later revealed to be for three single-muffle ovens, one of which was tested and set up in Buchenwald next to the special camp.

G. Pohl, Trade Group Berlin shows up again in Prüfer's records in March 1940, this time against a sales figure of 1,466 RM. Topf and Sons' historian Annegret Schüle, surmises that the 'G. Pohl' referred to in these early orders is Gruppenführer Pohl, using the cover of the Construction Industry Trade Group (a national body of which Topf and Sons were members) to disguise the fact that he was placing the orders on behalf of the SS. Both orders also state 'Wehrmacht Contract', which was standard practice when referring to SS orders for rationed building materials for the camps. In addition, Soviet administration documents produced in 1947 list the production of a mobile single-muffle oven in 1939, and a mobile double-muffle oven in 1940. Any early attempts to conceal the relationship were soon abandoned, however. From March 1940, Kurt Prüfer's records list the customer as SS Reich Office for Household and Buildings.

After securing his first commission from the SS for the mobile single-muffle oven, Prüfer got to work designing a mobile double-muffle oven which was sold to Dachau in November 1939. Prüfer's technical innovation with the double-muffle oven allowed two incineration chambers to be fuelled by one source of fire, through gaps left in the dividing walls between the chambers. This speeded up the incineration process, but the gaps and the single source of fire meant that the ashes and remains of the deceased intermingled – something that was illegal under German law where the ashes of each body were supposed to remain strictly separate.

Topf and Sons had proven themselves to be reliable suppliers to the SS and, having completed two orders for mobile ovens, began work on building permanent crematoria inside the camps. Oswald Pohl issued the order to build a crematorium at Buchenwald on the 11 December 1939 and, on 21 December 1939, Topf and Sons responded with a quote for a static, double-muffle oven with oil burner for 9,728 RM. This oven would be completely walled in and had to be installed in-situ. With better insulation and greater capacity, it would be able to burn more bodies more quickly. (With no slider or ornamental door, it would also badly burn the hands of those forced to open and close the ovens.)

On 21 January 1940, the Buchenwald concentration camp management unit submitted an 'application for building materials for the new build of an emergency crematorium in the KLB prison camp' to the SS main Office for Household and Buildings, and work commenced in the freezing winter of 1939–1940.

With temperatures dropping as low as -39°C all other work at the camp stopped, but the SS insisted that the building of the crematorium had to continue. 'All the SS Blockführer and foremen gathered together on the site,' an Austrian prisoner called Franz Bera recalled.

'The crematorium was built at speed, as the field crematoria that had been set up were no longer able to burn the bodies.'[35]

By summer that year the crematorium was up and running, and a crematorium manager had been employed at Buchenwald. Prisoner Eric Hasse remembers that the SS were so concerned with disposing of their ever-increasing number of victims that they would try to double the number of cremations per day by pushing in two or three bodies at the same time. 'It meant that larger bits of bone were left over; the SS people would wait until night and then throw them into the sewers. The prisoners in the camp only realised this was happening when the drains from the sewage treatment facilities became blocked.'[36]

Contrary to Topf and Sons' frequent boasts about ensuring 'smoke-free' cremation, smoke and flames often poured from concentration camp chimneys, and the smell of burned flesh lingered in the air. Curiously, it is a point that descendant Hartmut Topf feels most defensive about. Standing in Buchenwald next to the crematorium he says: 'If they say they saw that, I am not going to say they are lying. But that was one of the things that Topf and Sons was most proud of – being smoke free.'[37]

Of course, Topf and Sons' claim applied only to their standard practice in town crematorium – and as we know, in concentration camps, no rules applied. Smoke-free cremation is only achieved if bodies are burned individually over a long enough period of time. Burning multiple bodies too quickly meant that cremations in the camps were incomplete, and it was the unburned human remains and carbon that prisoners could see and smell.

In a statement given to Soviet prosecutors in 1948 in Moscow, Kurt

Prüfer outlines how the business relationship between the SS and Topf and Sons began:

> The Topf company started building ovens for crematoria in 1940 [Note: It was actually 1939]. The head of the SS construction management unit of the Buchenwald concentration camp, whose name was Grosch, approached the company about this. I conducted negotiations with Grosch on behalf of the company director, Ludwig Topf, for the construction of two ovens for the crematorium of the Buchenwald camp. Shortly afterwards a representative from the SS main office, whose name I've forgotten, visited the Topf company in Erfurt for negotiations with Ludwig Topf in connection with the construction of cremation ovens in other concentration camps. I took part in these negotiations by invitation of the company director, along with Mersch, who was head of the planning department. At the meeting an agreement was reached with the Reich Main Office of the SS that the Topf company would build ovens for crematoria in concentration camps, although the specific contracts in each case would be concluded with the SS construction management unit at the respective concentration camp, and these would also be the commissioning customer. And this is what later happened. [The 'Grosch' Prüfer refers to was SS-Obersturmführer Gerhard Grosch, a Weimar native and a construction manager at Buchenwald.][38]

Kurt Prüfer, as well as other engineers, fitters and the company management, must have been made aware of the conditions at Buchenwald after their very first visit to the camp when they were trialling the mobile single-muffle oven. Yet instead of being put off by the inhumanity, they saw the camp as an opportunity to attract more business from a previously untapped market. They dedicated themselves to cementing their relationship with the SS, in spite of the horrors they must have witnessed. For Prüfer, it was an opportunity to make more money and improve his status in the company – both of which were at a standstill. The motivation of Ludwig Topf, however, appears less straightforward.

Annegret Schüle speculates that a relationship with the SS appealed to Ludwig's 'lust for adventure and self-centredness'. Or, as his secretary, Johanne Bushleb, later recalled, his desire to be seen as a 'man of action' with a fiery temper and a need to get his own way.[39] Certainly Ludwig was operating in an area that he had already claimed as his own – cremation – and he was finally able to step out of his brother's shadow.

In the immediate aftermath of the war, Ludwig explained to the works council how Topf and Sons had formed a relationship with the SS. Setting the scene, Ludwig explains that Kurt Prüfer was in the process of repairing the Weimar civil crematorium when the dysentery epidemic broke out at Buchenwald, and the death toll began to rise.

'The epidemic naturally posed a problem for the transportation of the dead bodies, and it was decided to set up a crematorium oven right there on the site, which was totally the right thing to do from a hygiene perspective.' Ludwig then wrongly describes the administrative origin of the contract, before concluding 'and then other orders for ovens for Buchenwald and also for the other camps followed'.[40]

Schüle notes that in this meeting, Ludwig was 'at pains to conceal the true nature of the concentration camps,'[41] but he needn't have bothered, as the works council was already fully aware of camp conditions. The minutes from the meeting note: 'This background was quite clear to the men of the works council and they were of the opinion that it was not something they needed to be concerned about.'[42]

Despite describing the origin of Topf and Sons' relationship with Buchenwald as a public service, undertaken for health and safety purposes, the level of complicity between the company and the SS could not be denied. From 1940 onwards, Topf and Sons supplied the camp with the urns, urn lids, urn stamps and firebricks used in civil cremation (although they understood that these stamps and firebricks were a lie and a sham).

Still keen to conceal the true nature of life and death in the concentration camps, the SS ordered thousands of urns, stamps and firebricks to maintain the illusion that they were following the strictures of the 1934 Cremation Act which stipulated that 'the ashes of every corpse must be kept in an officially sealed container and laid to rest in an urn grove, urn plot or a grave'. As Topf and Sons were well aware, identifying individual ashes was impossible when multiple bodies were incinerated at one time in double-muffle ovens. Maintaining the façade, however, prisoners from Buchenwald, Dachau and Auschwitz would later describe how they assisted the SS in scooping up random dirt and ash, before shovelling it into individual capsules which could then be sealed, tagged and sent – for a fee – to the families of victims. (This 'service' was never offered to Jewish families.) Lilly Kopecky, a Slovak Jewish prisoner at Auschwitz explained: 'When German non-Jews died, their families were sent notice of their deaths along with a letter giving them the opportunity to purchase an urn containing the ashes of their loved ones.' Lilly's job was to accompany an SS officer, once a week, into the Auschwitz crematorium where she would then 'sweep up all the dirt I could find and dump it into the urns'. The SS officer would then seal each urn, before Lilly completed the process. 'I had a set of stamps on my desk with which I put three lines on the urn lids, one for date of birth and one for date of death.'[43] In 1997, a renovation of the attics at Buchenwald revealed hundreds of ash capsules, some empty and some filled – but all supplied by Topf and Sons.

The outbreak of war saw an influx of new prisoners to Buchenwald – including the arrival of thousands of Soviet prisoners of war between September 1941 and summer 1942. During this time the camp became a killing field, with 8,000 former Soviet soldiers and civilians shot dead in stables that had been made to look like a centre for medical check-ups. The prisoners would be led in to a room one by one and instructed to line up against a wooden ruler, which they were told would be used to measure their height. Unbeknownst to them, a member of the SS was standing behind them, concealed in a special cupboard, and would then shoot them in the back of the head through a slit in the ruler.

Once again this mass murder placed an unprecedented strain on the camp's abilities to dispose of so many bodies, and a double-muffle mobile oven from Topf and Sons was brought back into commission to assist with the gruesome task.

One prisoner, Max Girndt, described how the machine was stuffed with bodies in quick succession 'one body after another at intervals of just a few minutes. Just as in Nero's day, the burning was done publicly under a blue sky in bright sunshine for all the prisoners to see.'[44] He added grimly that 'since it was hot and there wasn't any wind, the ash of our cremated comrades fell as a shower of fine dust across the whole camp, even into the food bowls and pots in the barracks and the cauldrons in the canteen.' Girndt said the 'specialists' who operated the oven boasted that there were up to 200 such machines operating across Germany and the occupied territories.

To cope with the overload, work began to enlarge the Buchenwald crematoria – with two triple-muffle ovens designed by Kurt Prüfer. Later, Topf and Sons would name them the 'Auschwitz model', but they were put into operation at Buchenwald first.

One former prisoner, Hans Neuport, worked on the building of the enlarged crematorium at Buchenwald and vividly recalled the role Topf and Sons played in its creation.

When special orders were issued we had to leave the site for a while. Special orders were issued when newly arrived prisoners were to be liquidated in the crematorium at once ... for the most part these pitiable victims were Russian PoWs, officers and civilian ... I saw these proceedings with my own eyes from a hiding place ... I heard several earth-shattering screams one after another, so I looked through a gap in the wooden boarding and saw a Russian, still in his uniform, tied to one of the sliding shelves used with the crematorium chamber and pushed into the oven while he was still alive. His dying screams were the most horrific thing I ever heard in my life.[45]

This act was performed by three criminal prisoners employed in the crematorium and witnessed by a 69-year-old oven fitter from Topf and Sons named Martin Holick, who was 'completely shattered by what he had seen', according to Neuport. Holick was a fitter in Kurt Prüfer's department and later spent a year working on site at the concentration camp in Birkenau after building the first of the two three-muffle ovens at Buchenwald. Hans Neuport's devastating account vividly reconstructs the close working relationships Topf employees struck up with other workers in concentration camps – and how intimately they were involved with the most heinous of crimes.

For Kurt Prüfer, however, their work had been a triumph. In December 1941, he sent the following request for a bonus:

Erfurt, 6 December 1941

To Herr Ludwig and Herr Ernst Wolfgang Topf

Dear Messrs Topf,

As you know, I have worked up the three-muffle cremation furnace into an eight-muffle cremation furnace, mostly in my free time at home.

These furnace designs are also [indecipherable] and may I assume that you will grant me a bonus for the work I have done.

Heil Hitler!

Kurt Prüfer[46]

Now that the new three-muffle ovens at Buchenwald had been a great success – he followed up in November 1942 with a handwritten note to the Topf brothers demanding the bonus he had been promised.

Erfurt, 15 November 1942

To Herr E. and Herr L. Topf

Dear Herr E and Herr L Topf,

Following the discussion that took place between us last year, you agreed to make me a special payment for the new three-muffle cremation furnaces, to be paid as soon as they had been confirmed to be working perfectly.

The two Topf three-muffle cremation furnaces were put into operation in the Buchenwald crematorium twelve and six weeks ago, respectively.

The first furnace has already been used for a large number of cremations, the functioning of the furnace and hence the new design have been shown to work perfectly. The furnaces heat [to a temperature] a third higher than was demanded of me.

So far, eight three-muffle cremation furnaces have been completed and/or are currently being built. A further six are in progress. I therefore request that you kindly pay me the remuneration promised to me as soon as possible.

Your humble,

Kurt Prüfer[47]

The Topf brothers rewarded Prüfer's achievement with a bonus of 450 RM.

In December 1941, Karl Koch was accused of corruption and relieved of his positon at Buchenwald. He was replaced as camp commandant by Hermann Pister, who was commended by his superiors for his smooth running of the camp as a commercial operation.

'On 19 January 1942 he was given the camp, whose previous commander had made a complete mess of it,' concentration camp inspector Richard Glucks wrote. 'With great energy, never ebbing diligence and through his own example, he turned Buchenwald into a model camp.'[48]

After the outbreak of war the numbers of prisoners in Buchenwald rose dramatically: up to 20,000 in August 1943, 37,000 in December 1943, 82,000 by August 1944 and 110,000 in January 1945. By January 1945, Buchenwald consisted not only of the main camp, but also of eighty-seven satellite camps and places of work for inmates including the Gustloff II works next to the barracks, the nearby DAW plant that made carbines and the Mittelbau Dora works where prisoners laboured making V2 rockets.

In total, 238,980 men were committed to Buchenwald and 34,375 died there. Of the 27,000 women sent to sub-camps, 335 died. A further 8,000 Soviet prisoners were shot by the SS, and 1,100 hanged from hooks in the cellar of the crematorium. More than 12,000 people perished on the death marches and during transportation to other camps at the end of the war – bringing the final total for deaths attributable to Buchenwald up to approximately 56,000.

For many years, Goethe's oak remained the only tree standing in the camp at Buchenwald, casting its shade over the horrors committed there. When it was finally felled by an Allied bombing raid in August 1944, SS officers surrounded its smouldering trunk, distraught that they had been unable to save it. Later, its truncated remnants would come to symbolise Germany's ruin – and its people's journey from Goethe to the Holocaust.

CHAPTER FIVE

ALWAYS AT YOUR SERVICE

On 6 December 1943, Kurt Prüfer received an award for twenty-five years employment at Topf and Sons. As the somewhat curt language in the newspaper advert demonstrated, it was an honour grudgingly bestowed. Normally, German employees of longstanding could expect flowery, hyperbolic language and warm sentiments on such occasions. Topf and Sons' employees also sometimes received thoughtful letters and cards from the Topf brothers, commiserating on the death of a parent, wishing a spouse a speedy recovery, celebrating the birth of a baby. To commemorate Prüfer's twenty-five years at the company, he, too, received such a letter:

Erfurt, 6 December 1943

Dear Herr Prüfer,

It gives us great pleasure to be able to congratulate you today on your twenty-fifth anniversary with us.

In the last fifteen years you have been working with a great deal of autonomy in the cremation furnace division, which was founded before the World War of 1914–1918, and it is with both pride and satisfaction that we observe that your interest in crematorium construction is matched only by your success in it.

In addition, you took on the unpaid role of factory *obmann* [representative] for a time, and are still an active member of the consultative council. All this effort you devote to maintaining the well-being of the company of J. A. Topf and Sons gives us all the more reason to express our thanks and appreciation to you on your 25-year anniversary.

Hoping that many more years of fruitful labour will continue to bind you to us personally, we greet you with.

Heil Hitler![49]

Notably, this letter thanks him 'with pride and satisfaction' for having worked 'with great independence' in the crematorium construction department for the last fifteen years, and for dedicating himself to crematorium construction with 'both interest and success'. At the request of Ludwig Topf, the Erfurt Economic Chamber presented Prüfer with an award, and both the *Thüringer Gauzeitung* and the *Thüringer Allgemeine Zeitung* were asked to carry reports.

Yet this polite and formal letter contains none of the camaraderie or friendly backslapping that Prüfer must have hoped for. Much as he had done when demanding a pay rise or increased commission, Prüfer demanded recognition for his 'service' to the company, and, as usual, he received it, though never in a way that would prove emotionally satisfying. Prüfer would be incensed, like an insecure lover, at these perceived slights. He would repeatedly demand to know the depth of the Topf brothers' esteem for him, and always find their answers hollow.

The young Kurt Prüfer, who had been so keen to join the prestigious company Topf and Sons, had turned into a resentful man. A man who took dozens of sick days, formally requested to leave work ten minutes early and billed for the expense of snagging his suit jacket on a filing cabinet. Now, in the course of his four short years of association with the SS, he had mutated into something else: a monster. Prüfer had become a man who would not flinch when faced with heinous crimes; a man who would stand with a watch beside the ovens of Auschwitz like the devil's own helper.

Even in reading decades-old administration files, Prüfer's difficult personality, and the dislike and distrust between Prüfer and the Topf brothers, leap from the pages.

In July 1940, the Topfs received the most extraordinary call from one of Prüfer's neighbours, which Ernst Wolfgang carefully documents in a memo. On 6 July, a retired post office worker named Herr Kleinhans rang Topf and Sons and explained that: 'The Prüfers are our neighbours (worst luck) – they are utterly intolerable people. Frau Prüfer is hysterical and certifiable, and Herr Prüfer just falls out with everyone.'

It seemed that the Kleinhans and the Prüfers quarrelled often; Frau Prüfer accused Frau Kleinhans of gossiping with the Prüfers' maid. The Prüfers' maid was the niece of the Kleinhans' maid, Frau Daniel, whose husband also worked at Topf and Sons (it was a small world). This had led Kurt Prüfer to confront Herr Daniel, at work where he insulted Daniel's wife by claiming that she was 'un-German'.

'After Herr Kleinhans, full of outrage, had poured this all out like a waterfall, I asked what it all had to do with the Topf company,' Ernst Wolfgang writes. Kleinhans responded by saying that the company should ensure that Prüfer had no contact with Herr Daniel at work and take measures to stop Prüfer from 'exerting any influence over him [Herr Daniel] on company premises'.

With some satisfaction, Ernst Wolfgang noted: 'Herr Kleinhans's starting point here was that Prüfer is abusing his position in the company!' Rather than dismissing the call as a piece of overheated nonsense, Topf told Kleinhans that he would make a note of the call and look into the matter. For Ernst Wolfgang Topf, no piece of office gossip was too trivial to meddle in, and, usually, he loved to think the worst of his employees – and Kurt Prüfer in particular.[50]

Yet, on one crucial occasion, the Topf company was offered the chance to rid themselves of Kurt Prüfer: on 28 February 1941, he resigned.

Prüfer's main complaint was, as ever, money. Between November 1939 and February 1941, a period when Topf and Sons were supplying the SS, Prüfer's salary was 360 RM per month, with 2 per cent commission on the gross profit of his sales. On average this commission amounted to 66 RM per month, bringing his total pay to 426 RM. In comparison, Prüfer's colleague Paul Erdmann, who had worked longer for Topf and Sons, but who had less technical expertise, earned 900 RM per month.

In his resignation letter, Prüfer claimed to be in dire financial straits, and had been reportedly raiding his savings to make ends meet in order to look after his sick wife. The Topf brothers had promised to increase his salary at the time that they took over the company, Prüfer states, yet 'so far this has only happened to a very small degree'.[51] Although Prüfer had been promoted to the role of senior engineer in December 1935, he was given only a 10 per cent pay rise at the end of 1936, from then on he had been forced to actively request any further pay increases, which were granted rather grudgingly.

In 1937, the company argued with Prüfer over his sales calculations, pointing out that in four years his work in crematorium construction had not brought in any net profit. When Prüfer again requested a pay rise of 20 RM per month in June 1938, the company agreed to pay two-thirds straightaway, but the remaining third only at the end of the year. Prüfer asserted that he no longer wanted to be a '"supplicant" begging for money', so he used his resignation letter as an opportunity to remind the Topf brothers that 'I have my pride, after all'. He threatened to take up a job with another company.

The explanation for Prüfer's reward, or lack of it, lay less with his work, however, and more with his fraught relationship with Ernst Wolfgang Topf. After years of chilly formal relations, they had a serious falling out at Christmas 1939 over a dispute with a colleague in Prüfer's department, Herr Van Der Loo. The man had been summarily dismissed after allegedly insulting the company management, but, in an act of what Ernst Wolfgang Topf would term 'mutiny', Prüfer stuck up for his colleague, thus ensuring that he would never be deemed 'worthy' of legally representing the company as Fritz Sander and Paul Erdmann were able to do.

In two long and emotional memos, Ernst Wolfgang Topf lays out the full details of the complaint, and his frustration with Prüfer, who accused the Topf brother of acting 'rashly' in dismissing his friend.

Enraged, Ernst Wolfgang responded that Prüfer 'would never be able to become someone who planned and acted in the best interests of the company'.[52]

Given this exchange of hostility, the Topf brothers might have been expected to jump at the chance to get rid of Prüfer. Not only was he a demanding 'troublemaker', running a seemingly unprofitable department that was only a tiny offshoot of the main part of the Topf and Sons' business, but the company itself was facing liquidity problems. The war had led to a shortage of materials, which made it impossible to complete orders, added to which some clients were increasingly late in paying their bills. As a result, Topf and Sons was facing mounting debts with Deutsche Bank, Dresdner Bank and Commerzbank and could justifiably refuse demands for a pay rise. In negotiations with Prüfer, Topf and Sons should have held the upper hand – due to rules regulating the war economy, employees could not change jobs at will; a company had to approve an employee's request to leave – and Topf and Sons appeared to have every reason to turn down Prüfer's demands for more money, and accept his resignation.

Yet only a day after receiving his letter, the Topf brothers wrote back to Prüfer to tell him that they would not be accepting his resignation. 'You know better than anyone that you are working on essential tasks,' the brothers wrote, adding that, while normally the company would not consider a request for a pay rise, under these 'particular circumstances' it would make an exception. With mediation from the Trustee of Labour, the Topfs agree to pay Prüfer a fixed rate of 450 RM per month, with no added commission, bringing him an extra 24 RM per month. (This offer still amounted to less than half of what Paul

Erdmann was earning.) A company restructuring also worked in Prüfer's favour; his Department D became a separate department for Cremation and Waste Incinerator ovens.

If they had allowed Prüfer to leave, Ludwig and Ernst Wolfgang could have rid themselves of two problems: a difficult employee; and the issue of manufacturing ovens for concentration camps, the horrors of which had not escaped them. In letting Prüfer go, the brothers could have said, with justification, that they no longer had the technical expertise to continue working in the area, which accounted for only the smallest percentage of their firm's business.

Instead, the Topfs chose not to free themselves of their ties to the SS, but to use Prüfer as a conduit to deepening their association.

Looming over both brothers was the prospect of being called up to serve in the army. Although Ernst Wolfgang appears to have avoided a call-up due to his claims of ill-health, Ludwig's notice arrived on 19 September 1941, a few days after his thirty-eighth birthday. (The same month that Prüfer insulted the brothers again, by claiming that they had done nothing to help Topf employees sent to the Front – 'In the context of a discussion about parcels to be sent to the [called-up Topf workers],' Ernst Wolfgang writes, 'Herr Prüfer took the liberty of commenting that so far the company had done and paid nothing whatsoever for these people. I immediately set the record straight in the strongest terms.')[53]

Ludwig's great fear must have been that he would be sent straight into action on the Eastern Front – a likely death sentence. Instead he received a relatively soft posting, and was assigned to a construction regiment about 35 miles from Erfurt near Gotha. Despite this stroke of luck (no doubt secured by much manoeuvring behind the scenes), both brothers dedicated themselves to getting Ludwig out of the army altogether, applying after a month for him to receive Uk status, which meant he was needed for vital war work at Topf and Sons. This first request was denied outright and Ludwig was not even allowed the fourteen-day 'working holiday' the brothers had requested. Despite this, Ludwig persuaded his military superior to get Weimar Military Command to grant him one week's special absence on 10 November. During this week the brothers applied themselves earnestly to making a second attempt at getting Ludwig out of the army. On 13 November the Topfs applied again for Uk status, sending a letter to the President of Industry and Trade stating:

> It is our view that the military command is under the impression that the war work carried out by J. A. Topf and Sons is limited to the manufacture of grenades and repair of steering gear for the 'He III'. For this reason we are writing to you again to draw your attention to the war essential task we currently have in hand, i.e. orders with priority status S and SS, as well as construction priority O, which we are required to fulfil within the next few months.[54]

The Topfs listed their order for essential war contracts, totalling 7.8 million RM, which include parts and repairs, mines, aircraft, oil, light metal plants and agriculture and food. Finally they noted another customer – whose order only accounts for 150,000 RM, but which receives special emphasis: 'The Reichsführer of the SS (approx. twenty-five cremation ovens for prison camps in the East – extremely urgent!)

To back up this application, the Topf brothers played their trump card – their relationship with the SS. On the day before they submitted the application, someone from the company in Erfurt rang the SS Construction Management Unit at Auschwitz. Following this call, the camp's deputy construction manager, SS-Obersturmführer Walter Urbanczyk, wrote a letter to military command in Weimar outlining an expected arrival of 120,000 Russian prisoners, meaning that 'the construction of the cremation system has, therefore, become extremely urgent'. The person responsible for the installation of this system, Urbanczyk claimed, was Ludwig Topf, but 'we were today informed in a telephone conversation with Topf and Sons that they will be unable to install this cremation system because the above-mentioned Ludwig Topf has been called up as a construction soldier.' Urbanczyk requested that Ludwig be released from military duties for three weeks to oversee the Auschwitz work – but again military command ignored this request, perhaps seeing it for the fabrication that it was.

Faced with the stark reality of military service, Ludwig and Ernst Wolfgang must have been dismayed when they realised that only one man could save them: Kurt Prüfer. On 21 November Prüfer wrote to the head of construction at Auschwitz, Karl Bischoff, to discuss his recent visit to the SS Main Office for Household and Buildings in Berlin, before going back to the urgent and 'problematic' nature of the oven installation at Auschwitz. Under the circumstances, Prüfer writes, he has asked Ludwig Topf, 'who came up with the idea for the three-muffle cremation oven' to take an interest in the project and to visit the camp in person. To do this, however, he would need to be released from his military duties, and Prüfer suggests, Bischoff could write a telegram to Topf and Sons explaining why Ludwig is so vital to the project's success. Helpfully, he even provided Bischoff with an outline of what to say:

> Herr Topf is currently a construction soldier with the Third Construction Ersatz Regiment … since he is about to be granted a leave of absence, I would ask you to send a telegram to my company, and would suggest the following wording: 'Urgently request visit from Herr Ludwig Topf from 2 to 5 December for discussion new oven construction.'[55]

Ludwig's presence would allow him to see for himself the urgency of the operation, Prüfer concludes, 'this would then have a positive effect on our delivery times'.

This time the effort is successful. The SS send the telegram, which still exists with handwritten notes. Ludwig Topf is granted his leave and never returns to military service. Prüfer, meanwhile, has demonstrated the strength of his connections with the SS; he is recognised as an equal when bargaining with them. (It is something he attempts again when trying to secure the release of the son of a Topf and Sons' foreman from Buchenwald in 1943 – but on that occasion he fails.)

Prüfer and the Topf brothers never develop a warm relationship, but Prüfer now realises that he has a powerful tool at his disposal. In the fevered atmosphere of Topf and Sons in the 1940s, it is not surprising that an employee might use any leverage available.

During this period company memos and letters in the Topf and Sons archive reveal a snapshot of life in the company in one short space of time. From February to April 1942, the company was working with the

Nazi regime to begin implementing the 'final solution' of the total extermination of the Jewish race – but the Topf archives reveal not a hint of
this. Instead of documenting a business in a state of meltdown over such
a moral calamity, the files tell the story of a company riven by factional
fighting, fear and suspicion, with the directors themselves preoccupied
with petty disputes, and unable to control their employees' behaviour.

Over the course of six weeks, company files detail a range of volatile
and unpredictable revelations, beginning with allegations that Ernst
Wolfgang Topf had insulted his workers by turning up drunk one
night and calling them 'communist pigs'. On 16 February, the Nazi
shop steward Eduard Pudenz writes the following memo:

On the morning of 16 February 1942, the foreman, Nagel, came to my
office and told me the following:

Herr E. W. Topf had gone into the turning shop one night and had
called the operators working there 'communist pigs'. This had been discussed by the metal workers, and if true, 'people would be very angry
about it'.

Following an investigation, there is disagreement about whether Ernst
Wolfgang called his workers 'communist pigs' or actually said: 'Come
on, you communists! I want to go and have a bite of bread with you!'[56]

Many meeting and memos concerning this incident follow, but this
startling exchange reveals several things about life at Topf and Sons. It
suggests that the Topf brothers were aware of the communist groups
operating in their workshop; that Ernst Wolfgang's behaviour was
sufficiently questionable that the idea of him turning up drunk in the

middle of the night and hurling abuse at staff seemed plausible; and that even the lowliest workers regarded the Topf brothers with more disdain than fear.

Pudenz resolves to get to the bottom of the matter, but before he can investigate further, an even more worrying situation transpires. Later that same day, he discovers an explosive canister on the company premises:

FILE NOTE

Herr E. W. Topf

Re 'Explosive capsule' found on company premises

Shop steward Pudenz appeared at 15:15 and showed us a small capsule from which a number of fuses were hanging ... We reported it to the Security Service, via the fire authority, since we wanted to know the nature of the object, i.e. was it just a harmless firework or a device that had been set to explode? LT [Ludwig Topf] personally handed the explosive device to the security service. They will investigate its contents and, if appropriate, inform the Gestapo.

Erfurt, 17 February 1942[57]

No one seems particularly astonished that a member of the workforce would want to blow up the company – even taking into consideration the fact that Topf and Sons employed opponents of the regime.

There are now two serious staff issues under investigation, but dissent in the workforce, and questions about Ernst Wolfgang's treatment of his staff, raises its head again only ten days later in lengthy discussions concerning the resignation of Fritz Meier, a senior administrator who has been working closely with Ernst Wolfgang for over a year. Due to the war regulations, Meier must request permission to leave his job, and he makes it clear in a conversation with Ludwig exactly why he wishes to do so. At 10 a.m. on 27 February they sit down for a meeting: 'Meier replied that Herr E. T. had spoken about him in highly abusive terms. It was therefore impossible for him to remain in the company. When Herr L. T. asked Meier to repeat the defamatory word or words, Meier initially refused, before saying E. T. had called him an 'arsehole'.[58]

Ludwig immediately agrees to release Meier, but puts the reason down to his brother being dissatisfied with Meier's work. According to the file notes, Ludwig 'recognised that there was no longer any basis for successful collaboration with him – and not because of Meier's blackmail. (The arguments Meier made were of a downright blackmailing character!)'. However, when Ludwig speaks to his brother, Ernst Wolfgang says he wants to speak with Meier personally. Ernst Wolfgang and Fritz Meier then sit down for a meeting in the presence of a secretary – and argue back and forth at great length.

Ernst Wolfgang wants to carry out an investigation (one of the many that seem to be constantly underway at Topf and Sons) saying:

'You want me to believe I have insulted your honour! Without giving me any opportunity to defend myself.'

It was 'Serious abuse!' Meier insists. 'What kind of abuse?', Ernst Wolfgang demands to know. The memo notes: 'Meier replied that he couldn't say the word because there was a lady present ... Herr E. T. found it hard to understand this misplaced sensitivity. He didn't comment further, however, but began to guess what the word might have been. He hit upon the word, "arsehole", at random.'

Following this exchange, the two continue to spar over whether Meier will document his allegations and name those who had made him aware of the insult. This seems to send Meier in to a panic: 'Meier then gave every appearance of wanting to leave the room immediately, as if he wanted to run out of the building … Herr E. T. replied emphatically: "You are my employee; I do not give you permission to leave the building!"' By mid-afternoon, and after involving many other members of staff in the dispute, the Topf brothers agree to let Meier leave the premises.

With Fritz Meier's eventual, exhausted departure, both brothers have spent an entire working day embroiled in an argument about whether Ernst Wolfgang called a staff member an 'arsehole' – or, more to the point, whether he could prove it. Rather than address Meier's complaints, the brothers let their emotions run riot as they determine to discover who made such claims. And it seems Fritz Meier is not alone in his unhappiness – a few days later an anonymous letter about the company lands on the desk of the Weimar Military Command.

On 5 March, Ernst Wolfgang opens a file on the anonymous letter (which it transpires is the second such epistle), beginning with an account of a preliminary meeting between operations director Gustav Braun, representing Topf and Sons, and the Erfurt Chamber of Industry and Trade, who have been asked to investigate the matter and report back to Military Command.

The contents of the letter were approximately as follows:

1. J. A. Topf and Sons, Erfurt, is a complete shambles of a business. Everything's all over the place and no one has a handle on what's going on.

2. An acting director from Berlin therefore needs to be installed and the senior directors of the company need to be removed from their posts. A commission to investigate this scandalous state of affairs has already been formed. The writer merely wished to secure the agreement of the Military Command: this was supposedly required in order for the action to be implemented by Berlin...

3. The same conditions can be found in both the office premises and operations. Waste of materials, faulty work, discrepancies etc. – these all occur constantly.

4. Company director E. T. doesn't arrive until 11 a.m., and hardly bothers with the business at all. Pursues his own private interests. The same applies to company director L. T.

5. The financial situation is in complete disarray. The company is still living on down payments. When these run out, it will go bankrupt, causing monstrous harm to the state.

6. Production planning is just a completely disorganised, disordered group of people. To all intents and purposes it doesn't actually exist at all, it just swallows up a lot of money. And it's the same with the other departments too.

7. The firm continually does things that are not permitted; its manufacturing isn't actually war manufacturing.

8. The firm should be attached to the Gustloff Foundation.[59]

The Erfurt Chamber of Commerce asks Gustav Braun to address each of these points in detail, as well as provide examples. He does so and then reports back to Ernst Wolfgang, who seems most concerned by the allegation that he only arrives at the office at 11 a.m.:

On the subject of my late arrival ... It had been unreservedly confirmed by the Chamber of Industry and Trade that a company director is not required to keep the same office hours as his workers, but must be free to shape his office hours and other activities as he judges best ... They fully understood that my physical and nervous constitution meant that I chose to work different hours – with more emphasis on the afternoon and evening – and did not start at 8 a.m.

Regarding the claims of 'financial disarray' the Erfurt Chamber of Commerce reveals that it is already aware of Topf and Sons' reliance on bank loans. Braun then discusses the claims concerning the planning and construction department – and specifically mentions the dismissal of Fritz Meier and the allegation that Ernst Wolfgang had called him an 'arsehole'. The conversation again then turns back to the leadership of Ernst Wolfgang:

'Overall, then, Herr Braun responded to each individual accusation with examples and arguments showing how we work. He even dismissed the accusation that E. T. was never to be found in the company.'

Braun's role as operations director

made it possible for E. T. to be released from operational tasks of that kind. This was a fundamental working and business principle of the company, because E. T. was currently responsible for the entirety of the company administration and planning, and it would lead to fragmentation if he popped up everywhere. This, too, the gentlemen found understandable.

The meeting concludes with Gustav Braun informing the Chamber of

Industry and Trade about the existence of another anonymous letter, which they then ask Braun to forward to them so that they can try and identify the sender 'and punish him in a way that will make an example of him'. Included in brackets are Ernst Wolfgang Topf's musings '(I just wonder how they propose to do that; for no one knows who sent the letter, and it won't be easy to find out.)'

The difficulty of the task notwithstanding, Ernst Wolfgang begins an exhaustive process to do just that – he starts by accusing Eduard Pudenz of being the author. An alarmed Pudenz swears that he is innocent and does not agree with the letter's contents.

As the name of the letter writer appears to contain a 'Z', Ernst Wolfgang moves on to an interview with Herr Belz in the production planning department, and tried to get him to submit a list of names of those dissatisfied with the production planning process.

In an emotional outburst, Ernst Wolfgang explains:

Our work for the company is our life's work. We care for it as much as we care for ourselves and we are always available for it; and if it's in trouble, we are always the first on the scene. On the other hand, in normal circumstances, our working time is intended to be devoted to company management issues, so as to prevent our strength and energy being exhausted on everyday matters. We need time for planning and for reflecting on the effects of our work: we mustn't allow ourselves to be pushed and pulled about by events.

This seems ironic given that the Topf brothers are constantly distracted by every piece of passing gossip, but Ernst Wolfgang goes on:

Our goal is always to work in a planned way, even if personal circumstances occasionally make this impossible. It's not our aim to be 'popular', since popularity is usually achieved at the expense of actual success...

We draw no salary, on which savings could be made. No time-limited contracts for us: we're here to the end. That is our destiny and we are constantly aware of it.

As Ernst Wolfgang had so rightly surmised, the Topf brothers were certainly not popular, and a further series of meetings with staff revealed a deep dislike of company management. With some relief, the Topf brothers received news on 19 March that the Erfurt Chamber of Industry and Trade were consigning the allegations made in the anonymous letter 'to the wastepaper basket' and a relieved Ernst Wolfgang composed a long handwritten note for the file about the difficulty the brothers faced in running the company – along with the ultimate nobility of their cause.

Neither of us ever harboured the illusion that the fulfilment of these difficult leadership tasks would only ever meet with applause, or that general popularity would be the result of the work we did. On the contrary, no thoughtful employee, working for the benefit of the entire firm, will kid himself that he will therefore be the most popular person with every one of his workmates.

Nonetheless, Topf concludes, the company must continue to be run as it was – while always maintaining the sensitivity towards its workers for which it was renowned.

This brings us to a very important point that we have listed under the general heading of 'sensitivity'. Personal sensitivity is one of the main features of our entire workforce. This has been the tradition for many decades now, and we know of countless individual examples, not just from hearsay, but from our own experience, too. We absolutely must get it through to every individual person that no new organisational measure is ever directed at them personally, but has, rather, been conceived and ultimately implemented for their benefit.

Perhaps he was carried away with the relief of no longer being under investigation by the Third Reich – for it is not clear that Topf employees appreciated the brothers' sensitivity. Nor had the series of air-clearing staff meetings resolved the mutual distrust between workers and directors. With little settled and emotions still running high, the Topf brothers met again, in secret in June 1942, to discuss the results of their investigation into the anonymous letter writer – and their conclusions were far nastier in style and substance than some of Ernst Wolfgang's high-flown rhetoric: 'Regarding further investigations into the identity of the anonymous letter writer, we again discussed the likelihood that it was someone from within the company.'

The Topf brothers go on to discuss the 'dirty liars' in the company, working through the names of possible culprits one by one. Cyriax is 'dishonest', Geiling is a 'stirrer' who predicts that Germany is going to lose the war, Loffler was 'born to complain' and will 'seize any opportunity to drag the names of the company directors through the mud'.

These men have varied complaints and issues with management, but the Topf brothers conclude that they all have one thing in common:

Without a doubt, the main culprits responsible for the complaints and moaning, as well as the attacks on the honour of the company directors, are located in Department D. It is a sorry situation that can only be improved if one of them leaves the company and finds a better future for themselves elsewhere.[60]

In other words, the men the Topf brothers suspect of the greatest treachery towards the company all work in Department D – the most secretive location within Topf and Sons – alongside Fritz Sander and Kurt Prüfer.

CHAPTER SIX

AUSCHWITZ

'*When the doors opened for the last time we saw that the train had brought us to the place we dreaded the most – the flat, fetid swamp lands of South West Poland. We had arrived at Auschwitz, a death centre the size of a small city with thousands of workers busily dedicated to perfecting mass murder, and the extermination of the Jewish race.*'[61]

AFTER AUSCHWITZ, EVA SCHLOSS

Auschwitz-Birkenau was a world of its own. For its inmates it was a world of filth and depravity; starvation and death. For its captors it was a world of solidarity, comfort and varied pleasures. A world where life and death sat literally side by side, where tens of thousands of slaves laboured in appalling hardship to drive forward the Nazi war effort, while hundreds of thousands of others experienced the camp for only a few moments, a few hours, before they were led straight to their deaths in the gas chambers. It was a place where the children of the camp commandant, Rudolf Höss, could enjoy picking fruit from the garden of their family villa – so long as they remembered to wash the strawberries that were always covered in a strange grey soot that blew over the wall from the crematorium next door.

Although the concentration camp system had been a central feature of Nazi policy since 1933, its purpose and organisation had evolved – just as the Nazi policy towards the Jews had progressed towards its final, terrible conclusion. In truth, the Nazis were not as efficient, or monolithic, as they would have liked to believe – or as simplistic as historical accounts sometimes make them seem. Nazi policy was ever-changing and often subject to a surprising amount of internal criticism, although that criticism was about implementation and never about the ultimate objective.

All concentration camps came under the central control of the SS, but different camps had different designations. Some, in occupied countries like France and the Netherlands, were transit camps intended to dispatch Jews to the East, while others, like Dachau and Buchenwald in Germany itself, were officially 'work camps' where inmates were punished and subjected to hard labour. Tens of thousands of people died in these camps, but they were not technically designated as 'death camps'. After a series of discussions between Hitler and Himmler about the fate of the Jews in the winter of 1941, followed by a meeting about the implementation of this 'Final Solution', organised by Reinhard Heydrich at the Wannsee Conference in January 1942, four camps were built in Poland: Treblinka, Chelmno, Sobibór and Bełżec. The sole purpose of these camps was the killing of the Jews. People who were transported there were virtually all murdered upon arrival. These were the 'extermination camps', and they were actually very small in size. There was no need to build barracks or administration buildings as huge numbers of victims were led through the woods and gassed immediately.

In total, the Nazis operated more than 300 concentration camps across Europe, but the largest and, later the best known, of these was Auschwitz-Birkenau, which held a unique place in the concentration camp system.

Auschwitz-Birkenau was unique because it was both an extermination camp *and* a vast labour complex consisting of forty separate camps including an industrial plant operated by IG Farben, a coal mine and a farm. The Nazis were very proud of Auschwitz; it was the jewel in their concentration camp crown and, under the watchful eye of Himmler himself, who personally oversaw the camp's expansion and development, it became the engine of the Holocaust.

Until the autumn of 1939, Oświęcim was an unassuming town with 12,000 non-Jews and 5,000 Jews in an industrial part of Upper Silesia with good railway connections. But the German invasion of Poland on 1 September 1939 transformed the town's fate in unimaginable ways. Suddenly the Nazi regime had three large, and completely self-created, problems to solve: how to find homes and land for the resettlement of hundreds of thousands of 'ethnic Germans' that it had agreed with the Soviet Union would be allowed to emigrate from the Baltic states and northern Romania; how to manage a large Polish population (which the Nazis regarded as a sub-human species to be treated as slave labour); and what to do with Poland's two million Jews.

The first of these issues had been resolved by the spring of 1940. Poland was divided into two areas – the 'New Reich', technically a part of Germany where ethnic Germans would live in homes and on land Poles had recently been evicted from, and the 'General Government' an area that encompassed Warsaw, Kraków and Lublin where Poles would live. Jews would initially be 'relocated' to ghettos within the cities – starting with the Lodz ghetto in February 1940.

Oświęcim fell within the area designated as the 'New Reich' but its industrial landscape meant few 'ethnic Germans' would be resettled there. Instead the town was renamed Auschwitz, and its native population moved out to make way for a new concentration camp, initially planned on the site of an old barracks and horse-breaking yard. The Nazis had identified that building a concentration camp in the area would be important; they needed to incarcerate troublesome Polish prisoners and utilise a large slave-labour force, as well as create a symbolic location from which to terrify the general population. Yet, when Auschwitz's first and most important commandant stepped off the train on 30 April 1940; he surely had no idea that within the course of five years he would be presiding over the site of the biggest single mass murder in world history. Instead, the dream of SS Haupturm-führer Rudolf Höss was to create a model concentration camp, based on the lessons he had learned after six years' service in the SS, first at Dachau and then Sachsenhausen.

Höss, a forty-year-old ex-farmer from the Black Forest who had served as one of the youngest non-commissioned officers in the First World War, had been involved in violent right-wing politics since the early 1920s, and had joined the Nazi Party in 1922. Like many of his comrades, he later claimed his problem was not with Jews as individuals, but with the 'international world Jewish conspiracy' that he believed had brought Germany to its knees after the Treaty of Versailles (this rationale would crop up again when he later justified murdering Jewish children). Höss was a careerist Nazi who 'looked like a grocery clerk', according to the American lawyer Whitney Harris, who interrogated him at Nuremberg. Höss's first post initially appeared unremarkable – as camp commandant of Auschwitz, he would preside over a small camp in an eastern European backwater.

The first prisoners to arrive at Auschwitz were thirty German criminals who had been transferred from Sachsenhausen. These men, who arrived at the start of June 1940, would become the Kapos – they would preside over other prisoners, supervising the forced labour. Soon after, the first group of Polish prisoners arrived on 14 June. Previously held at Tarnów Prison, these were former university students, who were now charged with building the camp itself. As the Nazis had not secured any construction materials, the prisoners' first task was to try and steal some. 'I worked at demolishing houses that used to belong to Polish families,' Wilhelm Brasse explained.[62] 'There was an order to take building materials such as bricks, planks and other kinds of wood.' This method of stealing what was needed, even from other work gangs in the camp, also applied to Rudolf Höss himself, who drove as far as 60 or 70 miles to get kettles for the kitchen or straw sacks for bedding. 'Whenever I found depots containing materials that I needed urgently, I would simply cart whatever I needed away without worrying about the formalities ... I didn't even know where I could buy 100 metres of barbed wire. So I just had to pilfer the badly needed barbed wire.'[63]

This seemingly bizarre method of makeshift camp construction offers a much larger insight into Nazi policy – and its failings. Although the Nazis liked to present themselves as supremely organised and efficient, their policies were often dreamt up on the spur of the moment and were ill-thought through. For example, by the autumn of 1940, Oswald Pohl, head of the SS main administration office in Berlin, had visited the camp and instructed Höss to increase its capacity so that prisoners could be forced to labour in industries. This began with a plan to mine sand and gravel, while Himmler envisioned the camp as an agricultural utopia where 'every necessary agricultural experiment was to be attempted,' according to Rudolf Höss – this would include cattle breeding and massive plant cultivation experiments. Yet both of these policies proved to be pipe dreams. The prisoners of Auschwitz were engaged in slave-labour projects, both for the SS and private industry – but later studies demonstrated that even the IG Farben plant was massively inefficient, as its workers were weak and starving. Himmler's passion for farming, which he shared with Höss, was impracticable, as the marshy flat lands and flooding rivers near Auschwitz were completely unsuited to agriculture. But according to Laurence Rees, 'Until the day the camp closed Auschwitz prisoners would labour in pursuit of Himmler's vision, digging ditches, draining ponds, shoring up riverbanks – all because it was much more exciting for the Reichsführer SS to dream a dream than to discuss practicalities.'[64]

In 1941, the SS decided to increase the capacity of Auschwitz from 10,000 to 30,000 in order to accommodate the needs of the IG Farben plant. The number then grew to over 100,000 after a huge new camp was built at Birkenau, only two miles away from the Auschwitz main camp. This vast new camp was designed to accommodate the victims of the next stage of Nazi aggression.

The launch of Operation Barbarossa and the German invasion of the Soviet Union in the summer of 1941 would transform the role of the camp and its prisoners. Hitler's war against Stalin would lead to a vast influx of Soviet prisoners into concentration camps throughout the old Reich in Germany and the 'New Reich' in occupied lands. According to a letter he wrote to Italian dictator Mussolini, such a dramatic move left Hitler feeling 'spiritually freed' and he could now fulfil his most radical dreams. The fast progression of the German invasion surprised even senior Nazis who believed that the war against the USSR could now be won within weeks, a victory so vast that they believed almost anything was possible and within their grasp – and by that they meant the annihilation of the Jewish race.

Over summer and autumn several events happened almost simultaneously. In July 1941, the first 500 prisoners from Auschwitz were gassed – but these initial victims were not Jews and they were murdered not at the camp itself, but were transported instead to a former mental hospital near Danzig, several hundred miles away. These prisoners, deemed too sick to work, were the victims of the Nazi adult euthanasia programme which began in September 1939 and first targeted mentally ill and physically disabled Germans, before being extended to concentration camps two years later. (A similar law applied to disabled German children, who were perceived to be a drain on society.) It was not until August or early September, when Höss was away on a break that his deputy Fritzsch began experimenting with gassing prisoners using Zyklon B, a chemical made up of crystallised cyanide that was normally used to stop insect infestations. These first gassings occurred in Block 11, the barracks where prisoners were sent to be tortured. When Höss returned to the camp he watched the process, and deemed it highly satisfactory: 'Protected by a gas mask, I watched the killing myself. In the crowded cells death came almost instantaneously the moment the Zyklon B was thrown in. A short, smothered cry and it was almost all over.'[65]

In reality, death by gassing was neither painless nor instantaneous – but as Höss had realised, it was a solution to the mass murder the Nazis were embarking on. Einsatzgruppen death squads had been sweeping through Soviet territory killing at first all Jewish men, and then all Jewish women and children. Mass killing by firing squads raised some logistical problems, however, not to mention the fact that actually having to look their helpless victims in the eyes strained the nerves of many soldiers. The development of gassing as a means of mass murder, and the vast expansion of Auschwitz-Birkenau to accommodate large numbers of Jewish prisoners were both procedures Topf and Sons would become intimately involved in.

Rather than the swift victory they'd anticipated, by the winter of 1941 the German invasion of Russia had ground to a standstill, with German forces halted at the gates to Moscow. Realising that there was unlikely to be a fresh influx of Soviet prisoners, the SS recognised that those still alive and in captivity were too valuable a labour resource to waste.

Auschwitz-Birkenau would be transformed into the final destination for millions of deported Jews, starting with the arrival of Slovakian Jews in March 1942.

The camp at Birkenau eventually covered a vast area, more than 432 acres, and was teeming with many different groups of people. In the four years of its existence, the camp housed Jews of all nationalities from as far away as Norway and Greece, Roma and Sinti children, political prisoners and criminals – at one stage there was even a 'family camp' with a kindergarten for Roma children that had pretty pictures on the walls and story books. But this camp was eventually 'liquidated' and all of the children were sent to the gas chambers.

There was even a Birkenau orchestra, led by a Viennese violinist called Alma Rose, who was forced to play during executions and entertain the SS guards at camp concerts. Alma Rose was the daughter of the leader of the Vienna Philharmonic Orchestra and the niece of Gustav Mahler; she was known to exact the same professional standards that she had been used to before the war. In one memorable incident, she told some SS women guards to be quiet when they were chatting in the middle of a piece and, with German respect for 'authority', they recognised her role as the orchestra leader and fell silent. Like most things at Birkenau, however, Alma's story ended in tragedy, with various accounts suggesting that she was either murdered or died of botulism.

As at Buchenwald, and other concentration camps, there was a strict camp hierarchy with the criminal prisoners and Kapos at the top, and the Jewish prisoners at the bottom.

Over time non-Jewish prisoners accrued small concessions and benefits; they could receive food parcels, and in Auschwitz I some could even avail themselves of a rudimentary swimming pool (really a water tank with a wooden plank diving board created for the Auschwitz fire-fighters) and a brothel. Non-Jewish prisoners also received better medical care and sanitation – and could sometimes rise up the camp hierarchy into positions of authority in relation to other prisoners.

Jewish prisoners received no concessions – the Nazi goal was extermination by any means possible. For Jews the world was turned on its head, with all the normal experiences of life perverted. A non-Jewish prisoner might get a brief consultation with a doctor and some basic medicine; an ill Jewish prisoner receiving 'medical attention' was injected in the heart with a lethal dose of poison. Pregnant women were either subjected to late-term abortions, or had their babies killed at birth.

Of course, there were divisions between the Jewish prisoners, too. Kept in fenced-off areas of the camp depending on nationality, some groups fared better than others. Polish Jews, who were already accustomed to very harsh conditions in the ghettoes, usually outlasted Dutch and French Jews who had been living much more comfortable lives. Those who could not adjust to camp life acquired a vacant gaze, gave up hope and died. In camp language these people were called *muselmann*, because their lifeless stoop was perceived to resemble Muslims bent over in prayer.

As the first Polish prisoners of Auschwitz had quickly realised, survival very much depended on what work you were assigned. The main aim of every prisoner was to get a job with a 'roof', as being protected from the harsh weather could guarantee they would live longer.

Occupations varied from barbers to office workers (there were even German-speaking Jewish women working for the Gestapo) to manual labourers to the team of *Sonderkommandos* – prisoners who worked in the gas chambers sorting through possessions, pulling out gold teeth and clearing away the bodies. This was a truly horrible task, but these prisoners would usually be given extra food and had better living conditions (although they were usually gassed themselves after several weeks). Most workers were ordered to take part in different types of manual labour: some were sent to the laundry room, others joined an external labour unit making German ammunitions and many worked in the warehouses, sorting out the endless piles of clothes and belongings taken from people arriving on the transports.

Working in the warehouses, which were referred to as 'Canada' because they were the land of plenty, was a sought-after job for many reasons: women prisoners got to grow their hair back, take cold showers and could often pilfer extra food rations from the provisions that came in on the transports.

Eva Schloss remembers:

'Canada' itself seemed like a strange wonderland – full of surprising things. I approached one huge metal pile, glinting in the sunlight, and discovered to my amazement they were thousands of pairs of spectacles. Another warehouse was piled up to the ceiling with eiderdowns, while another housed nothing but false legs and arms.

There were shoes in every shape and size, and thousands and thousands of suitcases and trunks. 'One area had children's suitcases with their names and date of birth, usually carefully painted on to the front of the cases by their parents. Another room was filled with hundreds of empty prams – like a perpetual waiting room for a nursery that no babies ever returned from.'[66]

The purpose of 'Canada' was to plunder every conceivable piece of Jewish property and send it back to Germany, where it would be distributed to soldiers and their families, as well as ordinary people. "Canada" was nothing more than a gruesome graveyard of things,' Eva Schloss wrote.[67] German men were shaving with Jewish razors, while good German mothers pushed Jewish prams and grandparents put on Jewish glasses to read newspaper reports about the war effort. In July 1944, 2,500 wristwatches were sent to the residents of Berlin who had suffered damage from Allied air raids. A former Polish inmate named Wanda Szaynok remembered watching a transport of empty baby carriages, five abreast, making its way to Auschwitz station. There were so many prams it took an hour to go past.[68]

In a crazed effort not to 'waste' anything, the Nazis even piled up the hair they had shaved off prisoners, and made it into carpets and socks. All clippings over 2 cm in length were reused, and the proud Aryans of the Third Reich walked around wearing the hair of dead Jews.

It was theft and plunder on a truly mammoth scale. In the crematoria, teams of workers pulled out gold teeth from the victims, which were soaked in acid to remove tissue and muscle, and then melted down into gold ingots and shipped to Germany. This gold was supposed to be reused by the SS dental service (one year's supply from 1942 would have been sufficient for the whole of the SS for the full six years of the war), but, inevitably, much of it made its way into the hands of camp guards and Swiss bank accounts, including the International Bank of Settlements in Basel.

While institutional plunder was sanctioned, individual theft by guards was not. Nazis regarded stealing as a major problem – not to mention a deep moral failing. All officially plundered property was supposed to be accounted for in Berlin, but many soldiers posted in the camps were involved in brazen corruption – and made personal fortunes by stealing from 'Canada'. Later, in 1943, the Nazis launched a full-scale investigation into corruption at the camp and arrested many guards, as well as temporarily removing founding commandant Höss (He was in fact promoted to overseeing all concentration camps from Berlin, but he kept his family housed at Auschwitz, and returned to his role overseeing the camp in May 1944.)

In truth, though, the SS guards at Auschwitz-Birkenau did not need to steal to benefit from their time at the camp. Compared to other soldiers, they had an easy life, and most of the men were aware of their privileges and enjoyed themselves. The SS guards had a good canteen, a cinema and a theatre, plenty of plundered food and drink (including copious amounts of alcohol, rollmop herrings, and sardines to supplement the SS diet of sausage and bread). They also enjoyed frequent day trips which helped take their minds off any nasty activities that might be troubling their consciences. Very few guards who were questioned after the war admitted to being troubled at all by the horrors of Auschwitz: some had brought their families with them, and their children played innocently just outside the camp. Others enjoyed spa breaks at the Solahütte retreat in the nearby mountains. There they entertained women SS guards, and were photographed laughing, conducting tea parties and relaxing in deck chairs on the veranda. A few even went to church.

Twenty-one-year-old Oskar Groening arrived to take up a posting as an SS corporal at Auschwitz in the summer of 1942. On his first day at the camp he witnessed the arrival of a transport of Jewish prisoners; he later claimed that he was upset by what he saw. Up to 90 per cent of these arrivals were sent to be murdered at once in the gas chambers, but some stragglers were left behind. Sick people and lost children

> were simply killed with a shot through the head ... A child was simply pulled by the leg ... then when it cried like a sick chicken, they chucked it against the edge of the lorry. I couldn't understand why an SS man would take a child and throw its head against the side of a lorry.[69]

Groening claimed he protested to his superiors about the sadistic nature of the killing, though not about the murder itself, which he believed was justifiable: 'The children are not the enemy at the moment. The enemy is the blood in them. The enemy is their growing up to become a Jew who could be dangerous.'[70]

Despite initial qualms, Groening freely admitted that he grew to like life at the camp: 'Auschwitz main camp was like a small town. It had its gossip. It even had a vegetable shop ... there was a sports club, of which I was a member. There were dances – all fun and entertainment.' There were also his friends, his fellow guards, whom he grew fond of: 'The special situation at Auschwitz led to friendships which, I still say today, I think back on with joy.'[71]

Setting your 'qualms' to one side was something that all SS officers at Auschwitz became experts at (if they had ever cared to begin with). Even commandant Rudolf Höss, the innovator of so much death and misery, admitted that sometimes he had to have a few stiff drinks, or take a brisk gallop on his horse, to clear his head of the horrors he had witnessed. Occasionally, nothing could completely still the quiet voices, like the Jewish woman 'under the blossoming fruit trees of the cottage orchard', who was accompanying a group of unsuspecting children into the gas chambers and leaned over to whisper: 'How can you bring yourself to kill such beautiful, darling children. Have you no heart at all?'[72]

CHAPTER SEVEN

IS THERE ANYONE
LEFT TO BURN?

After five years of horror, the Red Army soldiers from the First Ukrainian Front arrived at the gates of Auschwitz-Birkenau on 27 January 1945. There had been intense fighting in the area for weeks, and SS forces had abandoned the camp, and then returned to it, before finally leaving for good. At the Auschwitz main camp 1,000 prisoners remained, while 6,000 people were still living at Birkenau and 600 at Monowitz, the slave-labour camp attached to the IG Farben plant. While German citizens reacted with fear and horror to the news of the Soviet advance, for the victims of the Nazis these men were liberators.

Eva Schloss recalls:

The door to the barrack was flung open and a woman shouted 'There's a bear at the gate – a bear!'... Nervously, we made our made down to the entrance and peered at the peculiar sight. Indeed, there was a 'bear'. A large man covered in bearskins, staring back at us with the same startled expression. Perhaps I should have been more cautious, but all I felt at that moment was unrestrained joy and I ran into his arms and hugged him.[73]

Another Eva who remembers the liberation is ten-year-old Eva Mozes Kor. She echoes the same sentiment:

We ran up to them and they gave us hugs, cookies and chocolates. Being so alone, a hug meant more than anybody could imagine because that provided the human warmth we were starving for. We were not only starved for food but we were starved for human kindness and the Soviet Army did provide some of that.[74]

The remaining prisoners had been existing on their own for almost two weeks. Earlier that month, the SS guards had blown up the camp crematoria, torn down electric fences and some guard towers, burned records in the administration building and dispatched thousands of those prisoners deemed well enough to walk on 'death marches' to other camps within Austria and Germany. But nothing could hide the appalling crimes. Two months later a Soviet commission produced a report into Nazi activities at Auschwitz, detailing the function of the crematoria, the fact that they were built by Topf and Sons and the method of mass gassing:

The Germans organised the Auschwitz concentration camp into a huge industrial complex for the mass annihilation of human beings. The murder was mostly carried out by means of the toxic substance, Zyklon

(B), with the bodies subsequently being incinerated in crematoria or fire pits. Transport trains arrived in Auschwitz from all German-occupied countries – France, Belgium, Holland, Yugoslavia, Poland, Greece and others – bearing people destined for annihilation. Only a small number of healthy people remained in the camp and were used either as manpower in armaments factories or as guinea pigs for various medical experiments, after which they were killed.

During the existence of the Auschwitz camp from 1940 to January 1945, powerful crematoria were in operation there, with a total of fifty-two separate chambers for the incineration of bodies. People were gassed to death in vast numbers in specially equipped, technologically perfect gas chambers that were in the same buildings as the crematoria, but separate from them. Incineration of the many corpses took place both in these perfectly equipped technical installations and in special fires. Here in the Auschwitz concentration camp, the Germans streamlined the processes and achievable scale of human mass murder.

The first crematorium with its six chambers, built in 1941, was soon unable to satisfy the appetite of Hitler's executioners, so four further crematoria were planned and built – at incredible speed – in the Birkenau part of the camp.

1. The technology of the mass murderers – gas chambers and crematoria

Crematorium I

The first crematorium at the Auschwitz camp (referred to as Crematorium I) was put into operation in early 1941. The crematorium had two furnaces with two chambers, heated by coke-powered generators.

Towards the end of 1941 (September, October), a third furnace with two chambers, of the same type as the first two, was added to this room. Each chamber could take three to five bodies at a time, and incineration took roughly half an hour. The number of incinerated corpses reached 300–350. The crematorium building contained a gas chamber with closable, airtight doors with viewing windows at both ends and four closable, airtight hatches in the ceiling. It was through these hatches that the Zyklon (B) gas was inserted to kill the people.

The crematorium was in use until March 1943, i.e. for two years.

The construction of new crematoria.

After Reichsführer SS Himmler had inspected the Auschwitz concentration camp in the summer of 1942, he ordered the massive expansion and technical improvement of the existing facilities for gassing people and destroying their bodies. (Letter dated 3.8.1942, No. 11450/42/BI/Ga) The company of Topf and Sons in Erfurt was commissioned to build the powerful crematoria. Work on the construction of four crematoria in the Birkenau satellite camp started immediately after this; on the general camp plan (drawing 2216) these are designated with the numbers 2 and 3, 4 and 5. Berlin demanded that construction of the crematoria be sped up and that all work be completed by the start of 1943 (letter from Auschwitz to the company of Topf and Sons, dated 22 December 1942, No. 20420/42/Er/L), letter dated 12 February 1943, letter dated 29 January 1943.

Crematoria II and III

Crematoria II and III (building plan nos. 932 and 933) were constructed identically and symmetrically on either side of the street. In the autumn of 1943, a railway line was rerouted to connect it directly to the crematoria; the sole purpose of this was to deliver the people from the transport trains straight to the crematoria. Coke and other materials were delivered by road. Each of the ten furnaces in the two crematoria had three chambers and two half-generator furnaces. A single chamber could hold three to five bodies, which could be cremated within twenty to thirty minutes. This means that, fully laden, the thirty chambers of the two crematoria could incinerate roughly 6,000 bodies in a day. To speed up the incineration process, the natural ventilation was supplemented with the installation of additional extraction fans. Each of these had a capacity of 10,000 cubic metres of furnace gas per hour. These fans were not in use for long, however, as they repeatedly and quickly broke down due to the extreme levels at which the furnaces were working. The extraction fans were therefore removed, after which only natural draughts were used...

Crematorium II was in operation from March 1943 to October 1944, i.e. for one year and seven months; Crematorium III from April 1943 to October 1944, i.e. one year and six months.

Both Crematorium II and Crematorium III had underground rooms that were shown on the building plans as 'corpse cellars' but which were in reality intended for gassing people.

People arriving on the transport trains were violently forced into the underground changing rooms (shown as 'corpse cellar no. 2' on diagram nos. 932 and 933) by the Germans. The changing room was 50 metres long, 7.9 metres wide (area: 395m²) and 2.3 metres high (volume: 910m³). The second underground room, designated 'corpse cellar no. 1', was 30 metres long, 7 metres wide (area: 210m²) and 2.4 metres high (volume:

504m³). It had four 45 x 45 cm hatches in its ceiling, in chessboard-style. There was a 30 cm long pipe above these, hermetically sealed with a layer of felt and a massive concrete cover. Between each hatch and the floor were tall columns, whose surface was of reticulated iron. In addition, dummy shower heads were attached to the ceiling.

Our investigations have concluded that these rooms, i.e. 'corpse cellar no. 1', were used in both crematoria as gas chambers for the murder of people. Each gas chamber had been fitted with a ventilator with intake and extraction functionality. With its 3.5 horsepower motor, the intake ventilator had a capacity of 8,000 cubic metres of air per hour. The extraction ventilator had a 7.5 horsepower motor, giving it a capacity of 16,000 cubic metres of air per hour.

If the people were standing as close together as possible, ten per square metre, between 2,000 and 2,100 people could fit into this kind of chamber at a time.

Crematoria IV and V

Crematoria IV and V each had one furnace with eight chambers (making a total of sixteen chambers). These crematoria were built in the Birkenau satellite camp, 750 metres away from Crematoria II and III, and were arranged symmetrically to each other. Each chamber could hold three to five bodies, and cremation took roughly 30–40 minutes. This means that, fully laden, 3,000 bodies could be cremated in the sixteen chambers of these two crematoria in a single day.

Crematorium IV was in operation from the end of March 1943 to August 1944, i.e. one year and five months. Crematorium V was in use from May 1943 to January 1945, a total of one year and eight months;

gassings of people took place there for one year and six months. Investigations have found that the Germans stopped using the gas chambers at the Birkenau satellite camp after October 1944, and took steps to have the gas chambers and crematoria removed. Crematoria IV and V had an annexe, 20 metres long and 12 metres wide, a total of 240 m².

This annexe contained three sections, divided from each other by walls; each of these was a gas chamber. Hatches had been built into the external walls of the gas chambers at a height of about 2 metres, to allow the Zyklon (B) to be poured in; these were covered with bars and had covers to hermetically seal them. The Zyklon (B) was let into the gas chambers through these hatches. Each gas chamber had two hermetically sealed doors. A corridor separated the gas chambers from the changing rooms which, together, were exactly the same size as the gas chambers.

It is significant that in official correspondence the Germans called the gas chambers 'special bathrooms' (Letter no. 12 115/42/Er/Ha dated 21 August 1942).[75]

Although some of the details of the Soviet report have since been revised (historians now estimate that approximately 1.1 million people were murdered at Auschwitz, 1 million of whom were Jews), the commission outlined in seven pages the entire process of the Auschwitz death machine as it was planned, established and expanded over the course of four years. It was a process that Topf and Sons chose to be intimately involved with from the beginning.

Since securing the first contract with Buchenwald, Topf and Sons had been keenly bidding for work supplying ovens to other concentration camps. They were not the only supplier, and faced stiff competition from their old rival, the Kori company in Berlin. Kori had always opposed the rules relating to human reverence in civil cremation, and also possessed strong personal connections to senior figures in the SS – meaning that they were successful in winning the contract to supply several camps. In 1940, for example, the SS ordered a Topf oven for the Flossenburg camp, but ultimately installed one from Kori.

As was the case at Buchenwald and Auschwitz, the purpose and size of individual camps were often in a state of flux. Frequently an order would be given to murder a large number of people. As circumstances in the camp changed, so did the requirements for disposing of the victims. Kurt Prüfer, in particular, proved adept at thinking on his feet. In July 1940, he discovered that the SS planned to use a mobile oven designed for Flossenburg at the Mauthausen satellite camp at Gusen in Austria instead. Upon hearing this, Prüfer took it upon himself to write and suggest that the SS take an identical mobile oven from Dachau, where it was not being used as the oil required to heat it was not available, and Topf would design a new coke-fired oven for Dachau. On this occasion the SS did not take Prüfer up on his offer – but it shows how Prüfer was prepared to do almost anything to accommodate SS demands.

Together with Auschwitz, Buchenwald and Dachau, the concentration camp at Mauthausen would make up a quartet of Prüfer's major SS clients and would play an important part in his plans right up until Germany's final moment of surrender. Mauthausen had been conceived as a 'Grade 3' camp for prisoners the Nazis considered impossible to 'rehabilitate' – and conditions were especially brutal. With an extremely high death rate, approximately half of the 200,000 people incarcerated there were murdered. Chosen for its proximity to several granite quarries, prisoners were often assigned to a 'penal company' for a trivial, or non-existent, reason and forced to carry 50 kg stone blocks on a wooden frame attached to their backs up the 'stairs of death' – while being beaten by guards. Many were pushed to their deaths over the top of the cliff, a practice known as 'parachuting' by the SS. The death rate at the sub-camp Gusen, which had three stone quarries and several industrial plants including one for Messerschmitt aircraft parts, was even worse. Mauthausen's commandant, Franz Ziereis, conducted the first experiments in gassing prisoners by driving a converted lorry, disguised as transport for sick prisoners, between the two camps. Thirty sick prisoners would be loaded inside at Mauthausen. Ziereis would then drive to Gusen, and the prisoners would be gassed with Zyklon B en route. Upon arrival at Gusen the dead bodies would be removed, and thirty more sick prisoners would be loaded and murdered on the return drive to Mauthausen. By the autumn of 1941, Mauthausen began building a static gas chamber and started gassing Soviet prisoners of war in the spring of 1942. Gusen never had a separate gas chamber, but gassed prisoners inside locked barracks.

Auschwitz was, therefore, far from being the only concentration camp where Topf and Sons plied their horrible trade – and, at first, it was probably not obviously different to other camps that Topf and Sons had secured contracts with. Annegret Schüle reminds us:

In 1941–1942 nearly 4 million Jewish men, women and children, mainly from eastern Europe, were murdered in places other than Auschwitz. All the same, Auschwitz was the apogee of extermination by the million, a place where the SS was constantly looking for ways to simplify the murder method, speed up the murder, and perfect the technical methods for hiding the evidence.[76]

Auschwitz evolved from a backwater camp for Polish prisoners to a site for Soviet prisoners of war and finally into a vast forced labour complex and the heart of the planned extermination of the Jewish race in Europe. And far from being mere 'camp suppliers', it was the innovation and flexibility of Topf and Sons that enabled this transformation.

The first Topf and Sons double-muffle oven was installed at Auschwitz in August 1940. It was located in what was later called Crematorium I in the main camp, a former ammunition depot half-buried underground. The death toll at the camp rose quickly, however, and soon a second oven was required. As they would for the duration of the camp's existence, the SS panicked when they realised their facilities could not cope with the ever-increasing number of corpses.

'The SS new-build management has already informed you by telegram that the first oven installation has already developed faults owing to high use,' SS Oberscharführer Walter Urbanczyk wrote to Topf and Sons on 8 January 1941. 'It is therefore absolutely vital that work on extending the system is begun. The start of the work … must not under any circumstances be delayed.'[77]

Topf and Sons installed a second double-muffle oven at the same site in February 1941, but, even with the extra capacity, it was not

Hartmut Topf with his parents, Albert and Irmgard.

Hartmut Topf with his sisters Elke (left) and Karin (right).

ABOVE Hartmut Topf in front of the Topf and Sons ovens at Buchenwald.

LEFT The Topf and Sons insignia, still visible today, on the ovens at Buchenwald.

TOP The exterior of Crematorium III at Auschwitz-Birkenau.
COURTESY OF AUSCHWITZ-BIRKENAU MEMORIAL

ABOVE LEFT The Auschwitz-Birkenau Commandant Rudolf
Höss moments before his execution.
COURTESY OF AUSCHWITZ-BIRKENAU MEMORIAL

ABOVE RIGHT Topf and Sons operations director Gustav
Braun (right) with his son Udo (left). COURTESY OF UDO BRAUN

LEFT Udo Braun as he is today. COURTESY OF UDO BRAUN

The entrance to the concentration camp at Birkenau, summer 1944.

COURTESY OF AUSCHWITZ-BIRKENAU MEMORIAL

The Topf and Sons ovens in Crematorium I at Auschwitz-Birkenau.

COURTESY OF AUSCHWITZ-BIRKENAU MEMORIAL

The Topf and Sons ovens in Crematorium II at Auschwitz-Birkenau.

COURTESY OF AUSCHWITZ-BIRKENAU MEMORIAL

Kurt Prüfer, head of the oven construction and cremation department at Topf and Sons.

Fritz Sander, co-head of the furnace construction division at Topf and Sons.

Karl Schultze, head of ventilation systems at Topf and Sons.

LEFT Ernst Wolfgang Topf (third from left) with his brother Ludwig (fourth from left) and other family members outside Ludwig's modernist villa in the Topf family park.

BELOW Topf and Sons employees at work in the main administration building during the 1930s.

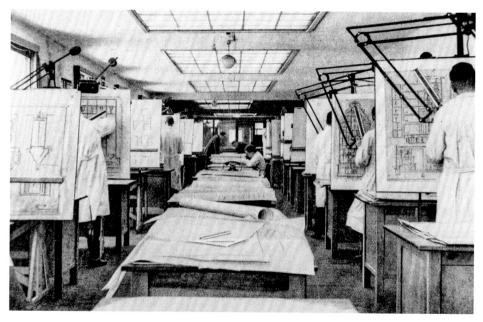

LEFT Ludwig Topf in army uniform in the early 1940s.
COURTESY OF LANDESARCHIV THÜRINGEN - HAUPTSTAATSARCHIV WEIMAR

RIGHT The main administration building at Topf and Sons as it was during the 1940s.
COURTESY OF LANDESARCHIV THÜRINGEN - HAUPTSTAATSARCHIV WEIMAR

The commemorative brochure printed for the sixtieth anniversary of Topf and Sons in 1938.

The founders of Topf and Sons: J. A. Topf (centre), Julius Topf (left), Ludwig Topf Sr (right).

ABOVE The Topf family in the early twentieth century.
COURTESY OF NIKOLA KUZMANIC

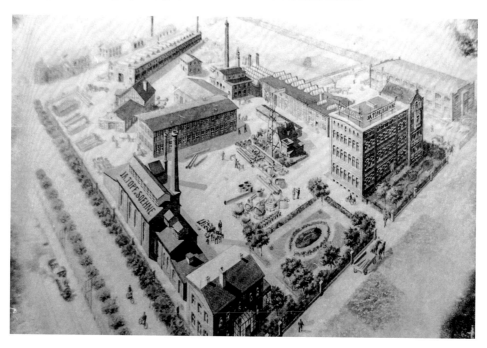

ABOVE Despite humble beginnings, Topf and Sons expanded and became a large firm in Erfurt.
COURTESY OF NIKOLA KUZMANIC

LEFT Ernst Wolfgang Topf and Ludwig Topf.
COURTESY OF TOPF & SÖHNE MEMORIAL

LEFT The remains of the 'Gotha oak tree' in the grounds of Buchenwald. © KAREN BARTLETT

RIGHT Wolfgang Nossen, former president of the Jewish community in Thuringia, and supporter of the Topf and Sons memorial site in Erfurt. © KAREN BARTLETT

The former Topf and Sons administration building, and now memorial site, in Erfurt.
© KAREN BARTLETT

A collection of ash canisters and fire bricks made by Topf and Sons for the SS, now on display at the Topf and Sons memorial in Erfurt.
COURTESY OF NIKOLA KUZMANIC

The drawing board and window on the third floor of the Topf and Sons administration building where Kurt Prüfer worked.

© KAREN BARTLETT

The small wooden house where Ludwig Topf stayed the night before he committed suicide in the Topf family park.

© KAREN BARTLETT

Hartmut Topf in front of what was once Ludwig Topf's modernist villa.

© KAREN BARTLETT

enough and Topf and Sons installed a third double-muffle oven in May 1942.

These first ovens were intended for the Polish and Soviet victims of Auschwitz, who were often murdered, or had died of disease. By the autumn of 1941, however, Auschwitz was beginning the final stage of its transformation. Prisoners were now being gassed with Zyklon B in the corpse room of Crematorium I that had been sealed and turned into a gas chamber. At the same time the SS had ordered the expansion of the camp by building Birkenau.

From the beginning, the SS assumed that high numbers of prisoners at Birkenau would die. The camp was originally intended for Soviet PoWs, and the Nazis had already drawn up plans that demonstrated killing millions of Soviet citizens would free up land and resources for German expansion. Therefore, following this rationale, these first Soviet prisoners of Birkenau could simply be worked to death – and disposed of in new Topf and Sons' ovens ordered for the task. Ultimately, of course, the expansion of Birkenau did not proceed along these lines, and the camp instead became the final destination for Jewish families. But, in either case, the requirement for the mass disposal of bodies remained.

On 4 November 1941, Ernst Wolfgang Topf signed a document confirming that Topf and Sons would supply ovens for the new camp. In this letter to the SS, quoted in Chapter Two, he explains that the oven chambers are larger – improving efficiency – and that the company has taken into account that 'some of the bodies to be cremated will be frozen', requiring more fuel and producing more 'gaseous waste'. The SS should 'rest assured', he adds, 'we shall supply an appropriate and well-functioning system'.[78] Kurt Prüfer, who is no longer on commission, sees this opportunity to ask for a one-off bonus – pointing out that he worked on the 'ground-breaking' design in his own free time.

By now Topf and Sons are well-known for supplying concentration camps with cremation ovens, with another contract in place. Just as before, though, the execution of that contract is fraught with delays, uncertainty and alterations.

The SS originally plan to build the new crematorium behind Crematorium I in the Auschwitz main camp – even though that means transporting bodies two miles from Birkenau. By February 1942 it appears that Hans Kammler, the SS officer in charge of the new camp at Birkenau, has realised the problems this poses and decides instead to build the new crematorium at the end of a railway siding in the Birkenau camp itself. There is little urgency to actually begin work, as there are far fewer Soviet prisoners than expected. Within months, though, the plan has changed again. As outlined in the previous chapter, the Nazi regime is now committed to the total extermination of the Jews and 1942 will become the bloodiest year of the 'Final Solution'.

In a telex to the inspector of concentration camps, SS Brigadeführer Glucks, Heinrich Himmler writes: 'Now that we are no longer expecting Russian prisoners of war in the immediate future, I shall send a large proportion of Jews and Jewesses who have been expelled from Germany to the camps.'[79]

With only one crematorium in operation, however, Auschwitz-Birkenau is as yet unprepared to play a major role in the liquidation of the first Polish Jews – those mass murders will take place in the newly opened death camps of Bełżec, Sobibór and Treblinka. The SS leaders at Auschwitz must now scramble, under high pressure, to prepare their camp to take up the mantle of killing. In the summer of 1942, plans for building the new crematorium begin at a frenzied pace.

Although early gassing experiments at Auschwitz have been carried out in or near Crematorium I, this is quickly deemed an unsuitable site for a gas chamber, as the screams of the victims can be heard by other prisoners. Camp commandant Rudolf Höss finds a temporary solution to this by deciding to convert two farmhouses on the edge of the camp into makeshift gas chambers. In May 1942, the first farmhouse, known as 'The Little White House' goes into operation – it will be officially known as Bunker I. Bunker II, known as the 'The Little Red House', follows in June 1942. The SS estimates that 880 people can be murdered at one time in Bunker I, and 1,200 in Bunker II. With the bunkers now in operation, the mass transport of Jews to Auschwitz can begin and between May and December 1942 180,000 Jews from across Europe arrive at Auschwitz – more than 70 per cent of whom are immediately taken to the gas chambers.

Laurence Rees writes: 'During 1941 the majority of the killing had been committed by special mobile units in the occupied Soviet Union; in 1942 the Operation Reinhard camps dominated the process of mass murder; but now three years after it was opened, it was Auschwitz's turn to assume a central role.'[80]

Yet, although Auschwitz is now ready to play a central role in the killing, it is still far from prepared for the disposal of the bodies of its victims. In July 1942, soon after the mass killings begin, the camp's only working crematorium, Crematorium I, breaks down, with an SS report stating that the chimney is so badly damaged 'due to constant overuse' that it must be replaced. More people than ever are being murdered at Auschwitz, but cremation of their bodies is no longer possible. Under pressure, the only solution the SS can think of is to bury 50,000 victims in mass pits. This hastily thought up method is soon abandoned, however, as the decomposing bodies poison the groundwater for the surrounding area, and cause an overwhelming smell that sparks Himmler to personally order the pits to be reopened.

In light of this, Höss and his top henchmen visit other extermination camps in the east to see how others are disposing of their victims. After some investigation, Höss orders that the bodies should be burned in enormous piles in the open air, stacked upon layers of wood and doused in methanol. This grim process takes two months to complete.

As the SS are well aware, the only permanent solution to the new scaled-up system of mass murder is to urgently build new crematoria – and in the summer and autumn of 1942, Topf and Sons is undertaking this work as fast as possible under the leadership of Kurt Prüfer.

An agreement has already been reached to supply a new crematorium, Crematorium II, with five three-muffle ovens – and the building commences in the summer of 1942. In August of that year, however, Prüfer attends a crucial meeting with the SS at Auschwitz to discuss plans to build a further series of Crematoria (III–V) and refurbish Crematorium I. The details of this meeting on 10 August, kept on file by the SS Construction Management Office, reveal just how confident Prüfer was in his dealings with the SS, and the extent to which he acted out his role as the man to whom they could turn to solve their technical problems.

Prüfer meets with the deputy in charge, SS Untersturmführer Fritz

Ertl, and two SS engineers Hand Kirschneck and Josef Janisch, as well as Robert Kohler who runs a local building company and has been commissioned to build the crematorium chimneys.

The meeting first discusses the deployment of Topf and Sons fitters Martin Holick and Wilhelm Koch to the camp to start work on installing the ovens for Crematorium II. Holick has been working on installing the three-muffle oven at Buchenwald, but Prüfer agrees that he can leave for Auschwitz as soon as that project is complete. Koch already has experience of working in Auschwitz after installing the double-muffle oven in Crematorium I in July 1940. These two men will work in the camp on the construction of all four crematoria.

The second item on the agenda picks up on discussions Prüfer has been having with chief of the SS Construction Office at Auschwitz, Karl Bischoff, about the ovens planned for the gas chambers at Bunker I and Bunker II. Prüfer has seen the technical drawings produced by the SS in which gas chambers are referred to as 'special baths' or 'special cellars'. At the meeting he suggests that instead of installing two new three-muffle ovens, the camp could install an eight-muffle oven in each bunker from an unused order Topf and Sons had made for a camp at Mogilev in the Soviet Union. Prüfer is keen to get rid of unused stock that has been sitting in the Topf warehouse, but he justifies the sale on the basis that Auschwitz will be getting 'the first large-scale oven' produced by the company.[81] Discussing this agenda item alone Prüfer reveals that he not only has knowledge of the gas chambers, but that he is an active and enthusiastic participant in the SS's plans for an even greater extermination programme.

The meeting then discusses the planned oven and ventilation system for Crematorium II, and concludes with Prüfer trying to persuade Auschwitz to keep an oven that has been shipped there mistakenly instead of to Mauthausen (the SS at Auschwitz decline to buy it).

All things considered, Prüfer must have left Auschwitz satisfied with the result of his negotiations. Three weeks later he makes a note of a phone call he has conducted with Hans Kammler, the deputy responsible for the SS Main Office in Berlin, in which Prüfer reiterates the increased performance the new ovens at Auschwitz will provide – using technical language to obfuscate the fact that increasing capacity from 250 per day to 800 per day refers to the disposal of the bodies of murdered human beings.

'Prüfer approached the problems of the SS as though they were his own,' Annegret Schüle writes. He 'willingly came up with innovative ideas for the disposal of the victims of camp conditions, murder operations and the increasing, systematic extermination of human beings; and the company management supported him in this'.[82]

Indeed, not only did the company management support Prüfer's department, Topf managers were even prepared to joke about it. With so much work outstanding at Auschwitz-Birkenau Prüfer calls a meeting with the head of the company's planning department, Mersch, and the Topf and Sons operations director Gustav Braun. Prüfer later claimed that on the way to the meeting Braun had joked with him: 'Boys, is there anyone left to burn there?'[83]

CHAPTER EIGHT

INNOVATORS UNTIL
THE END

Kurt Prüfer was nothing if not pushy with regards to his work – constantly reminding everyone about his role in the cremation department, his relationship with the SS and his innovation in developing an essential part of the technology for mass murder. Perhaps, given the lack of warmth towards him in the company, and his jostling for small financial rewards, he felt he had to be. Yet, much as he would have liked everyone to believe that he was the sole driver of innovation – the crucial role of Topf and Sons in devising the industrialisation of the Holocaust was very much a group effort. In this way, Topf and Sons was not just the provider of the ovens. It became something much more horrifying.

Take Fritz Sander – a long-standing and highly respected Topf employee. Sander was now a man in his sixties; he had worked for Topf and Sons for decades, had risen to become the manager of the furnace construction division, DI, which produced steam-boiler systems, and was an authorised company representative. This was someone held in such high esteem that Ernst Wolfgang would later describe him as a 'man of almost exaggerated integrity'.

Such a man, one would think, would not need – or desire – to stoop to dealing with the dirty business of disposing of the bodies of the victims of the Nazis. But it seems that the day-to-day work of over-seeing Kurt Prüfer's oven designs, and signing new orders with the SS, convinced Sander that he had something to prove. Why should Prüfer, a man he disliked intensely, be forging ahead opening up new areas of business for the company and not him? Not only did Sander believe that he too could design an oven – something that was not even his area of technical expertise – but that it would be more brutally efficient than any other oven in operation in a concentration camp. And so Sander dreamt up the 'corpse incineration oven for mass operation', and applied for a patent.

On 14 September 1942, Sander wrote to the Topf brothers explaining why his invention was necessary and how it would work: 'The high demand for cremation ovens for concentration camps – which has recently become especially apparent at Auschwitz ... led me to assess whether our present system with muffles is the best solution for the above-named locations.'[84] In a later interrogation in the Soviet Union, Sander claimed that Prüfer had said that the crematoria at Auschwitz 'could no longer cope with the number of corpses to be cremated,' and that two or three bodies were being crammed into a single hatch at one time. Sander then described how, 'as a specialist in firing technology, I decided on my own initiative to build crematoria with greater corpse-cremation capacity'. This, he explained, 'would be designed on the conveyor-belt principle, with bodies carried into the ovens continuously by mechanical means'. What Sander had in mind was a conveyor belt, continuously loaded with corpses, with the bodies providing the fuel themselves to burn other bodies. 'The bodies themselves served as additional combustion fuel.'[85]

This would address the 'basic problem' of muffle ovens, as Sander explained it: the cost of the materials, the space required, the amount of fuel needed and the frequency with which the ovens broke down. To rectify this, Sander had sold his idea to the Topf brothers by telling them: 'I propose an oven with constant feed and operation.' (In this topsy-turvy moral world, no one questioned that the 'basic problem' might in fact be the regime that was killing millions of people)

Referring to the bodies of the victims as 'cremation objects', Sander states: 'It is perfectly clear to me that such an oven is to be regarded purely as an elimination system and that the concepts of reverence, ash separation and any other emotional factors are entirely disregarded. However, all this is already the case with cremation with multi-muffle ovens.'

In one succinct paragraph, with a throwaway final sentence, Sander acknowledges that Topf and Sons have been openly flouting the law with regard to reverence in dealing with human remains in all of their work with the SS. He adds this statement to his patent application, dated 26 October 1942, first writing: 'This method does not, of course, allow compliance with the Reich Cremation Law of 10 August 1938.' (The statement was later amended to 'This method does not, of course, allow compliance with the legal requirements in force across the area of the German Reich.') In a triumph of Nazi administration-speak,

Sander described his invention as a way of 'restoring hygiene' in 'war-related conditions'.

In his patent application, he explains:

With the unavoidably high mortality rate in the assembly camps that have been set up in the occupied Eastern lands in response to the war and its consequences, it is not possible to bury the large number of inmates who die. This is partly due to lack of space and manpower, and partly a result of the clear risk posed to the immediate and wider environment by burial of the dead, many of whom succumbed to infectious diseases. It is therefore necessary to dispose of the bodies, quickly, safely and hygienically by means of cremation.[86]

Given the time-sensitive situation, the company had to act fast when applying for the patent, he informed the Topf brothers in his memo, otherwise they risked being overtaken by a rival competitor.

Later Sander would weakly justify his behaviour by claiming he was a 'German engineer', much like an engineer working in aircraft construction, who felt obliged to use his knowledge 'in order to help Hitler's Germany to victory, even if that resulted in the destruction of human life'.[87]

The fact was, however, that Sander was no Nazi. He was never recorded as expressing any anti-Semitic sentiments. Nor did he need to advance his career; he had risen as high as he could expect to and was close to retirement age. Sander's motives were driven by pure jealousy and dislike of Kurt Prüfer.

In response, Prüfer understood immediately that Sander was trying to muscle in on an area of work he had claimed as his own. He tells Sander that his design will not work as – in his own vast experience – scorched body parts stick to even steeply sloping surfaces. Sander, however, tells the Topf brothers that this can be easily rectified by adding openings where people outside can give the 'cremation objects' a push.

A cremation expert analysed Sander's design in 1985 and concluded that it was viable and could have cremated 1,200 bodies per day, but, ultimately, the patent was not granted and the 'Corpse Incineration Oven for Mass Operation' was never built. In principle, however, it had the full backing of the Topf brothers who initialled Sander's memo, apparently unperturbed by its contents, and requested a sketch of the new design.

The fact that Sander's gruesome invention did not come to fruition, did not deter Prüfer. Within six months he had quickly produced an equally heinous innovation: a 'Ring Cremation Oven', based on technology already in use for firing bricks.

On 29 January 1943 Prüfer visited Auschwitz-Birkenau and agreed with the chief of construction, Karl Bischoff, that the SS should plan a sixth crematorium, which was originally intended to be an above-ground 'open crematorium chamber' and later amended to an underground chamber (presumably to protect it from Allied airstrikes and reconnaissance flights) In a follow-up letter on 5 February Prüfer writes: 'The quotation for the large ring cremation oven will be with you by next Tuesday at the latest. If you wish to go ahead with this, we would request that you place the order as soon as possible.'

Prüfer's exact design is no longer in existence, but it appears to have been based on industrial ring ovens which operated a system of continuous combustion through one central source of fuel – reducing costs by up to 70 per cent. Using this system, Prüfer's oven, which his quote revealed to be twice as big and twice as expensive as an eight-muffle oven, would add coal from above, which would then land directly on piles of burning corpses.

In his trial after the war, Rudolf Höss confirmed that such a system was planned 'in the form of an enormous underground brick factory with a ring oven'. Although Prüfer's design was accepted, like Sander's it was never built. Initial plans to build in 1943 were put on hold as Ludwig Topf explained to the SS that the company was at full capacity, and could not take any additional orders for ovens. When the project was reconsidered in 1944, Höss claimed that the Allied advance meant the Nazi genocide had run out of time.

From the very beginning Topf and Sons was involved in helping the SS develop new means of disposing of its victims – but its complicity in the Holocaust went much further. From 1940 onwards, Topf and Sons took part in discussions and decisions about ventilation systems for the crematoria – and by 1943 it was developing ventilation technology for the gas chambers. In essence, Topf and Sons was devising more efficient ways of murdering people.

The person responsible for developing ventilation technology was 40-year-old Karl Schultze who originally worked in Department D, but was promoted in 1941 to run a department of his own , Department B, which developed industrial inward and outward ventilation systems, hot-air heating systems and dust-extraction systems. Schultze, who was married with no children, had joined the company in 1928 after being educated at technical college. Like Prüfer, he was not made an authorised company representative, so his business deals had to be approved by Fritz Sander or Paul Erdmann.

Between December 1940 and September 1941, Schultze submitted four designs for a ventilation system for Crematorium I at Auschwitz. In February 1941, the SS had bought and installed a temporary ventilation system from the Cologne-based Frederick Boos company, which was responsible for the heating systems in the camp. This, however, was deemed unsatisfactory, and hindered the Gestapo in their efforts to murder people in the room next door. 'The current system has become useless', complained the Head of the Political Department and Criminal Secretary, Maximilian Grabner, on 7 June 1941. Grabner, who was the second most powerful person in the camp after Rudolf Höss, went on to explain that 'When the second oven is in use – as is now the case on an almost daily basis – the morgue ventilation hatch has to be closed, as otherwise the hot air from the flue gets in, and this is the very opposite of the ventilation effect required.' Despite this, the temporary system remained in place, and the system supplied by Topf in April 1942 was not installed.

The greatest concern to the SS was the amount of time it took to decontaminate a room or building after a gassing had taken place – up to two days for the entire building in the case of the original gassings that were carried out in the Auschwitz cellars. To overcome this, Prüfer and Schultze were involved from the earliest stages in the planning for building Crematoria II to V. As Annegret Schüle charts in her book, there has been disagreement between historians about exactly when the SS decided to add gas chambers to each crematorium, but by the time of their completion in March 1943 each had a gas chamber attached to it.

Topf and Sons must have known about these plans no later than mid-1942, as Kurt Prüfer and the SS discussed plans for a ventilation system for Crematoria II and III at their meeting on site in August of that year. The minutes of the meeting specifically note that the construction of Crematorium II would have an inward and outward ventilation system – something that would only be necessary if there was a gas chamber. On 27 November 1942, SS Untersturmführer Wolter, a structural engineer at Auschwitz, notes that he has spoken to Prüfer on the phone in relation to Crematorium II, and that Prüfer had said that 'the company would have a fitter available in about a week's time to install the outward ventilation system once the ceilings of the special cellar are ready'. In SS terminology a 'special cellar' was a gas chamber. The SS later ordered two ventilation systems for Crematoria IV and V, where gas chambers had not originally been planned, but were added later. Karl Schultze prepared a quotation for each order in June 1943, and the ventilations systems were dispatched in December that year (though never installed in the case of Crematorium IV).

As the constant changes in plans for the camp show, Auschwitz-Birkenau was now being promoted at the highest levels of the Nazi regime as a 'showcase' elimination and work camp, and its development was progressing under the watchful eye of Heinrich Himmler himself. For the SS this added an extra pressure to a process that was often chaotic and prone to delays and breakdowns. Their response was to work ever more closely with Topf and Sons, consulting them in areas of work where the company had no expertise, and blaming them when things went wrong.

In December 1942, the SS construction unit at Auschwitz informed Topf and Sons that Himmler had personally set new deadlines for the completion of the crematorium. These deadlines were a month earlier than those the SS at the camp had originally suggested, but when the SS at Auschwitz replied to their masters in Berlin to say that the deadlines were impossible and could not be met, Hans Kammler agreed to a postponement only on the basis that he received weekly progress reports, and that every effort was made to meet the original deadline.

In January 1943, the new deadlines were agreed upon with Prüfer, giving the company two additional weeks to work on Crematorium II and an extra month for Crematorium IV. The reliability of Topf and Sons, and the efforts of all concerned to work under 'extreme pressure' was something the SS didn't hesitate to show off about in their self-serving reports to their superiors. They had deployed all labourers and 'worked around the clock' in sub-zero temperatures, and despite many difficulties, to complete Crematorium II, SS Hauptsturmführer Bischoff wrote to Kammler in Berlin – forwarding a report from Prüfer which stated that 'the inspection of the above-mentioned crematorium, complete with its internal fittings, showed that despite the scale of the task and the difficulties caused by bad weather and problems acquiring materials, the work was performed very quickly'. Bischoff concluded his report to Kammler by praising Prüfer, and informing the SS in Berlin that the ovens had been fired up in Prüfer's presence 'and are working perfectly'.

Despite Bischoff stressing that work on the crematorium was to be given 'the absolute top priority', with two teams of labourers working in shifts if necessary, the project was beset by problems caused by snow and permafrost, a severe shortage of materials and labourers being transferred to other work. To rectify this, the SS sent a telegram to Topf and Sons to demand that Prüfer work on site for at least two to three days per week as part of the construction management unit. By now, however, Topf and Sons, and Prüfer in particular, knew their power. The company replied by post, rather than by telegram, and stated that of course Prüfer would be available to frequently inspect the work at Auschwitz. This rather vague and leisurely reply showed that the company were not afraid of the SS, nor did they have any inclination to sacrifice other work or priorities to meet the demands from Auschwitz.

In January 1943, much anguished communication ensued over a missing blower for the ventilation system for the gas chamber, followed by a letter from Bischoff to Hans Kammler, blaming Topf and Sons for delays. The report of 12 February 1943 states: 'Problems with the company Topf and Sons of Erfurt … The many different promises made by this company, and their failure to deliver as agreed, are leading to serious problems.' Bischoff asks Kammler to respond by issuing 'the firmest possible warning'.

There was no doubt that Topf and Sons was now the SS's partner of choice in their extermination program, and that knowledge of this was widespread in the company with memos about discussion over ventilation for the 'gas cellars' passing through the hands of typists and secretaries, the administration office and company secretary Max Machemehl, operations director Gustav Braun, the purchasing manager as well as the engineers, and finally the company directors, Ludwig and Ernst Wolfgang Topf, who were ultimately responsible for every decision.

In February 1943, Topf and Sons was asked to source 'gas analyses' for the new crematoria that would measure the level of gas in the atmosphere and make sure no threat was posed to SS men working on site. Although this was an area where Topf and Sons had no experience, they obligingly tried to find a supplier, replying that 'two weeks ago we contacted five different firms about the display devices for cyanide residue that you need'. When interrogated in Moscow in 1948, Prüfer confirmed that he understood perfectly well what these devices were needed for. 'The head of SS construction management at the camp, Bishcoff, informed me that prisoners were being killed in these gas chambers using cyanide fumes, and it was at his request that I made contact with a number of German companies with a view to procuring the gas analysers for the gas chambers.'[88]

In addition to their existing orders, Topf and Sons had won the contract to supply the ovens for Crematorium III and a ventilation system for the gas chamber, an additional waste incinerator for Crematorium II, two lorries for ash transportation and a fumigator to disinfect prisoners' clothes. When the lifts, supplied by the Huta company, used to move the bodies up from the gas chambers to the ovens proved unsatisfactory, Kurt Prüfer was asked to source a temporary replacement for Crematorium II and '2x electrical corpse lifts' for permanent use in both crematoria. Prüfer did this by sourcing the order from the Gustav Linse Specialist Lift Company, a close neighbour to Topf and Sons in Erfurt that is still in operation today. The Linse lift was installed in Crematorium II by Topf fitter Heinrich Messing in May 1943, and Messing also repaired the lift in Crematorium II. The SS also ordered two new electrical lifts from Topf and Sons at ten times the price of the Linse lift.

Although he had stepped in to work on the 'corpse lift', Heinrich Messing was actually a ventilation fitter, and, as opposed to Prüfer's short visits, he was one of four Topf and Sons' fitters who spent a great deal of time at Auschwitz between 1942 and 1943. Messing was an Erfurt native, and still a relatively young man in his early forties during his time at Auschwitz. The seventh son of a shoemaker, Messing followed his oldest brother, Wilhelm, into a plumbing apprenticeship, and both became active members of the Communist Party of Germany, the KPD, and the *Rote Hilfe Deutschlands*, a charitable organisation that supported communist political prisoners. In 1933, during the first weeks of Hitler's reign, Wilhelm Messing was arrested and sentenced to two years imprisonment for 'preparation for high treason'. On 28 February 1933, Heinrich Messing was arrested on the same charge and sent to Erfurt's first temporary concentration camp at 18 Feldstrasse. Three other communist comrades, Bernhard Bredehorn, Friedrich Schiller and Hermann Kellerman were arrested in the same series of raids – but the four men were to meet again later, in the 1930s, all as employees of Topf and Sons.

It seems remarkable, and striking, that these four hardened communists who had between them been charged of the highest crimes of treason, and suffered long periods of imprisonment and unemployment, should all find employment in a company that was manufacturing technology for the SS – as well as aircraft parts for the Luftwaffe.

Heinrich Messing, now a married man with three children, took up his role as a travelling fitter at Topf on 13 August 1934; Schiller joined two years later as boilermaker in August 1936 and Bredehorn followed a month later in September as a welder. Kellermann was the last to join the company, taking up a position as a metalworker in May 1939. The four men would later claim they had been key members of the communist underground, using Messing's work as a travelling fitter to spread the word about new policies and bringing back new literature. Regardless of how successful their underground operations were, the men would always vouch for each other, with Schiller warning Messing to disappear to avoid interrogation by Soviet officers in 1946. The quartet provided each other with references during the years of East Germany's communist regime, with Schiller calling Messing a 'sincere fighter' and a 'role model' in communist activities.

The presence of active communists at Topf and Sons is a puzzling anomaly. Just as Ludwig and Ernst Wolfgang Topf were well aware of their political affiliations (how could they not be when, for example, Bernhard Bredehorn was even arrested and held in custody for 'small tasks undertaken for the left' as late as November 1944) so too were these supposedly underground communist fighters aware of the true nature of the work going on at Topf and Sons. As Annegret Schüle summarises: 'SS men were forever coming and going at Topf, the mobile ovens were made on the premises and were returned there for repair, and the customer addresses for deliveries were not a secret.' Bernard Bredehorn, she adds, was a welder who attached the brackets to the oven doors.[89]

The work of the Topf and Sons fitters at Auschwitz was crucial, not only to the installation of the crematoria and gas chambers – but also to Topf's relationship with the SS.

Between January and June 1943, Heinrich Messing lived and worked at the camp installing the ventilation system for Crematorium II, as well as an air fan and engines for the ovens in Crematoria II and III, and ventilation equipment for the gas chambers.

His Topf colleagues, Wilhelm Koch and Martin Holick, were installing the three-muffle ovens in Crematorium II from September 1942 onwards. Koch spent a total of nine months at Auschwitz, during which time he installed the waste incinerator in Crematorium III and the ovens in Crematoria IV and V. Martin Holick spent a year at Auschwitz, completing the construction of the ovens in Crematorium II, and the installation of the fumigators in the 'sauna'. A fourth fitter, Arnold Seyffarth, was dispatched to complete the ovens in Crematorium III, and stayed for several months.

These four men enjoyed a high status in the company, and in the camp. Although they may have exercised no control over their assignment, none of them used their advantageous position within the company to sabotage projects or oppose their work. They lived in comfortable SS accommodation during their stay, and were some of the 1,000 civilian workers on site who were cut off from the outside world during the typhus epidemic that occurred in the last months of 1942. 'The mass extermination carried out at Auschwitz-Birkenau cannot have escaped their notice,' Annegret Schüle writes. 'The flames from the incineration of tens of thousands of piled-up corpses were visible for miles around.'[90]

Kurt Prüfer, Karl Schultze and the Topf fitters were the men on the ground, and on 5 March 1943, the day finally came to try out the new ovens for Crematorium II. As predicted, the construction unit was running one month behind schedule, and that morning prisoners in the special unit (responsible for operating the crematoria and gas chambers) had been instructed by Prüfer to start heating the ovens early so that they could be operating at maximum efficiency later in the day. At about 4 p.m., a delegation of senior SS officers from Berlin, members of the political department and representatives from Topf and Sons drove up to the crematorium and took their places as the demonstration began.

Henryk Tauber, a prisoner in the special unit, described what happened next: 'Once the committee had arrived, we were ordered to fetch bodies from the morgue and throw them in the [muffle ovens].' In the morgue Tauber found the bodies of a large group of well-fed men, who had been gassed earlier in Bunker II. These men, with a higher proportion of body fat, had been specially requested by Prüfer to test the operating performance of the crematorium. 'Once all the bodies had been distributed across all the chambers of the five ovens, the committee members observed the process, holding their watches in their hands. They opened doors, looked at their watches, talked among themselves and expressed surprise that the cremation had taken so long.'[91]

Prüfer and his colleagues from Topf and Sons were surprised and dismayed. But these emotions were not provoked by the fact they had just witnessed such a horrific event; rather they were disappointed that the ovens, which had been heated since early morning, still had not reached the optimal temperature, and the cremation of one load of bodies had taken forty minutes. Initially, Prüfer had estimated that two full loads could be cremated every hour. Tauber added that 'senior overseer August told us that the calculations and plans for the crematorium had allowed 5–7 minutes per corpse.'

Annegret Schüle estimates that at the rate of three bodies per muffle every half hour, Crematoria II and III would have been able to cremate a maximum of 2,160 bodies per day, a figure that roughly tallies with one given by Rudolf Höss (the total cremation capacity across all of Auschwitz-Birkenau was 8,000 bodies over twenty-four hours). The SS was initially delighted with the 'highly efficient' running of the new crematorium, and commented on the reduction in coke consumption as a result of the continual use of the ovens. 'These are outstanding figures!' wrote one civilian working for the SS in March 1943.[92]

In reality, the 'efficiency' of the mass murder at Auschwitz-Birkenau was often derailed by a combination of unrealistic demands from Berlin, and the reliability of the people who worked in the crematoria on a day-to-day basis. These prisoners from the special unit had two compelling motivations: to keep themselves alive and make that life as bearable as possible. One way to do this was to shove four or five bodies into a single muffle to give themselves a break between cremations – but this increased the wear and tear on the ovens and led to repeated breakdowns, something that would strain the relationship between Topf and Sons and the SS.

Another strain was that while the ovens at Crematorium II had now been completed, work on the gas chamber had fallen behind schedule.

Topf fitter Heinrich Messing accumulated thirty-five hours of carefully recorded overtime, during the week beginning Monday 8 March 1943. Messing's job was to install the ventilation technology for the gas chamber and the undressing room in the cellar of Crematorium II. Although these were referred to officially by the SS as morgues I and II, Messing preferred to use the term 'undressing room' in his own notes, demonstrating that he understood the process, and the true nature, of the crimes planned for that location. As Annegret Schüle puts it, he was installing technology that would facilitate the 'speedy suffocation of hundreds of thousands of people'.[93] Topf's ventilation expert, Karl Schultze, was also working at Auschwitz during that same week, and tested the blower (the forced draught system) for the ovens on Crematorium II on Wednesday 10 March.

On Saturday 13 March, it was time to test the blower and the ventilation system for the gas chamber itself. On that day 1,492 Jews from the Kraków ghetto were transported to Birkenau to be murdered. The SS had recommended that the ovens should be working when the blower system was tested, as this was when temperatures were at their highest. That evening when the group arrived, the SS then selected between 150 and 300 men, women and children, and gassed them to death. The bodies were then moved upstairs to be burned in the ovens. During his interrogation by the Soviets, Karl Schultze disclosed the details of what happened:

At the moment when the SS people drove them into the gas chamber, I was in the crematorium, in the vicinity of the crematorium ovens. The bodies of these prisoners were burned in my presence. Once the killing of these prisoners in the gas chambers had been completed (which took no longer than fifty minutes) an SS man switched on the ventilation systems, with the help of which the contaminated air was extracted and fresh air blown in.[94]

This test showed that the ventilation system and blower were 'working perfectly', according to Schultze, and he returned immediately to Erfurt. Upon his return to Topf and Sons, Schultze 'gave Ludwig Topf a report on the work I had done in connection with the testing of the blower and ventilation systems in the second crematorium. As an aside, I informed him that the SS people had killed a group of prisoners in the gas chambers and that their bodies were then burned in the cremation ovens. L. Topf did not react to this.'[95]

Schultze's factual and emotionless account can be read in conjunction with another account, given by special prisoner Henryk Tauber, who also witnessed the gassing. In May 1945, Tauber recounted the scene to a Polish Commission of Inquiry. 'Once dusk had fallen, the first vehicles carrying people of various ages and sexes drove up. These included old men, women and several children. For about an hour these vehicles drove backwards and forwards between the crematorium and the railway station, bringing more and more people.'

Tauber and the other members of the special unit were locked in the doctors' room at the back of the building, from where they could hear people 'crying and screaming'. After two hours Tauber and his team were let out and ordered into the gas chamber.

> In this chamber we found piles of standing naked bodies, all collapsed into each other. The bodies were reddish in colour, in places a very pronounced red, in other places they were covered with greenish marks. They had foam round their mouths, some of them had blood coming out of their noses, and most had soiled themselves. I remember that many had their eyes open; lots of the bodies were hunched up together and most of them were huddled together around the door.

Tauber explained that it was clear people had tried to get away from the columns through which the gas had been introduced.

> We later realised that a lot of people in the gas chambers died of suffo-
> cation due to the lack of air, even before the gas had time to work. These
> bodies were the ones lying right on the bottom, right on the floor; the
> others had to run over them ... Before the Zyklon was poured in, the air
> was sucked out – that's what the ventilation in the chamber was for.[96]

Once the special unit had removed the bodies, they started to load them onto iron gurneys ready for the Topf ovens:

> Two prisoners put the bodies on them. They placed them so that the first
> body was lying on its back with its legs towards the oven and its face
> pointing upwards. A second body was put on top of the first, also on its
> back, but this time with its head towards the oven ... Once the bodies
> were inside the cremation chamber; the sixth prisoner would hold them
> in place using an iron rod while the fourth prisoner would pull the
> gurney out from under them.[97]

The prisoners would then have to open the doors to each cremation chamber so that an SS officer could check it had been loaded properly. This was the unvarnished truth of Topf and Sons' technology in action.

Innovator that he was, Prüfer suggested a further improvement to the murder process: piping off some of the heat from the forced draught unit Topf had installed in the crematorium to warm the gas chambers, and speeding up the diffusion of the Zyklon B. Although this idea was

seized upon by the SS, the heat from the continual use of the crematorium was so great that the forced draught unit did not work, and
it was eventually dismantled. Neither Prüfer, nor Karl Schultze, who
attended a meeting with the SS at Auschwitz to discuss the problem,
were in any doubt about what 'constant and without interruption' use
of the ovens meant. Schultze wrote: 'While we were with Prüfer in the
crematorium, the bodies of sixty dead prisoners were lying near the
cremation oven; I assumed they had been killed in the gas chamber.
Approximately twenty-five of these prisoner corpses were cremated in
our presence.'[98]

Despite the competition within Topf and Sons to provide the SS
with more efficient methods of murder, the building of the crematoria
and the gas chambers were not progressing smoothly. In March 1943,
fissures appeared in the eight-muffle oven in Crematorium IV after
only two weeks. Ernst Wolfgang Topf replied to the SS that repairing
this would only be under warranty 'if the alleged damage was the result
of faulty workmanship and not, for example, the oven being overheated, or metal tools being poked into the inner brickwork'. Although
Topf found a temporary fix for the problem, it seemed that the cause
of the problem was a design fault – the generator was too close to one
of the muffles. This put the ovens of Crematorium IV permanently
out of use, and meant the ovens of Crematorium V could only be used
with cool-down periods every four to six weeks.

Two months later, the SS was communicating its dissatisfaction once
again. Crematorium III was still not ready, Crematorium IV and V
were faulty, and Crematorium II (the only fully functioning crematorium) had broken down due to a faulty chimney lining. On 20 May, Kurt

Prüfer visited Auschwitz and was asked to find a solution to the chimney lining, which had been installed by a different company. Although he was accused by the SS of procrastinating, Prüfer eventually did this, but not in time to stop large parts of the lining collapsing into the flue.

In July, Prüfer contacted the SS with yet another complaint. Upset by the demands, Karl Bischoff, a member of the construction management unit at Auschwitz, demanded Topf and Sons repair the faulty lift in Crematorium II. Prüfer fumed in a letter: 'This lift was not built by us, but was assembled and installed by your own staff. We are therefore unable to understand why you are trying to make us responsible for a system that was not supplied by us.'[99]

Prüfer appeared to have no fear in dealing with the SS, or negotiating his way out of an unfavourable deal when it suited him. The issue of the faulty chimney was finally resolved when the SS was reluctantly forced to agree that the problem had been caused by overheating (i.e. overuse). A file note referring to a meeting with the chimney builder and Kurt Prüfer at Auschwitz on 10 September 1943 states:

> It has been brought to senior engineer Prüfer's attention that [the chimney builder] has come up with a different excuse for the collapse of the chimney casing each time he has visited. At his last-but-one visit he claimed in the presence of the commandant that the collapse was due to the high stresses caused by the over-heating of individual ovens.[100]

The chimney manufacturer, Robert Kohler; Topf and Sons; and the SS each agreed to each pay a third of the costs of the repair, with Ernst Wolfgang Topf concluding that the company was paying although 'our acceptance of the above-mentioned sum in no way constitutes an acknowledgement of a legal claim to do so. We simply agree to the payment as a result of our current shortage of staff, which makes it impossible for us to enter into further correspondence on the matter.'[101]

This neatly worded compromise by Ernst Wolfang Topf raises another question in considering those responsible for Topf's role in the Holocaust – the men and women who typed every letter, saw every order and recorded every phone call.

At the junior end of the scale was typist Annelise Hessler, who worked in the furnace construction division under Fritz Sander and Paul Erdmann. Hessler's initials appear on many of Kurt Prüfer's documents relating to his communication with the SS. A little higher up the pecking order were the technical draughtsmen who worked for Prüfer and Karl Schultze. Annegret Schüle names them as Hans Kohler, Walter Reinhardt and Sauerland from Department D, and Erich Krone and Horst Scharnweber from Department B (the ventilation department). Heading up the department were Fritz Sander and Paul Erdmann, who reviewed every order and often signed off on tricky correspondence. All of these people would have seen the design sketches, read the references to gas cellars, cremation capacities and corpse lifts. Overseeing all of Topf and Sons' business was the main administration office, run by the manager of the commercial department, Max Machemehl, who oversaw the invoices that were sent to the SS, as well as chasing up any overdue payments (a significant task, as the SS were often very late in paying their bills).

Max Machemehl was born in 1891 in Erfurt and, like Kurt Prüfer, had served in the First World War (though not on the Western Front). After leaving junior school, Machemehl joined Topf and Sons, where he would continue to work for the rest of his career, and was promoted to authorised representative in 1935. Like Prüfer, Machemehl was married without children. Also like Prüfer, Machemehl joined the Nazi Party at the end of April 1933. Both Prüfer and Machemehl held Nazi positions within the company during the Third Reich. Prüfer represented the German Labour Front within the company; Machemehl reported to the Security Services and the Gestapo on the mood and activities inside Topf and Sons. Gustav Braun reported that in 1944 Machemehl had approached him twice wanting to discuss production and the mood among the workers. When Braun questioned him, Machemehl produced a letter from the head of the Erfurt Gestapo, Reinhard Wolff, stating that Machemehl was required to submit reports about the situation at Topf and Sons. Wolff later explained that the Gestapo had spies inside every Erfurt factory – at Topf and Sons it was Max Machemehl.

The SS were late in paying more than half of their invoices, and in some cases they would delay payments by more than a year. In those instances, it was up to Max Machemehl to pen repeated reminders. On 2 July 1943, he wrote this letter in relation to late payment for the lifts at Crematoria II and III at Auschwitz, the fumigator for the 'sauna' and the waste incinerator: 'We hereby take the liberty of again sending you a list of the sums that still remain open on your account, from which you will see that the amount owing to us at this time comes to 32,732 RM. We have already written to you repeatedly about these outstanding sums on 16 April, 25 May, and 11 June 1943…'

Machemehl continues that he has been informed by Kurt Prüfer that these invoices have already been authorised and passed on to Berlin for payment. 'Since we are dependent on our accounts receivable, and the sums have now been overdue for some considerable time, despite our repeated requests for payment, we hope it will not be necessary to contact you again concerning this matter.'[102]

This letter had little effect apparently: the SS paid part of the invoices two months later, and the remaining part only in the summer of 1944.

Despite his involvement in all of Topf and Sons' deals with the SS, Machemehl insisted that his work at the concentration camps involved 'perfectly ordinary business' deals, and he moved seamlessly to forge a new career after the war in communist-controlled East Germany. His slipperiness is alluded to in a staff poem from the sixtieth anniversary commemorative booklet published in 1938:

> There, where the wax floor makes things slippy,
> On the first floor, sits Mache-Max
> Neatly behind glass and frame
> With his slim ladies…
> The door is never still here
> The telephone rings constantly
> This is where all the money decisions are made.[103]

Of course, Topf and Sons never made more than 2 per cent of its earnings from Kurt Prüfer's work with the concentration camps. At its peak in 1943, the annual earnings from Auschwitz never went above

1.85 per cent. Translated into today's money, Topf and Sons made only €30,600 per year in profit from developing the technology of the Holocaust.

The company had sold its soul for such little financial gain, hastening, in the case of Auschwitz, nearly 1 million people to their deaths in the gas chambers.

A large number of these people were murdered in the summer of 1944, when the arrival of Hungarian Jews pushed Topf technology to the limits. An agreement between the German-allied government of the Hungarian chief of state, Regent Miklós Horthy, and the Third Reich had kept Hungarian Jews just beyond Hitler's reach, until the German occupation of Hungary in March 1944.

The Hungarian government was itself one of the most anti-Semitic in Europe, and had passed hundreds of anti-Jewish laws in the 1930s. In November 1940, Hungarian Prime Minister Pál Teleki had advocated to Hitler that all Jews should be expelled from Europe, and the Hungarian government had murdered Jews on several occasions before the German occupation. In the summer of 1941, 18,000 Jews were deported to German-occupied Ukraine, with full knowledge that only death awaited them, and in January 1942, a further 1,000 Jews were murdered by the Hungarian military in Újvidék.

Despite this, the remaining presence of nearly 800,000 Jews in Hungary loomed large in Hitler's mind, and the German invasion of 1944, which aimed to keep Hungary loyal to the Third Reich by force, was followed by a *Sonderkommando* unit headed by Adolf Eichmann who was charged with implementing the Final Solution in Hungary. New anti-Jewish decrees were quickly passed: Hungarian

Jews were forced to wear the yellow star, Jewish businesses and properties were seized, and Jews were forced into ghettos. These ghettos, however, were short-lived ones, and between 15 May and 9 July 430,000 Hungarian Jews were deported – mostly to Auschwitz.

More Hungarian Jews were murdered in those two shorts months at Birkenau than in the previous two years. An average of 3,300 people were transported every day, rising to 4,300 on some days – and three quarters of those people were sent straight to the gas chambers. Eva Schloss, who arrived from the Netherlands that same summer remembered: 'The flames from the crematoria burned brightly, night after night, and all night long, but now everyone was dead – and we had sorted out the belongings that they had been forced to leave behind.'[104]

In total, nearly 440,000 Hungarian Jews were sent to Auschwitz, and on some days as many as 10,000 bodies were burned in either Crematoria II, III and IV or in open-air pits. These people were murdered and incinerated using the technology that Topf and Sons were so proud of developing.

Their clients and partners, the SS, were also pleased with the advances they had overseen in the more efficient murder of millions. Upon completion of the new extermination facilities, SS officer Perry Broad recalled that the SS had organised a photo exhibition of the new crematoria to be displayed in the entrance hall of the main building at Auschwitz. 'They forgot that when civilians were coming and going and they saw a large picture of the fifteen neatly set-out crematorium ovens, their reaction would be less likely to be admiration for the construction manager's technical skills than horror at the extremely dubious installations of the Third Reich.'[105]

CHAPTER NINE

TRIALS AND RETRIBUTION

With the Soviet forces closing in, the SS at Auschwitz realised that the end was near. In those final months they had murdered with a frenzy, sifting out those who could be sent on the 'death marches' back to Germany where they would be labourers, and dispatching those who remained: the young, the sick and the elderly. In just two weeks in October 1944, roughly 40,000 people were killed in the Birkenau gas chambers.

Then the gassing and burning of Auschwitz-Birkenau was over. On 25 November 1944, work started on dismantling Crematorium II and Crematorium III, but the Third Reich, aided by Topf and Sons, had still not given up on its dream of the total eradication of all Jews and prisoners. A member of the special unit notes that the following day, on 26 November:

It is strange that it is especially the counter-ventilation motor and its pipe that are being dismantled and sent to other camps – Mauthausen

and Gross-Rosen. Since these are required for the gassing of large numbers of people and there was never any such mechanism in Crematoria
IV and V, it seems that they are planning to recreate these facilities for
the extermination of the Jews elsewhere.[106]

Since the autumn of 1944 the SS had been looking for a suitable site
to reconstruct the extermination facilities of Birkenau at the camp at
Mauthausen – which was deep inside Austria, and much further from
the Soviet advance. Even as late as early 1945, when Auschwitz itself
had been liberated and Soviet troops were marching on Berlin, Kurt
Prüfer, on behalf of himself and Schultze's ventilation department,
was writing a detailed memo to the construction management unit at
Mauthausen:

REF: CONSTRUCTION OF CREMATORIUM (SPECIAL INSTALLATION).
Please find enclosed our drawing, reference D 61 654, showing half
of the total site area. The main building in the middle will have five
three-muffle cremation ovens, connected to two three-pipe chimneys.
The external side of the middle building contains the supervisors' room.
The coal store is on the opposite side. To the right and left are the rooms
for the waste incinerators with flue gas preheater. We have connected a
three-muffle cremation oven and the waste incinerator to this flue gas
preheater, which means that the waste gases from the two ovens are
fed through the flue gas preheater. The draft of the detailed design will
follow as soon as you have confirmed your agreement to the set-up.

Enclosed you will find a list of the terminology used in the naming of
the individual rooms. In the event of query, we request that you simply

give us the room number. In designing the facilities we have assumed that all components from the concentration camp Auschwitz should be reused.

This applies both to the iron components for the ovens and to the individual inward and outward ventilation systems. New pipework will be required; we will send you a quote for this once we have received your agreement to the construction of the new facilities. We have not included windows or how they should be distributed, since we do not know what will be sent to Mauthausen from A. The same applies to the roof trusses. A further on-site meeting with one of our team may be required before work on the new facilities can begin. If so, you would need to show the priority level on the contract, so that we can obtain the necessary travel permission. Possibly you would prefer to send us Wehrmacht tickets, second class, which you will obtain without difficulty from the Central Administration in Berlin.[107]

As this memo shows, Topf and Sons were now entirely used to planning gas chambers, in addition to crematoria, and were prepared to take on responsibility for constructing an entire extermination centre (an extension of their work at Auschwitz, where they had gone beyond their initial remit of ovens, to repairing chimneys, providing ventilation systems and sourcing 'corpse lifts'). Now all of this could come within Kurt Prüfer's orbit – and he could even resurrect his idea of using the heat from the ovens to preheat the gas chambers.

Although becoming chief architect of an entire extermination centre appeared to be a role that Prüfer tackled with some relish, his plans came to naught. Topf's chief fitter, Wilhelm Koch, was sent to

Mauthausen to oversee the project, but the planned centre was never built and within weeks the war in Europe was over.

On 7 May 1945 Germany surrendered to the Allies, and by 31 May Ludwig Topf was dead by his own hand. In the course of those few short weeks, the fortunes of Topf and Sons had collapsed, and those who had supported or played a role in the Holocaust were facing the bleak reality that they would have to answer for what they had always maintained were justifiable business decisions – but what others perceived to be heinous crimes.

American troops had reached the concentration camp at Buchenwald one month earlier on 11 April, and were shocked by the appalling conditions. Two months earlier, the camp had run out of coke supplies for the crematorium, which had resulted in several thousand bodies being hastily buried on the southern slope of the Ettersberg mountain, while piles of unburied corpses lay in the yard of the crematorium and rats ran wild throughout the camp. The last days of mass transports of prisoners from Auschwitz and Gross Rosen meant that the death rate at Buchenwald had soared, once again, in its final weeks of operation. In the last three months of operation, 6,000 people had died of starvation or disease; several hundred more died in the days after liberation. When American soldiers opened the Topf-branded ovens in the crematorium they found partially burned bones still inside.

One day after the liberation of Buchenwald, the US Army marched into the Erfurt offices of Topf and Sons and began a Counter Intelligence Corps (CIC) investigation into the company. Ernst Wolfgang Topf later gave his own account of what happened:

They had photographed the installations in the crematorium, together with our company signs. It was only a few days before we had a committee from the military government on the premises. Thorough and detailed investigations were carried out. They reassured themselves that all the files, drawings, parts lists, calculations etc. were all present. Nothing was missing, since every single document proved the only thing it could prove: that so far as we were concerned it had been just another perfectly ordinary business arrangement.[108]

To back this up, Topf representative Kurt Schmidt claimed that when shown a comparison between the oven doors at Buchenwald and the oven doors of a Topf civil crematorium, US Army Captain Faber could see that they were identical. (Of course, this was completely untrue. As Ernst Wolfgang Topf was well aware, every aspect of a Topf oven supplied to the concentration camps differed to those supplied to civil crematoria.)

Yet things were evidently not as cut and dried as Ernst Wolfgang sought to portray. Two weeks after the investigation began, Ludwig Topf met with the company's now communist-controlled works council to discuss Topf and Sons' contracts with the SS and address 'the rumours circulating about the Topf ovens'. In this meeting Ludwig attempted to agree a shared narrative for the company's involvement in engineering the extermination centres of the Holocaust – and to provide the most innocuous and benign justifications for their actions.

Ludwig begins by stating that the previous day he had spoken to Kurt Prüfer and Karl Schultze about the matter, and he was now talking to the works council in case they too were questioned as part of the investigation. Firstly, Ludwig explains, both the Kori company and the Didier company from Stettin also supplied ovens to the camps – the implication clearly being that Topf's role was not unique, or special, and that if they had not provided the ovens, another company would have. Moving on, Ludwig describes the origins of Topf and Sons' relationship with the SS:

> Several years ago the city of Weimar commissioned us to repair one of its crematorium ovens. Our senior engineer, Prüfer, travelled to Weimar to look at it. A typhus epidemic [it was actually dysentery] had broken out in the Buchenwald concentration camp, and the number of deaths was rising by the day. At the time, the dead of Buchenwald were still being sent to the Weimar crematorium. The epidemic naturally made the transportation of the bodies problematic, and so it was decided to install a cremation oven right there in the camp – which was absolutely the right thing to do from a hygiene perspective.[109]

The minutes of the meeting conclude that other contracts then followed from other camps, but that 'all members of the works council were completely clear about this sequence of events and all agreed that we had nothing to worry about'.

In this meeting Ludwig Topf followed the tried and tested formula, developed by the Nazis, of describing the most atrocious acts in the blandest possible terms – and it seems that the works council was perfectly willing to collude with him on this point. In a works council resolution they stated that:

Neither of the Herr Topfs were Nazis ... We have no complaints against the two gentlemen for the way they continued to run the business, and we are convinced that cooperating with them will be a good thing. Even in a communist-oriented economy, businessmen like these continue to have a place.[110]

Annegret Schüle writes that, 'Ludwig Topf took SS terror and extermination, and the Topf company's own willingness to act as eager accomplices to them, and made them sound like a logical, virtually inevitable and utterly innocent sequence of events.'[111] Yet both brothers knew that what they'd done was far from innocent, and that the investigation into their activities was closing in.

When the Allied forces arrived in Erfurt they evicted Ludwig from his luxurious villa, which they used as a base for themselves. Ludwig moved next door into a smaller wooden house, still in the grounds of the Topf family park. It was here that American army officers found him on the evening of 30 May, and broke the news that Kurt Prüfer had been arrested earlier that day. Ludwig was told that he could expect to be picked up for questioning the following morning at 10 a.m. A calmer man might have taken this, perhaps, as a warning to escape, or a chance to prepare for the day ahead. But in the final months of the war the Topf brothers had not been calm. Just as they had spent the war years engaged in paranoid company squabbles, the strain of knowing that the tide had turned, irrevocably, against the Third Reich, drove Ernst Wolfgang, Ludwig and their sister, Hanna, into an emotional, bitter dispute with each other.

Rather than attempt to escape, Ludwig went to one of Erfurt's oldest pharmacies, located on the corner of the cathedral square, and bought potassium cyanide. That night he used it to commit suicide. Before doing so he wrote a dramatic letter, steeped in self-pity, that captured his final thoughts:

If I have decided to avoid arrest, then it is for this reason: I no longer believe there is any justice in this world, after all the injustice and viciousness I have experienced at the hands of my family and everyone else. If I am arrested, gross injustice will befall me. I never did anything consciously and deliberately bad, but people have acted this way towards me. I was never cowardly – but I was proud. To put myself at the mercy of a foreign power is impossible for me, because I have learned the hard way that there is no longer any justice, any decency in this world. Therefore, as a decent man myself, I now have the opportunity to do with myself as I see fit. That means: to depart this world that has become generally unbearable and, that has persecuted me and been unjust to me in particular.

If I could believe that my innocence in the business with the crematoria – which is my brother's innocence, too – would be acknowledged and respected, then I would go on fighting for my vindication, as I have hitherto. But it is my belief that the *Volk* wants its victims. And so I would prefer to take care of this matter myself. I was ever decent – the very opposite of a Nazi – the whole world knows that. If I could still feel peaceful in the bosom of my family, then the fight would be worthwhile – but the Topf family does not exist anymore, the Topf attitude, essence and self-respect are all gone. In these respects, I was always its lone representative. I am so alone that there isn't even anyone I need to beg for forgiveness for my suicide.

In his new, and final, will, also composed that night, Ludwig explains why he has chosen to disinherit his siblings and make his lover Ursula Albrecht, company secretary Max Machemehl and the city of Erfurt his heirs: 'My two siblings have grossly misunderstood and insulted me, and it took infinite goodness and brotherly love and strength of mind on my part to be able to deal with the appalling injustice I have suffered at the hands of my relatives.'[112]

It was true that the Topf family had long been riven with petty infighting, dysfunction and mistrust (in his penultimate will, written in April 1941, Ludwig refused Ernst Wolfgang's pregnant wife, Erika, the right of residence in his home – and urged his brother to leave her). In the final year of the war, Ernst Wolfgang told company workers that the relationship between the two brothers had broken down to such an extent that Ernst Wolfgang stopped working in the office they shared in the administration building and withdrew from their joint partnership. From that point on, Ernst Wolfgang worked in a separate office some distance from Topf and Sons and acted as the company's commercial director while Ludwig now sat opposite executive secretary Johanna Büschleb – who took Ernst Wolfgang's side in the dispute, calling Ludwig short-tempered patronising and fault finding. 'In the last fifteen months or so, something became apparent in my brother that went far beyond any earlier differences and arguments ... namely, that he quite specifically couldn't work with me any longer,' Ernst Wolfgang told workers. 'It is too much if two people fail over a small issue, if they simply cannot agree, then the company needs them to decide that one of the two will leave the company, but in such a way that the company is not convulsed as a result.'[113]

It appears that the brothers had fallen out over their limited-partnership agreement, with Ludwig wanting to disinherit his sister Hanna and her children. But Ernst Wolfgang's account makes no mention of Ludwig's fears of the 'unjust retribution' he feared he would face for Topf and Sons' activities on behalf of the SS.

Of the two brothers Ludwig had taken the lead in developing the crematorium business for Topf and Sons, and when the Nazis came to power he had worked closely with his brother and Kurt Prüfer to ensure that every demand of the SS was met. He had involved himself in every intricate detail of the horrors of the Holocaust and the concentration camps, and for five years he had lived the blissful life of a playboy, all the while knowing that his technology was sending millions of terrified people to their deaths. Facing up to his actions would have required a maturity and composure that Ludwig did not possess, and choosing the coward's way out was a final testament to his character.

At 5.30 a.m. on the morning of 31 May, Ludwig's lover Ursula Albrecht woke Max Machemehl (who was also living in a house in the Topf family park) to tell him that 'Ludwig has gone!' Albrecht was overcome with emotion and proceeded to run around the park crying. In the midst of all the chaos, Machemehl got dressed and drove over to tell Ernst Wolfgang Topf the news. He recalled that 'shortly afterwards, Fräulein Albrecht arrived in the Daberstedt Strasse in the CIC [American Counter Intelligence Corps] car and screamed that L. had been found dead near the roofing felt store.'[114] Max Machemehl found Ludwig's farewell letter and passed it to the CIC. In keeping with Ernst Wolfgang's narrative that Ludwig's death was due to a personal matter, family doctor, Dr Karle, ruled that it was a case of suicide 'brought on by war-induced nervous shock'.

Above all, Ernst Wolfgang was determined to protect the family business, and his own fortune, by ensuring that Topf and Sons resumed production. In the early days of the American occupation, this seemed quite plausible. As far as Topf could see, the American investigation was going nowhere and the CIC seemed to accept the company line that Topf and Sons had spent the war conducting 'perfectly ordinary business'. Even Ludwig Topf's suicide appeared hasty when Kurt Prüfer was released from arrest on 13 June 1945, and went back to work at Topf and Sons. Those responsible, however, would have much more to fear from the Soviet forces, who would assume control of Erfurt and the surrounding area as part of the Soviet zone of occupied Germany.

With production at standstill, and the company still owed large amounts of money for aircraft parts it had produced for the Luft-waffe, Ernst Wolfgang Topf's most pressing problem was how to get his hands on a large life insurance policy for 300,000 RM which he could now claim after his brother's death. To do this, however, he had to travel to the Allianz insurance company in Stuttgart – something which required permission from the occupying government. On 13 June Ernst Wolfgang and his newly appointed deputy, Kurt Schmidt (formerly head of Department E for silo and storage construction) were granted permission to travel. Topf left Erfurt with his wife and daughter on 21 June and headed first to Wiesbaden, where his son was living with his in-laws. Once there, however, he was refused permission into the French occupied zone around Stuttgart. He then fell ill.

While Ernst Wolfgang was away, there was tumultuous change at Topf and Sons, as well as in Erfurt itself. One day after his departure, the American military informed Topf and Sons that they could resume production for systems related to foodstuffs and were allowed to employ fifty people – an announcement greeted with joy at the company, as a note in the file reflects: 'Sender: Military Government Erfurt. Content: Permission to resume Production. GREAT JOY!!!!!!!!!!!!'[115] Although furnace construction was excluded from the notice, the first order was for a crematorium oven for the city of Erfurt.

Ernst Wolfgang's absence, however, made the leadership of the company uncertain – with many questioning whether he ever planned to return, especially after the announcement on 3 July that Erfurt would be transferred from American to Soviet control (as had already been agreed by the Allies in September 1944). On 18 July Kurt Schmidt wrote to Topf: 'I don't want to write down here the rumours that are circulating in Erfurt about your absence ... but it would be very important for you to be here if you could.'

The change of control to a Soviet occupying force was one that Ernst Wolfgang had feared, and he had tried to seek assurances before his departure that it would not happen during his trip. However, it was clearly something beyond his control, and Topf now found himself in limbo – he had left Thuringia and was now unable to return. At the end of July Ernst Wolfgang was denied permission to re-enter the Soviet zone. He spent several months holed up in a schoolhouse near the border, while he petitioned to be allowed to return to Erfurt. When the new school year started in September, he moved in with his sister Hanna's daughter near Kassel for six weeks – but his efforts to return to Topf and Sons remained fruitless. Although Ernst Wolfgang was doing everything in his power to facilitate a return to Erfurt, he also used this time to lay what he hoped were the foundations for a new Topf and Sons in West Germany – building on the company's existing network of branch offices. While he continued to urge loyal employees like Kurt Schmidt to fight the expropriation of the company in Erfurt, he also urged them to join him in the west if those efforts were unsuccessful.

In the immediate aftermath of the handover from American rule, the Soviets wasted no time in assessing what role Topf and Sons could help play in rebuilding the Soviet economy – they also continued to make less overt enquiries into the links between Topf and Sons and the Nazi concentration camps.

In July 1945, the first month of Soviet rule, officers visited Topf and Sons on five occasions. Their first visit was to establish the size of the company, its production system and the raw materials that were being used. Officers were also keen to find out what had happened to an order for vertical kilns that had been destined for the Soviet Union, but which had been cancelled after the German invasion of 1941. They were mainly concerned with the food systems aspect of the business – including the possibility of producing field kitchens for the USSR (which was in fact the subject of a very large order in October that year).

At the same time Soviet officer Major Kriwenzow saw his visit to Topf and Sons as an opportunity to probe further about why Ludwig Topf had committed suicide. Kurt Schmidt, Gustav Braun and other representatives of the company's management reassured Kriwenzow

that Ludwig's death had had nothing to do with the company's relationship with the SS. 'The radio advertisement about the cremation
ovens at Buchenwald can be ruled out as a significant factor, since we
all knew that these were a perfectly normal order,' the Topf minutes
state. The record goes on to claim, untruthfully, that these ovens were
based on a 1911 design, and that they were the same as those supplied
all over the world, including the USSR. The Topf management seem
reassured that Major Kriwenzow shares their view: 'Major Kriwenzow
said that it was the view of the Russians that the supplying company
could not be held in any way responsible for the cremation ovens, since
so far as the company was concerned, it was a delivery just like any
other.' Kurt Schmidt agrees, adding that if one was to take the opposite
view, and hold Topf responsible for the atrocities committed in the
camps, you would also have to hold responsible every other trades-
person, including 'table makers, stool makers and cupboard makers'.[116]

These two strands of argument – that ovens were identical to those
supplied to civic crematorium and that Topf were just one of many
ordinary suppliers to the camps, in the same vein as table makers or
bread bakers – would prove enduring. In the case of the first argument,
all those involved knew that it was an outright lie, yet on 26 October
Ernst Wolfgang Topf granted his niece's husband, attorney Ernst-Otto
Keyser, the power to represent him – which he did, starting with the
following letter to the Soviet authorities:

> It is not as if they had been supplying mass-cremation equipment, it
> had just been the exact same cremation ovens supplied as standard to
> all crematoria; i.e. the ovens for the cremation of one body at a time.

The company of J. A. Topf and Sons had no way of knowing, and still cannot think, that the individual cremation oven could be abused for the purpose of mass cremation.[117]

This letter reveals the depths of Ernst Wolfgang's dishonesty, but it did nothing to stop the Soviets from taking control of Topf and Sons.

On 30 October, the Soviet military administration stated that all companies that were associated with the Nazi Party or the army were to be sequestered as 'ownerless property' and taken into the temporary administration of the state. Despite desperate last-minute wrangling by Kurt Schmidt, Topf and Sons was declared ownerless and taken into Soviet administration on 20 November.

Meanwhile, Ernst Wolfgang had discovered that he might be granted permission to return to Erfurt, but, fearing for his own safety no doubt, he decided ultimately to remain in the American zone, where he could urge his workers to rally behind him. In the month following the expropriation, Topf urged his loyal members of staff to support him in trying to get the company takeover reversed by writing letters stating that the Topf brothers had never been Nazis, and detailing their anti-Nazi activities. Some obliged, including the executive secretaries and long-serving administrative staff as well as Willy Wiemokli, the half-Jewish bookkeeper whose own father had been murdered at Auschwitz, and who was likely to have been incinerated in a Topf oven.

This effort was a failure, and the company remained in Soviet hands – with the first order of the Soviet administration requiring Kurt Schmidt to provide a full list of the company's assets, bank accounts, machinery, raw materials and semi-finished goods. Despite claiming that Topf's 'perfectly ordinary' supplies to concentration camps were identical to their deliveries of civic cremation ovens, the inventory carefully lists the patents applied for by Department D, including the 'cremation oven with double-muffle' registered on 6 December 1939 and developed for Buchenwald, as well as Fritz Sander's hideous innovation for Birkenau, the 'continuous operation corpse incineration oven for mass use'.

Whether they were aware of it or not, the net was now closing in on those engineers and managers who remained in Erfurt. Topf records reveal that on 11 October a Soviet officer had visited the company looking for Kurt Prüfer, but that he had not been on site that day. But this was only a temporary reprieve for Prüfer. Between the fourth and seventh of March 1946, Kurt Prüfer, Fritz Sander, Karl Schultze, Gustav Braun and Max Machemehl were arrested by the Soviet authorities.

Max Machemehl was released eighteen days later without charge. Topf fitter Wilhelm Koch was interrogated as a witness, as was Paul Erdmann and executive secretary Johanna Buschleb. Heinrich Messing went underground for two weeks after being tipped off about the Soviet investigation. The remaining men were sent to the headquarters of the Soviet Army Command in Berlin-Karlshorst, and were subjected to an initial round of interrogations. Fritz Sander had been through four interrogations when he died of heart failure on 26 March 1946, only three weeks after his arrest.

Kurt Prüfer, Karl Schultze and Gustav Braun were transferred to Butyrka prison in Moscow where, more than two years later, they were subjected to a second brief round of interrogations in February–March 1948. All three were then charged.

The indictment against the men began:

Deputy Minister for State Security of the USSR

General Lieutenant

15 March 1948

INDICTMENT

On 7 March 1946, the following employees of the German machine-engineering company Topf and Sons was arrested by the counter-espionage organs of the Ministry for State Security of the USSR on the basis of criminal responsibility for their participation in the horrific acts of the Hitlerites in the concentration camps:

Prüfer, Kurt – manager of the cremation furnace planning and construction group

Schultze, Karl – manager of the ventilation construction group; and

Braun, Gustav – company operations director

The investigations established that:

Between 1940 and 1944 the machine-engineering company Topf and Sons maintained contacts with the organs of the SS, on whose behalf they built crematoria and gas chambers in the concentration camps, which were intended for the mass extermination of citizens of the USSR, Poland, Yugoslavia and other states under the yoke of fascist Germany.

The accused Prüfer, Kurt; Schultze, Karl; and Braun, Gustav were specialists in the field of the design and construction of cremation facilities and gas chambers for the company. Between 1940 and 1944 they built and equipped crematoria in the Buchenwald, Mauthausen, Dachau, Gross-Rosen and Auschwitz death camps.

In Auschwitz alone, in the Auschwitz main camp and Birkenau

satellite camp, five powerful crematoria and four gas chambers, in which more than 4,500 wholly innocent people were murdered every day, were built and equipped by them.[118]

The charges against Prüfer were that he had led the negotiations with the SS, planned and overseen the construction and installation of the ovens, and taken the initiative to develop and improve existing designs.

> The accused Prüfer represented the company of Topf and Sons in discussions with the SS administration about issues relating to the construction and equipping of the above-mentioned crematoria and gas chambers. He participated in the development of technical projects and crematorium drawings, led consultations and monitored the construction work.
>
> Prüfer was directly in charge of the assembly work during the installation of the twenty-one cremation ovens designed by him for the crematoria.
>
> Despite knowing the true purpose of the crematoria and gas chambers in the camps, Prüfer, on his own initiative, gave thought to how the technical equipment and crematorium facilities could be improved so as to increase their capacity, before devising ways to do so.
>
> In addition, he entered into written correspondence, on his own initiative, with various German chemical companies relating to the manufacture of gas analysers for the gas chambers in Auschwitz.[119]

Karl Schultze was charged with building and installing the ventilation systems for the gas chambers, and for overseeing a test run during which prisoners were killed in the gas chambers – as well as increasing the capacity of the ovens through fitting specialist blowers.

The accused Schultze, K., designed and installed powerful ventilation systems in four gas chambers at the Auschwitz death camp, on behalf of the SS.

During commissioning of these systems, he personally carried out a test run in which prisoners were killed in the gas chamber.

In order to increase the capacity of the cremation furnaces in the camp crematoria, Schultze designed special fans and personally supervised their installation.

In early 1943, the accused Prüfer and Schultze tested a cremation furnace in Auschwitz. In the course of the test run, the bodies of approximately twenty prisoners who had been specially killed in the gas chambers for this purpose were cremated in the said furnace.[120]

Gustav Braun was charged with sending fitters to the camp, fulfilling SS orders and for forcing 300 'foreign workers' into slave labour.

The statements each man made during his interrogation contain factual errors. No doubt they were extracted under duress. But, nonetheless, they provide telling insights into the attitude and mindset of Topf and Sons employees as each man worked to advance his position through enabling the worst kinds of atrocities.

Fritz Sander begins his 1946 interrogation by confirming his name and basic details, including how long he has worked for Topf and Sons. His interrogator then asks him how he designed the 'corpse incineration furnace for mass operation'.

As chief engineer in the company, I presided over the cremation construction department, which was managed by Prüfer. In 1942 (I can't remember the exact date), he mentioned that the crematoria at the Auschwitz concentration camp couldn't handle the number of corpses that needed to be cremated. He told me that he had witnessed two to three bodies being shoved into a single chamber, and that the crematoria still weren't able to deal with the number of corpses they had.

As a specialist in incineration technology, I then took the initiative to build crematoria with greater corpse incineration capacity.

In November 1942, I presented my design for a crematorium for the mass incineration of corpses – the corpse incineration furnace for mass operation – and applied to register it with the state patent office in Berlin.

[This] would work on the conveyor-belt principle, meaning that bodies could be brought to the furnaces mechanically and continuously.

The interrogator then asks Sander who designed the crematoria at Auschwitz and Buchenwald, to which Sander replies that it was Kurt Prüfer, but designs were approved by Sander himself and then overseen by Ludwig Topf. When asked what he knew of Prüfer and Schultze's visits to Auschwitz, Sander replies:

In the summer of 1942 Prüfer and Schultze told me that large numbers of people were being killed in the gas chambers of Auschwitz and that their bodies were then being incinerated in the crematoria. There were so many of them that three bodies were being pushed into a chamber at a time.

'So you knew that innocent people were being murdered in the Auschwitz concentration camp?' the interrogator probes.

'Yes, I knew [that] from the summer of 1942. Prüfer told me about the mass transportations of people being brought to the Auschwitz concentration camp from Poland, Greece and other countries, who were then murdered in the camp.'

The interrogator later returns to this line of questioning to confirm that Sander knew specifically about the gas chambers. 'At what point did Prüfer tell you that the crematoria could not handle the incineration of the bodies? Did you ask him out of interest where all the bodies were coming from?' he asks.

Sander replies: 'Yes, I did ask Prüfer why there were so many bodies in the camp; he replied that they were killing people there in gas chambers and then cremating their bodies.'

But before this the interrogator asks: 'Knowing that the concentration camp crematoria were being used for the annihilation of innocent people, how could you – on your own initiative – suggest the design of an even bigger crematorium for the mass incineration of bodies?'

Sander replies: 'As a German engineer and employee of the Topf company, I felt it was my duty to use my knowledge to help Hitler's Germany to victory, even if that resulted in the annihilation of people – just as every engineer in aircraft construction did.'[121]

Some of Sander's inconsistencies regarding the dates of his conversations with Kurt Prüfer have been seized upon by Holocaust-denying historians as evidence that his statement was fabricated. Of course, it's likely that Sander was confused. But while he may have mixed up whether the conversation with Prüfer took place in 1942 or 1943, there can be no denying Sander's chilling description of the 'corpse incineration furnace for mass operation' – and his rationale that it was his duty to help Hitler's Germany achieve victory, even if that resulted in the annihilation of a population.

When Karl Schultze is interrogated, he formulates a slightly different defence. Initially, Schultze confirms the details of his employment and admits that he made three trips to Auschwitz in 1943 in connection with fitting the ventilation systems for the crematoria and gas chambers.

The first time I was there, I was summoned to see an SS man who worked at the camp and who warned me that the construction and outfitting work that our company was doing on crematoria and gas chambers in Auschwitz was an extremely important state secret. He made me sign a confidentiality agreement. I had already had to sign a similar agreement for Ludwig Topf, since I came into direct contact with the work that the company was doing for the SS construction management unit at Auschwitz.

After detailing how he witnessed the gassing of the first prisoners at the crematorium, Schultze then states that he reported this to Ludwig Topf upon his return to Erfurt and that Ludwig 'did not react to this [information]'. The interrogator points out that in Schultze's first questioning in 1946 he claimed to have also told Kurt Prüfer about the gas chambers. Schultze admits that he may have done, 'but it's a long time ago and I can't remember the exact circumstances and nature of our conversation'. Schultze agrees that he and Prüfer travelled to

Auschwitz together in early 1943 to fix the broken fan in Crematorium II, and that during this visit 'there were around sixty prisoner corpses lying next to the cremation furnaces. I assume they had been killed in the gas chamber. About twenty-five of these corpses were incinerated in our presence. After that I didn't go to Auschwitz again.'

The interrogator asks Schultze what he would like to say in reaction to a document that shows that '4,756 prisoners were murdered every day' in gas chambers built and equipped with his involvement.

'I have no reason to doubt these official figures. The document really does show [that],' Schultze replies.

Does he realise, the interrogator asks, that this means he was working on the mass extermination of innocent people?

Schultze responds:

I must admit that [...]. However, when I was doing this work, I assumed that the SS wouldn't be killing innocent people in the crematoria and gas chambers, but that they would only be killing criminals who had been sentenced to death for their actions against German troops and authorities in Poland and other occupied territories.

The interrogator says that, in addition to Jews and other non-Aryans, the SS did murder people who were fighting for liberation from German rule of their homelands – but why does Schultze consider these people criminals?

'I was and am a German, who is loyal to the German government and its laws,' Schultze replies. 'That's why I considered those who had fought against this government and its measures, including those in the

German-occupied territories, to be criminals. They were condemned in line with German laws, because they had murdered representatives of German authorities and the German military.' Although he was never a member of the Nazi Party, Schultze adds that he 'believed it to be my duty to respect and obey the laws of my land'.

The interrogator concludes by stating that Schultze had already confessed in 1946 to his role in building the gas chambers and crematoria, and he urges Schultze to 'tell us what led you to pursue this criminal path?' At this point Schultze diverges from the strict explanation of 'wartime duty' that his Topf colleagues have so far adhered to.

> I did not get involved in the building and equipping of crematoria in concentration camps and the gas chambers in Auschwitz on my own initiative, but did so on the orders of the boss of Topf and Sons, where I was employed. If I had refused to carry out this work, I could have been dismissed as a saboteur and been subjected to reprisals. It was out of fear of this that I never asked the company boss Ludwig Topf to refrain from using me for these projects.[122]

This is the first time a Topf defendant has claimed that they carried out their work for the simple reason that they were afraid not to. If true, it might be a plausible justification – but all of the evidence demonstrates that this wasn't the case. At no point did any senior member of staff at Topf and Sons, or either of the Topf brothers, appear to be afraid of the SS. To the contrary, they often expressed frustration and annoyance and were tardy when completing work if it suited them. As the previous chapter outlines, Topf and Sons would occasionally turn down SS commissions if the company was too overstretched to fulfil them – without any fear of reprisals.

When interrogated Kurt Prüfer, the instigator and innovator for all of Topf and Sons' work with the SS, attempts a similar blend of detailed fact and obfuscation, confusion over dates and lies about knowledge and motive.

Prüfer begins by stating:

Until 1943, I didn't know anything about the real purpose of the crematoria in the concentration camps. I only found that out when I visited Auschwitz. Until then, the people from the SS construction management units who led the discussions with the Topf company had always said that the concentration camp crematoria were for the cremation of corpses of prisoners who had died a natural death as a result of epidemics.

I only found out about the existence of gas chambers at Auschwitz when I visited the camp in 1943. Until then I knew nothing about either their existence or their purpose.

I would also like to emphasise that the Topf company never built any gas chambers in the concentration camps. I only know that the Topf company fitted two ventilation systems for the gas chambers in the Auschwitz concentration camp.

The interrogator asks Prüfer what he specifically discovered about the nature of the gas chambers and crematoria during his visit to Auschwitz in 1943. Prüfer replies:

I discovered that the mass murder of people, including women, children and the elderly, was taking place in the camp. Hitler's people were bringing them to Auschwitz in transport trains from German-occupied European countries. The prisoners brought to Auschwitz were sent to the gas chamber by the SS, where they were killed. Their bodies were then incinerated in the crematoria and special fire pits.

Asked if this implies that he was aware the crematoria he was building were for the disposal of the bodies of innocent people, Prüfer replies: 'Yes, I knew that.' Why, then, the interrogator queries, did he continue to work on their construction? This time Prüfer points the finger of blame at Ludwig Topf:

> After I'd discovered the real purpose of the crematoria in the Auschwitz concentration camp, I considered refusing any further involvement in their construction, and I said this to the company boss, Ludwig Topf.
>
> Ludwig Topf replied that the construction of the concentration camp cremation furnaces was a commission from the Reich HQ of the SS, and that if I refused to work on them, I could be arrested and sent to a concentration camp myself for sabotage.

Prüfer adds that he feared losing his job and suffering reprisals from the Nazis. After a disagreement over the date upon which he became aware of the true nature of the gas chambers and crematoria, Prüfer explains that the conditions were first described to him on a visit to Auschwitz in 1942.

Claiming to have come upon this revelation 'by chance', Prüfer says:

In early 1942, the Auschwitz SS construction management unit asked me to go to the camp to assess a design for a new crematorium in the Auschwitz section of the camp and to view the proposed site for it.

I viewed the proposed site with one of the SS men. As we drove past Crematorium I, I saw through the half-opened door a room with human corpses lying on the floor in various poses; there were more than ten of them. When I approached this room, someone quickly slammed the door shut from inside. Since I didn't know what this room in Crematorium I was used for, I asked the SS man about it. He said that there was a gas chamber in there, where prisoners were gassed to death.

In answer to my next question about how the gas chamber worked, the SS man answered evasively, claiming that he didn't know anything about it, before telling me that he knew there were gas chambers in the city of Lodz, in which the SS had carried out gassings using vehicle exhaust fumes. At some point they had accelerated this process through the use of some kind of gas. The SS man said that the use of gas in the Lodz gas chambers had reduced the killing time from 10–15 minutes to 1–2 minutes.

The SS man told me that the killings in the Lodz gas chamber went as follows: the prisoners were forced into the gas chambers, the doors were hermetically sealed, and then gas balloons were thrown in through special openings. On the basis of this description, I concluded that prisoners in the gas chamber that the SS had built in Crematorium I at Auschwitz were being killed in the same way.

As the interrogation progresses, Prüfer admits that while he was not responsible for the installation of the ventilation systems, he did assist the SS in their attempts to source gas analysers that were used to measure the cyanide level in the chamber – something far beyond his remit as a furnace engineer.

> When Von Bischoff came to me with this request, he explained that hydrogen cyanide fumes still remained in the gas chambers after the prisoners had been gassed, even after ventilation, leading to the poisoning of people working there. Von Bischoff therefore asked me to find out which companies were producing gas analysers, with a view to using them to measure the concentration of the hydrogen cyanide fumes in the gas chambers and thereby avoid endangering the workers.

Prüfer adds that, on this occasion, he was unable to help the SS, as he had struggled to find companies who produced gas analysers. The interrogator then asks if Prüfer himself was involved in testing the crematoria on site. Prüfer responds:

> No. That was done by fitters from the company who were carrying out building and assembly work in these crematoria under my direction. On my visits to Auschwitz I observed and checked the functioning of the cremation furnaces in operation. During this checking, bodies of prisoners killed in the gas chambers by the SS were incinerated in my presence.[123]

Prüfer changed many details in his interrogation and obfuscated on many points – but he never deviated from his justification that he had only ever acted out of fear of reprisal. Yet his avid attempts over many years to cement himself as the key to Topf and Sons' relationship with the SS proved otherwise. Extermination had become his life's work, but Prüfer was shameless enough to claim that he had only ever acted out of fear of reprisal. Nothing could have been further from the truth.

Kurt Prüfer, Karl Schultze and Gustav Braun confessed to the charges outlined against them in the indictments, and were found guilty without ever facing trial. Each was sentenced to twenty-five years hard labour. Despite his attempts to cast his behaviour in a more favourable light – for Prüfer it was the end of the road. On 25 October 1952, he died of a stroke while still incarcerated in the USSR. But both Braun and Schultze were released from prison after nine years, in October 1955, as part of a prisoner amnesty between Germany and the Soviet Union. Schultze's future and fate after this point are unknown – unlike Gustav Braun he left no family behind to cope with the aftermath of his actions. Gustav Braun returned to Germany where his son Udo picks up the story of his father's last years.

CHAPTER TEN

A CHANGE OF SCENERY IN THE USSR

The Soviet indictment against Gustav Braun read as follows:

As operations director of the company of Topf and Sons, the accused Braun, Gustav sent installation teams and other specialists to the concentration camps to set up and install cremation furnaces and gas chambers. He ensured that the company took all necessary steps for the timely completion and dispatch of the SS's orders for the production of equipment for the camp crematoria and gas chambers.

From 1941 to the day of the German surrender, Braun was directly responsible for up to 300 'foreign workers' who had been abducted by the Hitlerites from the occupied territories of the USSR and other countries to work in the production facilities of the company of Topf and Sons.

Braun despised these workers, had them guarded in the company's own camp and forced them into slave labour.

From 1941 Braun was a deputy counter-intelligence officer in the company of Topf and Sons. He carried out counter-intelligence work against sabotage and diversion activity and informed the organs of the SD [intelligence agency of the SS and Nazi Party] about the various moods of the company's workers and employees.[124]

Gustav Braun never visited a concentration camp, nor did he oversee the work of any of the engineers, but his senior role in the company meant that the Soviet authorities were persistent in building a case against him.

Braun was unusual among the senior management at Topf and Sons in that he had only joined the company in 1935. Recruited directly by Ludwig Topf, Braun was forty-five years old when he joined the company, and married with one older son. He was a highly qualified engineer who had spent eight years in the USA and South America and, in his years at Topf and Sons, he would demonstrate both his engineering and management skills.

One of Braun's sons, Udo, remembers how his father met Ludwig Topf:

He was on his way back [to America] in 1934 or 1935 when he met Topf. According to my mum, he met him in Hamburg, just as he was about to emigrate for good. He wanted to go back to America, but when he met Ludwig Topf they started talking and he cancelled his departure and decided to take the job managing a building site associated with Topf and Sons. Apparently Topf suggested that once that job was finished, he should join the firm in Erfurt as plant manager. So he agreed, and turned down the job in America.[125]

Braun had worked abroad due to the poor state of the German economy and the lack of opportunities – but he believed that the job with Topf and Sons would be advantageous. While working on the building site, Braun met the woman who would become his second wife – and Udo Braun's mother.

> He was married to his first wife, but they got divorced. He met my mother up on the building site, where she worked. She was an office clerk and stenographer. My father was retained by Topf to finish the job. The building site was already in progress – and there was a lot of time off in the evenings, right? And in any case, my mother was a very positive person – and she was twenty years younger.

Braun began working for Topf and Sons in the storage construction division, but was quickly promoted to operations manager, and then operations director in charge of managing and fulfilling all the orders. At the onset of the war, he was made responsible for 'Uk' matters – deciding which workers were indispensable, and should therefore be released from service in the army. He also took on the role of company defence officer, monitoring the workforce and reporting those findings to the Gestapo.

Despite being promoted to such a senior position in such a short space of time, Braun's tenure at Topf and Sons was marked by angry disputes and conflict – particularly with Ernst Wolfgang Topf.

'My father had a very confrontational relationship with Ernst Wolfgang, but not with Ludwig,' says Udo Braun.

> My parents talked about it, and later I found some documents from my

father and read about it. Ernst Wolfgang Topf was a *Korinthenkacker* [a petty man] and my father had difficulties with him. Not with Ludwig. Ernst Wolfgang Topf was a nit-picker who mainly wanted to hurt and dominate others. Ludwig was a gentleman.

To this day Udo still has fond memories of Ludwig Topf:

As a little boy I was invited to the Topf family park and I went to their villa, holding my father's hand. Naturally I was very impressed by the expensive furnishings and found it all very exciting. The gardener came along and brought some cherries. Ludwig Topf was very nice to me, and that is important for a little boy. My father was very strict and a bit old for a father. He was forty-seven when I was born in 1936. I like to think about Ludwig Topf; I remember him as a very nice man.

Throughout the 1930s and 1940s, Topf and Sons' files document the tense relationship between Gustav Braun and Ernst Wolfgang Topf, which would often descend into outright hostility and name-calling.

The first complaint in the Topf files about Gustav Braun appears in 1937:

Report by Herr Machemehl

Erfurt, 27 November 1937

Re: Foreman Görlach's complaint about Herr Braun, operations director. Foreman Görlach came to see me today to say that working practices in the company could not go on as they were. Although Herr Görlach didn't want to go into too much detail and repeatedly stressed that he was telling me this in confidence, it was clear that his comments were directed towards Herr Braun. He criticised the fact that, among other things, Herr Braun had issued instructions behind his back that he really should have been aware of. He also complained that in some cases the formalities necessary for good order in the company were not being observed. For example, in agreement with Herr Braun he had instructed that the silo crew should work on Sundays, and had informed the gatekeeper and the crew leader of this in writing, naming the individuals concerned. But on another Sunday, Herr Braun issued a similar instruction and summoned the new foreman, without informing Herr Görlach.

Herr Görlach repeatedly emphasised that he had only come because he was worried for the company and was afraid things would turn out badly if things carried on in this way. He even spoke of 'bankruptcy' in connection with Herr Braun.[126]

As was common at Topf and Sons, the report contains long accounts of fairly trivial matters, undercut with an element of hysteria (the warning of 'bankruptcy').

In October 1938, Ernst Wolfgang Topf composed another lengthy file note about a dispute between himself and Gustav Braun over the replacement of a technician. Topf wants to promote someone internally, a man named Habel, but immediately complains that 'from the very first moment, Herr Braun took against the idea (facial expression, etc.)'. When Topf explains why he thinks an internal promotion will be quicker than advertising in the newspaper, he states: 'This, too, [was] met with icy rejection. When I asked why he was opposed to the idea, and whether he was familiar with Herr Habel's work, Herr Braun just replied, "I want to find someone *myself*!"' Topf agrees to drop the matter – but then writes a further page-long note in the file about why he finds it impossible to work with Braun. Topf writes:

> I would like to add to this record that Herr Braun's desire to put himself on a throne has been commented on many times before … Herr Braun still retains his character faults, and even displays them in his dealings with me. I must make it completely clear that I was as courteous as I could be. My behaviour was like that of a Pope blessing a supplicant. I didn't make *any* demands at all – I just put the idea to him. I did, however, speak very clearly and concisely, and Herr Braun's decision to send me away, as though I were some junior employee in my own company, just highlights his defective character.

Ernst Wolfgang Topf's complaint about Braun's lack of respect, and his belief that Braun was his brother Ludwig's ally, runs throughout the file references to Gustav Braun. When Braun is given an air defence position in the company in October 1940, Topf records another highly excitable memo about Braun's supposed high-handedness in dealing with his staff. Ernst Wolfgang fumes:

> Herr Braun heartily dislikes order. He's all for confusion and a totally subjective, impulsive style of management that is subject to neither order nor any kind of plan. Everything of an ordering or organising nature is wholly alien to him, for the simple reason that he can rule better in a state of disorder, disorganisation and chaos, and that a lot of things can be hushed up that way. When your operations management is based on

shouting instructions without any order behind them, you can get away with almost anything and no one will ever be able to call you out.[127]

Between the time of this letter in 1940 and the end of the war, Topf and Sons was embroiled in producing the machinery of the Holocaust (as well as overseeing a large slave labour force, and manufacturing aircraft parts – in addition to their main business matters). Yet, as ever, the leadership of the company was consumed by petty rivalries and disputes. As the records show, the enmity between Ernst Wolfgang Topf and Gustav Braun worsened as the years passed.

On 30 January 1943 (while Topf and Sons are in the midst of constructing the crematorium at Birkenau), Ernst Wolfgang takes the time to write a two-page memo about Braun's behaviour – this time in relation to the redundancy of someone called Röder. He sets the tone by marking the note 'strictly confidential' and then adds – 'Theme: Only buffoons [Hanswürste] can co-exist as officers of the company alongside the operations director.'

The memo outlines a farewell conversation between Topf and Röder, but as expected with Ernst Wolfgang, it quickly descends into gossip. 'He is very depressed about his redundancy, since he has enjoyed working here. He lets it be known that this redundancy is just the last in a series of attempts by Braun to "neutralise him" and make him surplus to requirements.' Röder then explains to Ernst Wolfgang why he believes his poor performance and redundancy is in fact the fault of his manager, Gustav Braun. Topf writes:

In summary, Röder is convinced that he and every other production engineer could only survive in the operations division shadow-like, as a subpar employee. Braun simply refused to tolerate those around him; he always wanted to make all of the decisions and do everything himself, right down to the smallest detail, it just wasn't possible for any equivalent specialist to exist alongside him. We have already previously experienced this. Our response to all this is that Braun's nature and temperament – and also his character – have been well known to us for a long time.

On 2 March 1943 things appear to come to a head between Ernst Wolfgang Topf and Gustav Braun, when Topf openly confronts Braun – this time in a dispute over a new roof for the plumbing workshop yard.

FILE NOTE

By Herr E W Topf

For the Braun personnel file

2.3.1943

SECRET

The statement I made to Herr Braun today:

I told Herr Braun that open enmity towards him seemed to me to be the simpler and better course, and that he should assume me to be his declared enemy. This was the result of the last few weeks, in which he has indulged in his scheming to the point where I am just sick of it.

The events leading up to my declaration this lunchtime (to which I added, that he was a devil and his behaviour correspondingly devilish – something I totally stand by), were as follows…

Topf then details the nature of the disagreement, which is over the length of the new roof – and whether workers should be deployed to work on that, rather than building a new wall. Braun, states that he has already called off the work on the wall. 'Braun responded to my astonishment as follows: "I called it off, because nothing's allowed to be done without the approval of Herr Ludwig Topf!" At this point all four of us fell silent. I was quite naturally astonished at this audacious and tactless manner and attempt to put me down.'

The row continues, in detail, about whether or not to continue building work on the wall, before Ernst Wolfgang becomes almost incoherent with rage:

Torpedoing the discussion we'd had on Wednesday ... has to lead to open enmity between Braun and me. All the more so, given that he succeeded in playing my brother off against me, since the latter agreed to Braun's project. Since Braun clearly felt quite comfortable doing this, I've made this tactic easier for him in future. So now we'll see where this open feud between us will lead.

Everyone knows that Braun is a chop-and-change kind of a person who never plans anything and who has wasted our company's money over and over again these last five years with his impulsive actions. He has overturned everything from one day to the next: started this, abandoned that, never seen anything through. I have been on his case for months and that doesn't suit him at all. He wants to see me off, and thinks he'll find it easier dealing with the other one [Ludwig Topf], whom he can still impress with his fast and short-lived actions. At any rate, Braun reckons he hasn't been rumbled yet. But he knows full well that I have seen through him and that I disapprove of his constant chopping and changing. This is why he has been avoiding me for weeks and hides behind my brother with evident malice. This shamelessness is intolerable.

What I have always known about this man – that he doesn't know how to behave in any way other than dishonestly and maliciously, and that he's an appalling schemer – has now been definitively proven.[128]

What this memo proves most clearly, perhaps, is not that Braun was an 'appalling schemer', but rather that both Topf brothers were afflicted with a strong strain of mental instability (especially bearing in mind that Ernst Wolfgang was the brother who did *not* commit suicide). Given such sentiments, however, one might wonder why Braun was not sacked. On the contrary, despite the mutual loathing that existed between Braun and Ernst Wolfgang, Braun's position at Topf and Sons was firmly established, and, in 1943, he was awarded a large bonus of 800 RM. No matter how much Ernst Wolfgang fumed and vented, the reality was that workers as qualified as Braun were neither found nor replaced easily.

Udo Braun remembers his father in these years as an old-fashioned, duty-bound patriarch – a man typical of the time:

He got up very early to go to work. He drank his ersatz coffee standing up and didn't sit down for breakfast. He took the same route to work every day and greatly enjoyed his walk. He wanted to be early and the first to arrive and the last to leave. [On one occasion] there was an air raid. I was tired and sat on the stairs. My father was already in the cellar with the rest of the family. So he came back up, picked me up and just shook his head. [On another occasion] I was crossing the street with him. In the middle of the street I stopped to look at some flowers and I got into trouble. When you are in the street you have to cross it! ... There were rules and you had to obey them. He was an authority figure and very distant from me. I can't say that we liked each other. There was a distance. That is what I meant when I said he was an 'old' father. He was too old for a cuddle. I needed that.

Although Udo heard that his father told humorous family stories at work, at home he was serious and authoritarian.

In the company of his colleagues he was very jovial. Apparently he used to tell stories about my little brother and I – like the one where my mother took me by the scruff of the neck and my little brother bit her on the bum. Despite being quite senior in the company, he was still a very humorous man – but I saw little evidence of his humour myself.

Although Braun divorced his first wife and married Udo's mother, his second marriage did not prove particularly happy either.

'My mother was born in Oldenburg. My father was from Swabia. That's a terrible combination if you ask me,' Udo Braun says. 'I don't mean to sound horrible, but we used to joke "that's the maximum sentence".'

Udo remembers his mother once asserting her authority over his father when he refused to build her a second potato rack for two different types of the vegetable. To get her own back his mother mashed the two types together into a horrible concoction, and served it up for dinner. As a result, Gustav Braun built his wife a second potato rack.

In 1936, the family moved into a middle-class, three-bedroom apartment in a house on the street next to the Topf family park, where Udo Braun still lives. They were joined by Gustav Braun's son from his first marriage, Hans, who the family believed needed some paternal discipline. Udo's older brother joined the Waffen SS, and there is a photo of him in his uniform holding hands with little Udo. Despite his military position, Hans formed a secret romantic relationship with Ruth, the youngest daughter of the Jewish Stein family who lived in the same house.

In another example of how the horrible work of Topf and Sons often went hand in hand with complex relationships with Jewish friends and family, both Ruth and her sister escaped from Nazi Germany, but their parents, Leopold and Elly Stein, were murdered at Auschwitz – possibly gassed, and almost certainly burned, in machinery Gustav Braun had knowingly overseen the construction of.

All the evidence suggests that Gustav Braun knew all about the SS's orders of ovens for the concentration camps, as well as the ventilation systems for the gas chambers.

When the SS placed a new order for five three-muffle ovens which would be housed in Crematorium III at Birkenau in September 1942 (in addition to the five that had previously been ordered for Crematorium II), Kurt Prüfer discussed the details of the order with Gustav Braun.

Later in February 1943, a typed note in the Topf and Sons file refers to a conversation between Karl Schultze and Fritz Sander who were discussing the missing blower for the ventilation system and ovens at Birkenau. In the note, Topf employees set aside SS convention and refer directly to the 'gas cellars'. This note is then read and signed by purchasing manager Florentin Mock, Max Machemehl, Ludwig Topf – and Gustav Braun.

When the war ended, Braun colluded with the Topf brothers and their senior employees, perpetuating the myth that all of the company's business dealings with the SS had been 'perfectly ordinary'. Braun also agreed with the assessment that Ludwig Topf's suicide on the eve of his arrest had been due to overwork and 'excessive stress'. Despite his second-hand role in developing the technology of the Holocaust, Braun was arrested alongside Prüfer, Sander and Schultze on 4 March 1946.

As a nine-year-old, Udo Braun knew very little about his father's work and the reasons behind his arrest:

I was too young and too 'far away' from him. Shortly before he was arrested my mother said: 'Dick [Braun's nickname because he had spent time in America], why don't you leave for a couple of days. I've got a funny feeling.' Then my father shouted – I heard his voice from my room – 'What do you want, you old hag, I was not even a member of the [Nazi] Party. I have not done anything. I am not leaving. I don't even know why I should leave!' My mother didn't know either, but she had a feeling – and a couple of days later they came to take him away.

When interrogated, Gustav Braun initially admitted to knowing about the deliveries to the concentration camps, before changing his story and denying he had any prior knowledge. During an interrogation on 12 February 1948, he is presented with a company diagram that shows him overseeing the production of machinery for the gas chambers and crematoria. In response, he states:

> The Topf company organigram you're showing me wrongly lists my position as company production director. I only managed the company's machine-engineering operations. Company departments such as production planning, assembly, standards, purchasing and dispatch did not report to me, and I had no connection with their work. Those departments reported directly to the company boss Ludwig Topf.

The interrogator admonishes Braun: 'It is a known fact that the Topf company assembly department built crematoria and gas chambers for use in concentration camps, and that the overall management of this work rested with you as operations director. Tell the truth!'

Braun responds to the interrogators' remarks by stating:

> I am not denying that the assembly department built and equipped crematoria and also equipped some gas chambers in German concentration camps over the course of a few years, especially from 1941 to 1943. However, as I have already stated, I was not involved in this work, as the assembly department did not fall under my competence.[129]

In the face of his denial, the Soviet authorities decide to bring Kurt

Prüfer and Gustav Braun together for an explosive face-to-face encounter on 25 February. It is clear from the meeting that the two men dislike one another – and Prüfer's determination to point the finger of blame at Braun is also evidenced. According to the interrogation record, the meeting lasted an astonishing seven hours, beginning at 11:40 a.m. and finishing at 6.30 p.m. After noting that Prüfer and Braun have known each other in a professional capacity since 1936 and that 'there had never been any personal bad feeling between them', Kurt Prüfer gives a long account in which he firmly implicates Braun as a guilty party in all of Topf and Sons's activities:

Gustav Braun was operations director of Topf and Sons. He was a close confidant of the company owner, Ludwig Topf, and also reported to him directly. He was in charge of all of the company's production activity.

Sometimes Braun would deputise for Ludwig Topf, if he and his brother (and co-owner of the company), Ernst Topf, were out of town for longer periods.

The following departments, offices and units came under Gustav Braun's jurisdiction as operations director: production planning office, assembly department, standards office, dispatch department, materials warehouse and operations.

Topf and Sons started carrying out construction and outfitting work for the concentration camp crematoria in 1940.

The commissions for these works always came from the responsible organs of the SS, specifically, the SS construction management units at the Buchenwald, Gross-Rosen, Mauthausen, Dachau and Auschwitz concentration camps.

These commissions were included in the company's general production plan, which was drawn up by the planning office together with Gustav Braun.

As operations director, Braun would work with the planning office to set the timescales for carrying the commissions out, depending on the company's production capacity at the time. He therefore always knew which organs of the SS the company had accepted commissions from, and what kind of commissions these were. He arranged whatever was necessary to ensure the commissions were carried out on time.

The Topf company carried out these commissions in the following way: the factory manufactured the required equipment, supplies and parts. These were then sent to the relevant concentration camp by the dispatch department. Foremen and workers were sent from the assembly department to carry out the construction and assembly work on site, i.e. in the concentration camps.

These works were carried out with Braun's knowledge and on his instructions – company operations, assembly and dispatch all reported to him directly.

Normally, the Topf company only built cremation furnaces in the concentration camps I named above; it was only in Auschwitz that the company was involved in setting up four gas chambers alongside the crematorium.

The following equipment and parts were manufactured in the Topf factory for the named crematoria: mountings, ventilators, steel floors for the cremation chambers. In addition, the company's turning and metalworking workshops produced cast-iron doors for the cremation chambers/muffle furnaces, as well as iron grids.

It was Braun who ensured the production of these parts and fittings, since he was directly responsible for the work done in the workshops.

At this point, the interrogator turns his attention to Braun, and asks him to confirm his position at Topf and Sons, and whether he knew that the company was carrying out work in concentration camps on behalf of the SS. Braun replies:

I found out about it, quite by chance, in 1940, in the course of a conversation with one of the Topf and Sons's fitters. I'd asked him where he was working and he replied that he was building crematorium furnaces in the Auschwitz concentration camp, along with senior engineer Prüfer.

The second time, I was informed by workers in the dispatch department, which was under my authority. It happened like this: one day in 1940, I went into the dispatch department and saw several SS men there. When I asked what they were doing there, the department manager responded that they were negotiating the dispatch of building materials to the Buchenwald concentration camp, since the company's senior engineer, Prüfer, was building a cremation furnace there.

In general terms, I knew as operations director that the company was building cremation furnaces, but I didn't know where or for what purposes – I wasn't interested in that.

The interrogator then asks Prüfer to respond to Braun's statement. Prüfer claims that Braun is lying:

> Braun's claim that he didn't know who Topf and Sons were building cremation furnaces for, and for what purpose does not correspond to the truth. As operations director, Braun was informed about the furnaces and almost all the construction work on the cremation furnaces in the concentration camps was carried out with his knowledge.
>
> As evidence for this I would like to make clear the following facts:
>
> 1. In 1940–41, two cremation furnaces for the Dachau and Mauthausen concentration camps were assembled in the Topf and Sons factory, with Braun's direct involvement. Braun personally designated a location in the factory where the furnaces were to be assembled, and assigned workers to carry out the assembly work on these furnaces. In addition, individual parts (metal racks) and fittings for these furnaces were manufactured in the factory workshops on Braun's instructions. Once the furnaces had been assembled, they were delivered – on Braun's instructions – one to the Dachau concentration camp, the other to the Mauthausen concentration camp.
> 2. In autumn 1940 or early 1941 (I can't remember the exact date), an SS man from Berlin visited the company to find out why one of the cremation furnaces was not yet ready and on schedule, as well as to inspect the assembly work on the furnace. As a result of this visit, company boss Ludwig Topf called a special meeting to discuss the construction of this furnace. In addition to L Topf and the SS man, this meeting was attended by both Braun and myself, and Braun

actively participated in the discussion of the deadlines for construction of this cremation furnace for the SS. On the instructions of the SS organs in Berlin, the company dispatched this furnace to the concentration camp at Mauthausen.

3. As company operations director, Braun held a meeting with the factory foremen every morning after breakfast to review the work plans for the day. Thus Braun was not only aware that parts and equipment were being manufactured in the factory workshops for cremation furnaces that would be used in concentration camps, at these meetings he himself issued the instructions to the factory foremen to produce the necessary parts or equipment within the specified time frame.

4. In autumn 1942, I personally agreed the delivery of an eight-muffle cremation furnace to the Auschwitz concentration camp for Crematoria IV and V – the parts of which had been manufactured for the Berlin SS organs and deposited in the factory warehouse. Braun assigned a worker to help me check that all parts for these furnaces were present; and he instructed the dispatch department to send these cremation furnaces to the Auschwitz concentration camp, which they did.

5. In the course of 1941 and 1942 I approached Braun several times in his capacity as operations director with the request to send specialist workers to the Auschwitz and Buchenwald concentration camps so that they could carry out a series of works relating to the construction of the cremation furnaces in these camps. In each case, Braun approved the request and assigned me the required specialists for the work in Auschwitz and Buchenwald...

6. As company production director, Braun was involved in every last detail of the work being done in the factory workshops, and also in the departments and offices that reported to him. He was interested in everything they did and would check their work. It is therefore impossible that he did not know what was being produced in the factory or where it was going to be sent.

Prüfer's statement is so clear and well-argued that it can only have been agreed in advance with the Soviet authorities. Having marshalled this evidence, the interrogator then tells Braun:

The statements of the prisoner Prüfer during this head-to-head encounter are sufficient proof that the construction and outfitting carried out by the Topf company in the concentration camp crematoria was not only done with your knowledge, but also with your direct participation. Drop your stubborn denials and tell us the truth.

Braun refuses to back down, however:

The statements made by the prisoner Prüfer during this head-to-head encounter are not what happened in reality, so I cannot confirm them. I again stress the fact that I was aware Topf and Sons was producing cremation furnaces, but I neither knew nor cared who for or on whose behalf.

In response, Prüfer states he stands by his account and that he would like to ask Braun two direct questions:

Does Braun remember the following incident? In the summer or autumn of 1942, we received the second order from the SS construction management unit at the Auschwitz concentration camp for the construction of five three-muffle furnaces for Crematorium III in Birkenau. Since the written order did not specify a priority level or the sequence in which the work should be carried out, I told Braun about the order when I met him in the company secretariat, and showed it to him. Braun immediately went with me to see the company's planning department manager Mersch, with whom we then reached an agreement on the matter. On our way to Mersch's office, Braun asked me the following question in jest, or more specifically, he stated in a jokey fashion: 'Boys, is there anyone else to burn there?' I replied in similarly jokey fashion.

Secondly, Prüfer says:

Does Braun remember that in early 1942, the company was visited by a SS officer from Berlin who wanted to negotiate the construction of new cremation furnaces for the SS? The company boss Ludwig Topf called a meeting to discuss this, in which Braun, Mersch and the SS man participated.

At this meeting it was said that the company was fully occupied with the fulfilment of urgent orders for spare parts for military aeroplanes and could not accept any new orders from SS organs for the construction of cremation furnaces.

In response, Braun simply states that he is 'unable to recall these incidents'. The following day, when Gustav Braun's solo interrogation resumes, he appears to have realised the futility of maintaining his denial. Braun now states that while he did not oversee plans for the crematoria, he was aware of their existence:

I'm not claiming I didn't know anything about them. Whenever the company had a major order, the company boss Ludwig Topf, or his co-owner Ernst Topf, would inform me of it and we would agree an achievable deadline.

In individual cases I was consulted about things such as deadlines and stocks of materials for various orders. The orders received from customers were processed by the company's technical departments. In addition, as operations director I carried out briefings of the foremen every morning, in the course of which their work for the next few days was discussed. This was based on the requirements arising from the current status of the work that needed to be done for individual orders, which the planning department had already passed to the workshops.

These briefings were also attended by the manager of the production planning department, who passed the orders to the workshops and managed the deadlines for their completion. Thus I was always informed about the company's operational plans, even though I was not [officially] informed about the plans created by the general planning office.

The interrogator responds: 'So that means you were informed that Topf and Sons had accepted and carried out orders from the SS organs for concentration camps?'

Braun says: 'Yes, as operations director I knew that the company had accepted and carried out orders for the Buchenwald, Dachau and Auschwitz concentration camps.'

Braun goes on to admit that these orders were for crematoria and that, as operations director, he provided the space in the factory to assemble the furnaces, as well as arranged for metal workers to complete the installation. In the final part of his confession he states: 'Under my directorship, the Topf and Sons factory produced ventilation systems with inward and outward ventilation which I later learned had been installed in the gas chambers.'

'Why did you deny these facts during your head-to-head encounter with Kurt Prüfer?' the interrogator asks.

Braun responds: 'Because I couldn't remember clearly and also I was afraid that admitting it would [make things worse for me]. After the head-to-head I thought about it all and decided to tell the truth here.'[130]

As his interrogation shows, Braun always maintained that he was initially unaware that Topf and Sons were producing ventilation systems for Auschwitz-Birkenau that were intended for the mass murder of millions in the gas chambers. Yet, the evidence of the Topf and Sons internal memo of 1943, referring to the 'gas cellars' at Birkenau, contradicts this.

In addition to the charges laid against him relating to his knowledge of the production of machinery for the crematoria and gas chambers of concentration camps, the Soviet authorities also questioned Braun rigorously over his role reporting on company activities to the Gestapo, and his treatment of foreign labourers. As Annegret Schüle points out in her book on Topf and Sons, it is difficult to single Braun out for his relationship with the Gestapo – all companies were required to have a surveillance officer and Braun was appointed to this role by Ludwig Topf.

Similarly, there is no evidence that Braun mistreated the foreign workers who came under his area of responsibility as operations director at Topf and Sons. Braun claimed that he had intervened on their behalf when they complained about poor food provision in 1943, and Udo Braun says some of the forced labourers went to the Braun house to say goodbye at the end of the war.

At the end of his interrogation, Braun 'confessed' to the charges against him and was sentenced to twenty-five years' hard labour – as were Kurt Prüfer and Karl Schultze. As an engineer, Braun was sent to work on the railway line 428 km south of Moscow at Kuybyshev. A fellow German prisoner reported that, even in an international group of highly skilled workers, 'his work is the best'. After nine years, Braun was released and returned to Erfurt in October 1955.

Udo Braun remembers that 'Those nine years were horrible for our family. I was the son of a war criminal. Nobody said that directly to me, but they insinuated it by not letting me go either to secondary school or to university.'

During his father's absence, Udo had stepped in to offer his family emotional and financial support – particularly his mother, whom he adored. In 1955, Udo was working in the Wismut mines to earn money for the family.

One day I received a telegram: 'Can you come home, please. Father is back.' I took the telegram to the Russian shift manager. He was very decent and gave me time off. He knew I always met my quota, which was very important to the Russians. So I got a week off to go home. My brother met me at the train station and showed me a passport photo of my father. He told me, 'This is how he looks.' I was shocked.

The Gustav Braun who stepped off the train was, in his son Udo's eyes, a broken man.

When I got home there was a man standing in front of me who resembled my father. By now I was a big lad, built like a brick shithouse, and he couldn't cope with me. And I couldn't cope with him. Our communication was dire. Neither of us knew what to say. I didn't even know how to address him. Should I call him 'Papa'? Or 'Father'? 'Papa' was customary in our house. 'Mutti' and 'Papa'. But I just couldn't say 'Papa'. Once I very nearly addressed him with 'Sie' [formal address for older strangers].

For the rest of Gustav Braun's life, he never discussed his work for Topf and Sons, or his time in Russia, with his son.

I missed out on vital years. I was nine when he 'went away' to Russia. In his papers, he used to refer to his time in Russia as 'a change of scenery in the USSR'. Otherwise he wouldn't mention a single word about it. And it wasn't like anyone would have said to him 'Come on, tell us all about it.' No way. He once told me that he'd been imprisoned with criminals, and that sometimes they were forced to sleep with a big plank of wood chained across their legs. So that was pretty drastic. But when the Russians realised what he could do, they moved him to an engineering office where he could work on construction projects and he did much better there.

Above all, Udo sensed that his authoritarian father was now a frightened man. 'My mother told me that my dad went downstairs one day and saw a railway worker walking past wearing a uniform.' Gustav Braun was now afraid of men in uniforms. 'My dad ended up hiding behind a pillar. He was a completely broken man. My mother said: "What's the matter with you? It's just a railway worker."'

Shortly after returning to Erfurt, Gustav Braun moved back to his home town of Heilbronn, where his eldest son Hans was living. Although Udo's mother and younger brother also went to Heilbronn, Udo stayed behind in Erfurt – and began working for Topf and Sons as a fitter.

We didn't talk much. It was simply impossible. There was no common ground. Later, he wrote to me from Heilbronn saying it wasn't good enough for me to be just a fitter. So he sent me some formulae that he thought I could use in my career. Just imagine, he was a brilliant structural engineer himself – and he sent me these formulae and said I shouldn't get married, even though my mother wanted me to get married because in communist East Germany getting married meant that the government would allocate you an apartment and furniture.

On occasions when they did meet, Udo felt that his father continued to torment him. One day when Udo was visiting his parents in

Heilbronn, his father announced that he was going to take Udo out for an afternoon snack. This consisted of some sausage, bread and a quart of wine. Udo remembers the scene well:

> I had grown up without drinking wine, so when he went to the toilet I got the sugar and put some into the wine. That was a mortal sin. When we got back home he said to my mother: 'I won't go out with this *Rindvieh* [moron] anymore. He doesn't know how to behave.' That was my father.

As the son of a *Republikflüchtling* (a refugee from East Germany), Udo Braun found himself persecuted by the authorities. Yet despite this, he worked his way up the company ladder until he held his father's position at the company that was once Topf and Sons, but which had now been renamed VEB Erfurter Mälzerei- und Speicherbau (EMS).

On 11 May 1958, three years after his release, Gustav Braun died of cancer in Heilbronn. For Udo, his father's death offered a chance to hold the kind of conversation that had never been possible during his lifetime:

> A couple of years after he died, I went to the cemetery and talked to him. I said: 'Father, we can end our war. I accomplished everything that you accomplished. Even a bit more than you did. You can be nice to me now. I have made up for what was lost.' We worked in the same office without knowing it. First him as director and then me – years later – as head of production. That is quite ironic.

During his years living and working in what was then East Germany,

Udo visited the camp at Buchenwald – and witnessed some of its horrors:

> I have been to Buchenwald several times. Normally, I went with other employees from the company. It smelled very bad. Terrible. I saw the furnaces; terrible. There are images and the machinery … It is very moving and upsetting. It really does get to you. There is no room for laughter or for jokes. You can't imagine it happening again – one couldn't bear that. This is particularly true when you have not only seen Buchenwald, but also the pictures published by the media. Terrible, terrible things. Many people should see the camps, but, above all, it's the sabre-rattlers who should make the trip. Buchenwald is horrifying.

Despite seeing this evidence with his own eyes, Udo says that he still struggles to accept the fact that his father, or Topf and Sons, were totally culpable – especially given his own long career with the company after the war.

> I was an apprentice when I first heard about their having built the crematoria, or rather machines for the disposal of corpses, but I didn't gather the extent of the measures taken to perfect the process. East Germany was not so keen on dwelling on the past. I only really began to understand it all later. I've always had problems, even to this day, with the apportionment of blame. Yes, the company built the furnaces and they shouldn't have done that. They built the furnaces with German thoroughness –this is an enormous disgrace – but they also built good machines. Other machines. Good people participated, including skilled

German craftsmen who built malting plants and silo facilities, some of which are still being used today. When I was working in a senior position at the company, I came across many Topf installations. This gave rise to a kind of inner conflict. The fact that Topf and Sons built those 'perfectly efficient' furnaces is very, very bad. But the Krupp steel and armaments company acted badly as well by building canons. And those who built other guns were bad, too. As were all the other people who supplied war materials. I cannot say that it was solely the fault of Topf and Sons. But what happened at Buchenwald was and remains atrocious.

Working for the renamed Topf and Sons after the war, Udo Braun found himself having to defend the company more frequently as the decades passed. On one occasion, a Jewish group told him they believed the company should be taken into Jewish hands – something Udo rejected.

It's not a question of too much or too little culpability. I feel it's like this: they built the furnaces and now everybody has come down on them. I took a senior position in the company afterwards and then we built our machines. History is a great burden for us … The allocation of blame had exceeded any limit. Everybody thought that they had to say something against us. This was very difficult for the subsequent employees who had played no physical part in constructing the furnaces. Our name was *Erfurter Mälzerei* und *Speicherbau*. But people kept saying: 'Ah, these are the Topfs who built the furnaces.' Why should this shame be heaped on us? We didn't do anything wrong. Do you understand?

That bothered me terribly ... I am not capable of attributing the right amount of blame. There is always guilt if this kind of thing happens, but there has to be a limit to it.

Nor does Udo Braun accept his father's personal role in developing the technology that fuelled the Holocaust.

'I have always wondered why my father was attacked and dragged off, while the Topfs got away unscathed. They just went for Braun, Erdmann, Prüfer and Schulze. That doesn't seem right to me.' Later, he added:

You can accuse my father of being in charge of war defence within the company. The question of his guilt ... in relation to the ovens, is something that I don't see. His role in war defence – yes, he's guilty where that's concerned. But he played no part in the construction of the ovens.

History, however, takes a different view. After the fall of the Berlin Wall in 1989 and the collapse of communism in Eastern Europe, Gustav Braun's conviction was reviewed again by the public prosecutor's office of the Russian Federation in accordance with a new law 'Governing the Rehabilitation of Victims of Political Repression'. After reviewing the files, the public prosecutor's office reaffirmed the original charges against Kurt Prüfer, Karl Schultze and Gustav Braun, stating that all the men 'were correctly convicted and are not eligible for rehabilitation'.

CHAPTER ELEVEN

POWER WITHOUT MORALS

'No one in our company was guilty of anything at all, either morally or objectively. It is no empty phrase when I describe my company and the entirety of its conduct throughout the twelve years of the Hitler regime with the phrase: 'Morality without Power.'

ERNST WOLFGANG TOPF, 1958[131]

Despite lengthy wrangling, Topf and Sons of Erfurt officially passed out of Topf family hands on 10 May 1947, when it became a state-owned enterprise and no compensation was awarded to its former owners. On 1 June 1948, sequestered companies in the area of Soviet occupation were deemed 'people-owned' – and renamed VEB.

For the remaining members of the Topf family, this was a setback. Yet, it was far from the end of the story. For Ernst Wolfgang Topf, the loss of the company was merely a waypoint in the ongoing efforts to clear his name and re-found Topf and Sons in the West. He would dedicate the rest of his life to achieving this goal.

Together with his sister Hanna, Ernst Wolfgang had set up a new company in Gudensberg, a small town near Kassel, as early as 2 November 1945 – while he was still actively fighting to retain control of Topf and Sons in Erfurt. The new company, J. Topf GmbH, was listed as a hardware retailer and Johanna Topf, Ernst-Otto Keyser and Heinrich Mersch were all shareholders. (Mersch, the managing director of the new company, was a former head of planning at Topf and Sons and was in a relationship with Johanna Topf.)

From the beginning, however, the Topfs' new enterprise was dogged by revelations of their business dealings during the war. On 6 March 1946, local Kassel newspaper *Hessische Nachrichten* published an article titled 'Soap from human fat', detailing how the Nazis exploited the murder of millions for profit, including breaking teeth and melting down gold fillings, stuffing mattresses with women's hair and stealing all of the belongings of those sent to concentration camps (although they did not make soap from human fat). The article, which was based on prosecution documents presented at the first Nuremberg trial, goes on to name companies which supplied cremation ovens: the Kori company, Didier-Werke and Topf and Sons. 'In the offices of the Auschwitz concentration camp, members of the Soviet State Commission found extensive correspondence between the camp management and the company of Topf & Sons, Erfurt.'[132]

Even at a time of such political upheaval and revelations, it appears that one reader of the *Hessische Nachrichten* was paying attention, lodging a criminal complaint against Ernst Wolfgang and leading the US Counter Intelligence Corps (CIC) to reopen its investigation.

This 'dirty denunciation from a Gudensberg resident,' as Kurt

Schmidt described it,[133] had far-reaching consequences. On 25 March 1946, Ernst Wolfgang was questioned by the CIC and issued a statement where he claimed upon his 'sacred oath' that Topf and Sons was never involved in the 'horrors, such as the recovery of gold teeth and hair,' and that the company's 'perfectly normal' transactions with the SS were extremely urgent war orders that he would have been 'severely punished' for delaying or sabotaging. Clearly Topf and Sons had never thought it had anything to hide, he added, otherwise the company would never have stamped its logo on the cast-iron fittings for the camp crematoria. 'Had we known or suspected that they were to be used for anything evil, my brother would have omitted the company logo from the parts lists.'[134] More truthfully, perhaps, he would have stated that neither brother thought he would have to face the consequences of his actions.

After holding Ernst Wolfgang Topf under arrest for two or three weeks, the American CIC released him without charge, after failing to locate the crucial evidence needed to prosecute him. Soon after, however, Topf was to become embroiled in the much longer process of a denazification tribunal, which would last from April 1946 until March 1950.

Not long after the denazification investigation against Ernst Wolfgang began, J. Topf GmbH collapsed. Topf himself had left Gudensberg (probably as a result of the notorious newspaper article) to live with his parents-in-law in Wiesbaden. The company that Kurt Schmidt reported was in a 'desolate state' had been taken over by Heinrich Mersch, who had fallen out with the Topfs and renamed the company after himself.

The denazification process applied to everyone living in the American-occupied zone – and began with a requirement that every citizen fill out a notification form about their relationship to the Nazi Party. Ernst Wolfgang Topf did this on 26 April 1946, stating that he rejected national socialism – and that he had actively opposed it for the entire twelve years of Nazi rule. In a statement he claimed that he had joined the party at 'the last moment' in 1933 and had done so to prevent the 'anti-Semitic demon' that had already broken out at Topf and Sons.

As a member of the party, however, his case was put forward for investigation at a denazification tribunal – which were lay courts largely implemented by Germans themselves under guidelines laid down by the American military. Those incriminated were called before a hearing and assigned to one of five categories: major offenders, offenders, lesser offenders, followers and exonerated persons.

Ernst Wolfgang's case came before the Fritzlar-Homberg denazification tribunal in Hesse. Topf began preparing his defence by asking the works council at Topf and Sons in Erfurt to issue him with another Certificate of Political Innocuousness, as they had done in 1945 – but there is no record that they did this. By August that year, however, the charges levelled against Ernst Wolfgang Topf were beginning to seem more serious, with three people writing to Topf to tell him that he was accused of producing the inward and outward ventilation systems for the gas chambers.

Ernst Wolfgang replied in his usual, slightly hysterical and disingenuous manner, claiming that he was a 'deceived victim'. Topf replied that even the fitters themselves could not have 'divined that an inward and outward ventilation system could be abused!' and added that the system in itself was 'the most innocent thing in the world'.[135]

In his defence, Ernst Wolfgang then told a further series of outright lies. He began by stating that his brother, Ludwig, who he said was 'always open with me about his struggle with suicidal thoughts', had never implied 'any kind of connection between the ventilation and that "procedure".' Neither of the brothers had known any of the people responsible, either in the camps or in Berlin. 'There was never even a single personal visit to Erfurt for the purposes of discussing the orders with us. They didn't even know we existed.'[136]

Although evidence existed, the complicated course of Ernst Wolfgang's tribunal demonstrates the difficulties of acquiring true information, especially working across different occupied zones, and with people and organisations that often had their own agendas in terms of protecting themselves or accusing others.

Ernst Wolfgang Topf's tribunal began in December 1946 with an initial aim of obtaining sworn statements about him from two non-suspect witnesses. In July 1947, the public prosecutor and president of the tribunal wrote to the SED (the Socialist Party of East Germany that would rule the DDR from 1948 until 1989) and the Erfurt police requesting information about the Topf brothers. A police employee, Kurt Ziegenbein, replied in August that year, reiterating that Ludwig Topf had committed suicide before questioning by the Allies and that Ernst Wolfgang had fled to the West. Both these events had occurred due to 'installation of crematoria in all of Germany's concentration camps at the behest of both brothers'. Ziegenbein added that the brothers had 'definitely' been 'informed of what was happening in the camps'.

As a police officer, Ziegenbein had been a colleague of former Topf worker and ex-communist resistance member Bernhard Bredehorn, and former Topf fitter Heinrich Messing (Bredehorn had briefly been head of the police force in Erfurt, before being forced out in 1947, and Messing also occupied a prominent police position for a time). As such, Ziegenbein clearly knew where his loyalties lay, as he also stated that the Topf brothers had forced the workers to install the crematoria against their own wishes – and went on to make other, unproven allegations against Ernst Wolfgang. Contrary to all other reports, Ziegenbein said that Ernst Wolfgang had been a member of the Nazi Stormtroopers, the SA, involved in carrying out pogroms against the Jewish population of Erfurt and was a '200 per cent' Nazi who liked to run around in a uniform.

When the denazification tribunal replied to the letter, asking for verification of these allegations, they waited several months before receiving a reply on 3 February 1948 that it was a case of mistaken identity with another Ernst Wolfgang Topf in Erfurt (there was no other Ernst Wolfgang Topf – the Erfurt police were clearly trying to seal the case against Ernst Wolfgang with false accusations).

A lack of interest and support for the denazification process meant that the tribunal was severely hampered by a lack of reliable information. The American-controlled document centre in Berlin replied to a request for information, but did not mention either of the two CIC investigations that had been conducted against Ernst Wolfgang. The Russian consulate, the mayor of Erfurt and the Erfurt police did not reply at all. In February 1948, the works council at the company that was once Topf and Sons replied to the tribunal, stating that the company had supplied crematoria for the concentration camps, but then added a series of allegations that the Topf brothers had been drunken brawlers, and had once hit each other with clubs in front of the workers.

In March 1948, the case against Ernst Wolfgang was passed on to the Wiesbaden tribunal, where he was now living, and the public prosecutor followed a new line of inquiry that Topf and Sons had developed and produced a mobile oven for Buchenwald. This mobile oven was illegal – and was perhaps the most incriminating evidence in the entire case presented against Ernst Wolfgang. By letter, a former Buchenwald prisoner, Werner Munchheimer said that he had read many times in his work with the Buchenwald camp construction department that the Topf company had built the cremation ovens. Munchheimer referred this to his former departmental head, Alfred Ingehag, who confirmed the company had installed static and mobile ovens, but this letter of 5 January 1950 was the last letter in the denazification file.

The advent of the cold war meant that, by 1948, the Americans had lost interest in pursuing the long-running denazification process – and it was wound up in 1950. In March that year the denazification case against Ernst Wolfgang Topf was dropped, because 'the accused was only an ordinary member of the NSDAP from 1933, and never held any office or rank in the party'.[137]

By the end of the war 8.5 million Germans were members of the Nazi Party. Of that number, nearly one million (950,000) found themselves before a denazification tribunal. (The class makeup of the group in itself was interesting – nearly half of civil servants went before a tribunal, whereas only 3 per cent of workers did.) Yet the tribunals were placed under competing stresses from the beginning; all those who were assigned to the most serious categories were forbidden from engaging in anything other than 'ordinary labour' until the tribunal process was complete. As a result, the tribunals were torn between 'the two equally pressing obligations of freeing the little Nazis from discrimination at the hands of the law, and punishing the big Nazis as quickly as possible'.[138]

At the end of the denazification tribunal process only 1,654 people were classified as category 1 – major offenders. A further 22,122 people were classified as category 2, while 106,422 people were deemed 'less interested persons'. As one observer put it: 'The system had run the sea through a sieve, in order to catch a couple of big fish.'[139]

One of those fish who had escaped the net was Ernst Wolfgang Topf. The denazification tribunal had failed to hold him to account just as it failed to hold many others to account. But the evidence of the illegal mobile oven at Buchenwald was sufficient for the public prosecutor to hand over Topf's file to the criminal authorities. This time Topf faced a charge of accessory to murder.

Despite the severity of the charge, the criminal case proceeded with as much confusion and as many obstacles as all of the other attempts to hold the Topfs accountable for their actions. The Wiesbaden state prosecutor's office opened file number 3Js 737/50 against Ernst Wolfgang Topf and, at the beginning of 1951, it wrote to the state prosecutor in Erfurt asking for information.

In Erfurt, however, a strange turn of events, meant that four Topf employees (now working for the renamed Topfwerke Erfurt VEB) were arrested on suspicion of crimes against humanity after a socialist party group within the company alleged that they had been seen burning sensitive documents relating to Topf and the SS in the steam-heating system – in the middle of summer.

The allegation itself was a strange one: why would anyone draw attention to themselves, by doing something so conspicuous, when they could have removed and disposed of the documents in a much more discreet way? The burned papers turned out to be personal documents, and the claim itself appears more like a trumped-up charge indicating a rift in the workforce, and the breakdown of the conspiracy of silence that had held strong at Topf since the end of the war, with former colleagues now turning on each other.

Two of the four men who were charged, Max Machemehl and Paul Erdmann, had certainly known about Topf and Sons's relationship with the SS and the supply of crematoria and gas chamber ventilation equipment to the camps. Charges against the other two, Herbert Bartels (the director of Topfwerke VEB) and commercial assistant Wilhelm Gleitz seem less explicable.

Nonetheless, all four were immediately dismissed from the company without notice and their files passed to the criminal police. Here again, however, the case stalled. The police officer in charge of the case insisted that nothing would come of the matter as the Soviets had no interest in it, and sure enough the investigation was halted in mid-February 1951.

All the men were released from custody on 23 February, but the case had at least succeeded in proving Erdmann's involvement and knowledge of Topf and Sons's actions. Erdmann had always maintained that he never supplied installations to Auschwitz, and that there was no correspondence on this matter. A search of his office for the investigation in 1950 proved otherwise. Investigators discovered a signed letter to the SS Reichsführer construction management Auschwitz, the copy of an operating manual for mass extermination systems and a drawing showing the feed between the gas chambers and the ovens.

Max Machemehl – immortalised in Topf's sixtieth anniversary celebration booklet as the man in the upstairs office who knew everything about the running of Topf and Sons – also steadfastly maintained that he knew nothing about the 'technicalities' of the supplies to the SS:

'Technical matters were dealt with solely by Department D ... So far as orders for cremation facilities were concerned, I was merely informed that such orders existed.' He had nothing to conceal, he added, 'because the connections were not known to me'. Challenged by the police officer leading the investigation about why he had not turned his back on Topf and Sons when he discovered they were supplying ovens to the concentration camps, Machemehl replied: 'If I had known back then what we found out after the war about the crematoria in the concentration camps, then I wouldn't have hesitated – I would have given up my job at once, in keeping with all my decades of conscientious conduct in all aspects of business life.'[140]

After the Erfurt case was closed, and the four men had been released, the state prosecutor replied to the inquiry from Wiesbaden stating, untruthfully, that the investigation was still ongoing and that they had secured statements from Topf oven fitters claiming that they had repeatedly asked to be removed from working on the installations in the camps – but that these requests had been rejected by the Topf brothers. The Wiesbaden prosecutor responded to this letter, asking to see copies of the statements as they were of considerable importance in determining 'whether or not the accused knew of the criminal purpose for which the cremation ovens supplied to the concentration camps were to be used'. Although the Erfurt prosecutor general instructed the office to send these statements to Wiesbaden, they were never delivered.

In an interim report of 6 June 1951, the Wiesbaden prosecutor, Dr Konig, stated that they were unable to demonstrate that Ernst Wolfgang Topf had had dealings with the SS at Buchenwald, or other camps, or that he knew about the criminal use of the ovens.

Without access to the SS files at Auschwitz that documented correspondence between the camp and Topf and Sons, witness statements from camp survivors, or the Soviet interrogation reports for Kurt Prüfer, Fritz Sander or Gustav Braun, the investigation largely accepted Ernst Wolfgang's version of events. On 10 June 1952, the criminal case against him was officially closed, with the prosecutor noting that 'it had not been possible to disprove the accused's claim that he had never dealt with technical matters and had not been informed about the real purpose of the cremation ovens supplied to the Buchenwald camp'.[141]

Topf and Sons's copies of the files detailing their work with the SS have never been discovered. While the controversial amateur historian Jean-Claude Pressac (more of whom later) claimed that Kurt Prüfer had disposed of the files prior to his arrest, Annegret Schüle suggests that Ernst Wolfgang Topf actually passed the files to the American CIC at the end of the war – before they mysteriously disappeared. Even without the files, the evidence of what Topf and Sons had done was always in plain sight – the Topf name was branded across the ovens in iron letters, and Buchenwald survivors testified to the role Topf and Sons played in building the crematoria. Yet the American forces seemed relatively disinterested in Topf and Sons, perhaps because they were so overwhelmed by the horrors that they had seen in the camp and the other, more obvious, perpetrators of war crimes.

With the conclusion of the case, Ernst Wolfgang Topf was free from the prospect of a life in prison. The long-drawn-out denazification case, which was followed by criminal proceedings, had done nothing to deter him from trying to re-establish his business in West Germany – and he demonstrated that he intended to restart Topf and Sons using a patent for the 'process and device for the incineration of bodies, carcasses and parts thereof'.[142]

This patent was not, as is sometimes reported, based on the techniques Topf and Sons employed, or had planned to employ, in the ovens of the concentration camps. But the very fact that a new company run by Ernst Wolfgang was intending to make money from 'carcass incineration' outraged Holocaust survivors and the families of victims.

In December 1947, Topf applied for a business permit in Wiesbaden and opened an engineering office in Recklinghausen, hiring an engineer and some shared work space in a wooden barracks. From the outset, the company focused on furnace and oven construction, as Ernst Wolfgang probably surmised that a lack of capital would make it more difficult to break into the bigger malting and storage businesses. There is no doubt that Topf planned to recreate an almost exact replica of the business he'd presided over in Erfurt, even wanting to assign the same departmental letters, including the infamous Department D for oven construction and furnace constructions. A

1953 brochure proudly proclaimed 'Seventy-five years of Topf' ovens, which were 'of first-class quality' and 'the product of long years of experience'.

Yet, although some of these ovens were sold to civic crematoria in West Germany during the early 1950s, the new Topf company struggled under insurmountable debts. Soon the company office and Topf's family home were relocated in an unsavoury part of town in nearby Mainz, where potential customers were put off by having to run the gauntlet of 'prostitutes, ex-offenders and drunks' to get to the office entrance.

By 1956, the Topf company had given up selling cremation ovens, and was focusing on making municipal incinerators, while Ernst Wolfgang employed desperate measures to stave off insolvency and apply for loans. These efforts proved to be nothing more than sticking plasters: two years later, the Topf family was registered as living on state welfare, with Ernst Wolfgang marked down as unfit for work on health grounds. The new Topf company was economically dormant from 1959 until its final dissolution in March 1963.

These economic difficulties faced by a small, failing company, which Ernst Wolfgang Topf likened to 'the life of a tiny creature'[143] were severe, but they were just a small fraction of the problems Topf was facing. However grandiose his plans, Topf was constantly forced to respond to damaging accusations aired in books and the media, and his denials appeared to do nothing to stem the tide.

Ernst Wolfgang had first compiled a long company and family history in 1950, in a document which made no mention of dealings with the SS or concentration camp ovens. Annegret Schüle notes that

Ernst Wolfgang glosses over his brother's suicide, almost as if it was a family tradition, stating that 'on 31 May 1945 Ludwig Topf chose to end his life – as his father had done in 1914'. Ernst Wolfgang then adds that both brothers were in grave danger during the war as 'passionate enemies of Hitlerdom'.[144]

By the mid-1950s, with the denazification tribunal and the criminal case behind him, Topf might have been lulled into a false sense of his security; he may have allowed himself to believe that his past actions were well and truly buried. But in 1957, just as Ernst Wolfgang's financial woes are at their worst, former Dachau inmate and journalist Reimund Schnabel published a book called *Macht ohne Moral* (*Power without Morals*), which printed documents linking Topf and Sons directly to the SS and the Holocaust. Schnabel had spent time in Dachau for opposing the Nazi euthanasia programme and had written the book to drum up opposition to a plan to allow former Waffen-SS officers, up to the rank of lieutenant colonel, to join the West German army. The book contained photos of piles of bodies of the victims and the ovens themselves, a letter from Topf and Sons to the SS construction management at Mauthausen concerning the incineration capacity of the double-muffle oven, and a letter to Auschwitz from 1 April 1943 quoting a price for building a giant ring cremation oven.

Topf and his wife Erika immediately understood the book would have a 'devastating impact on anybody who picked it up', and drafted a 21-page typed response to the main allegations levelled against Topf and Sons. As the archive files show, they took pains to revise and edit the draft several times to ensure that their justifications were exactly right.

Topf began by questioning whether the letters in the book were genuine, and then criticised their inclusion 'as though this had formed part of the horrendous crimes'. The Topf company carried out its business in 'exemplary fashion', Ernst Wolfgang continued, and had always provided technology 'for the best possible attainment of the greatest possible reverence, as required by the laws relating to cremation'.

Topf continues with what are now familiar justifications for the company's actions, before claiming that Topf and Sons was a well-known protector of Jews, and the Topf brothers represented 'a family with the qualities of humanity, especially chosen to protect its persecuted Jewish fellow citizens and colleagues to the very best of its ability, and that we demonstrably did, to the point of self-sacrifice, right up to the end of the war'.

In what he knew was an outright lie, Topf claims that no 'service personnel from the SS or from any concentration camp were ever received or seen' in the company, and there had never been 'any meeting with the SS ... in Berlin or anywhere else'. He then goes to great pains to prove that neither of the Topf brothers were Nazis, and that they hadn't benefited from the Third Reich:

Between 1933 and 1945, we did not take on a single new member of staff with good 'party connections', nor did we recruit any such staff from operations. Throughout the twelve Hitler years, we carried out all our customer commissions but did not sympathise in any way whatsoever with either the NSDAP or its affiliated organisations, economic enterprises or functionaries. We deliberately assigned a non-party member to deal with all agencies. We consciously swam against the tide, and consequently encountered serious difficulties with all authorities and party agencies.

We also strictly adhered to our policy relating to treatment of staff, i.e. all staff, whether German or foreign nationals, were treated with equal decency, without any discrimination on the basis of religion, race or language. We also consciously avoided either recruiting, transferring or promoting active party members or other pro-Nazi elements. We rigorously adhered to this principle, even though it put us at a disadvantage when it came to the assignment of white- and blue-collar workers by the Labour Office and State Labour Office. As a consequence of this, our company became a meeting place for opponents of the Hitler system. Of the approximately thirty people we made departmental managers, only three to five were nominal party members.

The 'political unreliability' of the Topf brothers can be demonstrated by the fact that neither brother received a war service medal, something handed to many other business owners in Erfurt. In addition, the 'foreign nationals' (slave labourers) left the company at the end of the war in an orderly and friendly fashion:

No plundering or destruction of any kind in their camp, the administration block or workshops. No red flag raised. No fighting with Germans … Groups marched off in orderly fashion over a number of days, having first taken their leave of us through spokesmen. Many individual groups of Russian, French and Italian backgrounds thanked us with handshakes.

It is in this document that Ernst Wolfgang Topf refers to the respectable and honourable heads of department who worked for Topf and Sons, and specifically calls Fritz Sander a 'man of almost excessive integrity'. A succession of investigations had proven that 'no one in our company had been guilty of anything at all, either morally or in practice'. Challenging the very title of Schnabel's book, Topf stated that he could 'describe [his] company and the entirety of its conduct, throughout the twelve years of the Hitler regime, with the phrase: 'Morality without Power'.[145]

Yet none of this lengthy justification did Ernst Wolfgang any good. When Schnabel's book was published, in 1957, Topf was already under investigation for promissory note fraud (a crime that involves two or more people sending each other promissory notes as a means of proving that a business is solvent, when there are no actual deals to underpin them). The publication of *Macht ohne Moral* was the final nail in the coffin for the new Topf company. A loan that had been previously agreed on from the burden sharing office was abruptly turned down. Commerz-und Credit Bank and Deutsche Bank followed suit by refusing to administer a state loan.

The J. A. Topf company of Wiesbaden continued to limp along in its final incarnation until 1961, when a groundbreaking West German TV documentary series *Drittes Reich* highlighted that 'the company that supplied the cremation ovens used in the concentration camps' was now headquartered in Mainz. A few months later, a book by Robert Neumann called *Hitler: Aufstieg und Untergang des Dritten Reiches* brought even more unwelcome attention from the foreign press after publishing a copy of the Topf and Sons patent for the 'continuous operation corpse incineration oven for mass use' and a copy of correspondence with the SS at Auschwitz about the ventilation systems for the gas chambers.

Topf had escaped another police investigation in January 1960 in connection with 'gassing ovens at concentration camps', by offering up his usual justification that 'anything burned in these ovens was already dead', but as a result of the new television series and book, Ernst Wolfgang found himself referred back to investigators from the Central Land Judicial Administration Office for the Investigation of National Socialist Crimes who passed the case to a special unit preparing for trials in relation to Auschwitz.

Despite the many efforts to bring Topf to justice, he never faced any further prosecution for the actions of Topf and Sons during the Holocaust. The immediate consequence of the new media revelations was that J. A. Topf and Sons was finally deregistered. J. A. Topf and Sons was dissolved on 18 March 1963 and the last Topf brother was out of business for ever. Ernst Wolfgang's wife Erika died a month later on 23 April.

Despite living on in a state of some dereliction, Ernst Wolfgang survived for another sixteen years – dying on 23 February 1979 in the northern German town of Brilon. He was seventy-four years old, an age many of his victims never reached. He had defiantly evaded justice to the very end.

CHAPTER TWELVE

ATONEMENT

When Hartmut Topf was sixteen, he borrowed five marks from his young teacher Heinz Bunese and caught a bus from his home in Falkensee in the Soviet zone to West Berlin. In the autumn of 1950, eleven years before the Berlin Wall was built, it was still possible for workers with the right papers to cross the city, but Hartmut did not have the right papers and it was a nerve-racking journey; he knew that he would be arrested if caught. The new East German communist police and customs officers were often on the commuter buses, on the lookout for the wrong people, but they couldn't apprehend every passenger. And, much to Hartmut's relief, he made it.

> I went to Spandau. I didn't know where to go, so I asked the first policeman I saw and he told me that there were places that welcomed refugees. I went to one of the places he mentioned, got registered, answered some questions, had a medical test and after a few weeks I was accepted as a political refugee – and then I was sent to West Germany.[146]

As a teenager, Hartmut had been involved in small acts of rebellion against Soviet rule, refusing to sign a telegram for Stalin's birthday, and smuggling in airmail copies of West Berlin newspapers to secretly distribute in school text books. But eventually he had been exposed, and his choice was to flee or be sent to prison. Now that he had made it to the West he was free to build a new life for himself, but in many ways he was still a young boy away from his family for the first time.

While his mother understandably missed him, his sister Karin remembers being pleased about inheriting Hartmut's bicycle. 'I didn't really notice his absence. Perhaps it was even a relief, because I was also a bit difficult. I had my own ideas, and my own ways.'

Not only was Hartmut leaving his family behind, but also his home town. With refugees flooding into West Berlin from the Soviet zone, housing was horrendously overcrowded and priority was given to families with children. There was no place in Berlin for a sixteen-year-old with few skills, and Hartmut was sent to Hanover where he boarded with other young men. Eventually he managed to secure an apprenticeship with his father's old company, Siemens, and began a career as a telecoms engineer.

Life in the West was about far more than work, however. Although Hartmut completed his three-year apprenticeship, living in Hanover opened his eyes to theatre and music, and he began to envision a different future for himself:

I met very interesting people in Hanover. I met lots of people involved in theatre and I sang in a choir. I went to the theatre almost every evening. I cut a strange figure wearing my leather shorts and carrying a ceremonial knife while I wandered around in the theatre canteen after the show with the actors ... I even celebrated my twenty-first birthday on a concert tour of the *Matthäus-Passion* by Johann Sebastian Bach. We performed in Belgium and in Aachen. It was another world. That would have never happened in Falkensee.

Even so, Hartmut longed to return to West Berlin, and eventually managed to do this, working a string of day jobs while indulging his passion for the theatre in his spare time. At work, Hartmut was often preoccupied, thinking about the theatre, and the day jobs seemed to inevitably end with his dismissal. As the years passed, Hartmut married and divorced his wife, becoming a single father to their son, Till. Eventually he vowed never to take another full-time job that he woke up dreading, and embarked upon a freelance radio, journalism and theatre career that sustained him for the rest of his life.

In 1956 there was a Soviet military intervention in Hungary, and the army crushed the revolt. My friends, who were actors and artists, were desperate and cried. They were all so involved. I said I have to be closer to the action – and I decided to go to Berlin. I hoped I would also get the chance to go to a theatre school there, but I wasn't accepted to any. Then I got a job in a small Christian theatre: the Vaganten. The director, Horst Behrend, had four children and was very conservative. He was a bit of a dictator in his theatre, but very devoted to it. He was a Christian and secretly he was a homosexual. He allowed me to work there as an assistant and I learned a lot. It was the best theatre experience I ever had; we put on beautiful plays and I was respected. Later I organised big theatre events, and I also helped organise the filming of *Katz und Maus* by Günter Grass in Poland in the '6os.

In the 1960s, Hartmut also began working in puppet theatre – something he had been drawn to since his experiences with his childhood friend Hans Laessig decades earlier:

I like to call it an infection. Puppetry was contagious in my early years. Then I rediscovered it after meeting a puppeteer called Steinmann in Berlin … and I assisted him on the technical side of things in his little theatre, like the sound engineering and the light equipment. I stayed backstage and did all that, and through that I met many, many puppeteers, and I wrote critiques about puppetry festivals. I joined UNIMA, the reformed *Union Internationale de la Marionette* that was founded in Prague in '29 by a puppeteer's friends. I became a notorious festival-goer and the nickname I earned is pretty accurate – I am a puppet diplomat. I connect and I bring people together.

Puppetry, theatre and politics were becoming intertwined in Hartmut's world, especially in Berlin where everyone was either a dissident or refugee, or an American agent or Stasi spy. His puppet theatre work took him across the border into Poland and Czechoslovakia, and ultimately back to East Berlin, where he reconnected with his family and learned what little he could about the history of Topf and Sons.

My theatre career and journalism absorbed me completely – but of course I read all of the important books, like Eugen Kogon's work on the SS system and the concentration camps. I was familiar with a lot of political literature. I had my own political education, but there was a big lapse of time before I could look into Topf and Sons in Erfurt.

The lapse Hartmut mentions refers to the decades when Topf and Sons continued to operate as a company in East Germany. There appears to have been no appetite, either under Soviet occupation, or East German rule, to account for the company's role in the Holocaust (other than the rather strange criminal case of the 1950s, which was dismissed almost as soon as it emerged).

Under the leadership of Willy Wiemokli, who became the head of the company in 1946, Topf and Sons continued to make payments to the wives of Kurt Prüfer, Gustav Braun, Fritz Sander and Karl Schultze while they were under arrest in the Soviet Union, and in 1948 both Paul Erdmann and fitter Martin Holick received fifty-year anniversary commemorations for their dedicated services to the company. Payments to the wives of the four arrested men stopped when Topf and Sons became a state-run enterprise in 1949, and all mention of the war and working with the SS was whitewashed from the company's history.

Until 1952, Topf and Sons was known as Topf Works VEB, but the company was renamed in 1952 to remove the Topf family name, and then again in 1957 when it became known as VEB Erfurt Malting and Storage Construction. The crematorium division had been closed down two years previously in 1955, with all drawings, documents and models sent to another company in Zwickau, and the new company focused instead on grain malting equipment which was exported to

Eastern Europe and the Soviet Union, and then later to Libya, Angola, Cyprus and other countries sympathetic to East Germany.

Just as the old Topf administration building was still the heart of the company, the Topf family park was also still in use – housing a company clubhouse and restaurant in Ludwig Topf's villa, and at various points, a hostel for apprentices, swimming pool and kindergarten in the grounds.

The expropriation of the Topf family park and villa is referred to in a 1980s company history, as an example of the triumph of the workers in beating their capitalist bosses.

> When Hitler came to power, the company experienced a brisk upturn in productivity. It started producing parts for ships and aircraft, as well as grenades and cremation ovens. During the Second World War, the concentration camps were equipped with cremation ovens produced by 'Topf and Sons'. However, the workers employed by the company at that time did not know what the ovens were being used for. They had only been told they were incineration ovens for animal innards. This inhumanity was only uncovered after the end of the war and the liberation of the prisoners from the concentration camps.

The company brochure continues with an account of the foreign workers forced to work for Topf and Sons during the war, stating: 'The workers had to work under a piecework system so that the factory owner could hold orgies in his luxury villa, now the Erfurter Mälzerei- und Speicherbau clubhouse.' Next to this statement is an illustration of Buchenwald and the oath of the Buchenwald survivors swearing to destroy fascism.[147]

In such a way, the history of Topf and Sons had been rewritten to serve the propaganda of communist-controlled East Germany. Annegret Schüle writes that:

> Even though the Topf fitters spent long periods of time in the camps; even though the mobile ovens were built in the Erfurt company and were returned there for repair; even though the staff involved spoke quite openly of the equipping of the gas chambers; this version of events, with its abstruse reference to the incineration of animal innards, declares the entire workforce collectively innocent [creating] the impression that the Topf villa, which was expropriated and placed at the disposal of the workers after the war, could now serve as a symbol that the oath taken by the Buchenwald survivors had now become reality at VEB Erfurter Mälzerei- und Speicherbau.

The fall of communist East Germany and the reunification of Germany in 1990 spelled the end for many state-owned enterprises – including the VEB Erfurt Malting and Storage Construction (EMS), the company that was once Topf and Sons. Now under the leadership of Gustav Braun's son, Udo (who had finally surpassed his father's achievements), EMS was placed under the administration of the 'Trust Agency' which sought privatisation. Ultimately, Udo Braun's efforts ended in failure; the company was initially sold before it petitioned for bankruptcy on 19 June 1996.

'They gave me eight months to find an investor in Germany who would be willing to buy Topf and Sons,' Udo Braun says.

> I accepted and did my best, because I didn't want the company to die

and people to lose their jobs. Lots had to leave anyway. Of the 700 employees only 100 stayed. Since I had spent my entire working life there, my heart was also in it. The company was bought. The new owner got 70 per cent, I got 10 per cent – that's what they wanted – and there were two other partners. That went on for two or three years. We then found out that we didn't have enough money to construct new premises since we were not allowed to sell land that we owned in order to finance it. So the inevitable happened. The investor had difficulties of his own and in 1996 a liquidator took over and filed for bankruptcy. That was the worst day for me, when I had to go to the court. But I had to do it. I had to take care of everything.[148]

The administration building where the Topf brothers and their engineers had plotted how to build the technology for mass murder fell into decay, the family park slipped into leafy ruin. In its final company history, written in the 1990s, EMS had not mentioned the period of the Second World War at all – but still some important documents remained in the company archives, including Fritz Sander's memo about his patent application, and the note about the dispute with the SS over the missing blower. Other documents had been retained by the former East German state archive in the Document Centre for the Prosecution of Nazi and War Crimes where Western researchers could look at them under Stasi supervision. These papers formed the basis of a file that was used at one stage to try to persuade Hartmut Topf to become a Stasi agent – an offer he refused.

Hartmut had been visiting Erfurt and staying with his cousin Dietrich since the 1970s. During one of these visits he visited the concentration camp at Buchenwald for the first time:

I wanted to see what was left of the camp. That was the first time that I walked through the small crematorium building that Topf and Sons had built. It was a shocking encounter. You walk through a very sad environment, and I found it hard to digest. I think I was speechless for a while. I saw things that I'd only seen before in photographs or in the newsreels. Then I wanted to know more, but at that time there was nobody to ask, not in Erfurt and not anywhere else.[149]

Hartmut began piecing together his family history, discovering the Topf and Sons commemorative brochure and old letters, while at the same time reconciling his much more immediate relationship with his father.

I grew into researching and asking questions slowly, step by step. I knew that the Nazis had killed so many people and that Topf had played a part in building the machinery. And of course they earned a lot of money from the Nazis, and my first thought was that they should not have touched this dirty money.

I was good friends with Jewish people over the years in Berlin, and I read all the important books, and I wanted to understand when people told me their stories. I wanted to know the whole system and framework, and the framework of the dictatorship too. I felt obliged to warn people who follow ideology, because I had the example of my own 'good' father, who also believed in Nazi ideology.

I loved my father, and I felt so sorry that he had served the Nazi movement with all of his good manners and his devotion to social tasks and neighbours. He was a naïve believer perhaps. I wanted to discuss all these questions with him: why did you join this movement? Perhaps you did it to help your brother, to protect his half-Jewish wife? In my father's case, I think he was partly convinced that this really was a way of national socialism, of building a community for all. He must have believed that. That was his profound error. As a boy, these were the questions I wanted to ask him, but he wasn't there so I could only dream of how he might have responded.

My aim is not to blame people, or to put them in jail or punish them, but to understand how it happened, why it happened, the road to this disaster. And, of course, within that at least name who was responsible, and make people liable for whatever they did.

So back then my priority was not so much the concentration camps, my first task was to warn people to look at the motives of those 'bag-pipers' who led you to catastrophe, and into an abyss, because you believed them and supported them. That was my first course of action. Later, of course, I got into the precise and exact story of the Topfs in Erfurt, and this crystallised as the main topic.

Two events in the early 1990s forced Hartmut into taking a more active and public role in discussions about Topf and Sons: the fall of the Eastern bloc and the reunification of Germany meant that many former residents and business owners were seeking to reclaim the homes and businesses they had been forced to abandon during East Germany's communist era. More than 2.5 million claims were filed, one of which was registered by members of the Topf family, who were seeking ownership and financial restitution for the company of Topf and Sons and the Topf family park in Erfurt.

At the same time, more information about the company's role in the Holocaust was coming to the attention of the international media due to the publication of a book by Jean-Claude Pressac on the crematoria of Auschwitz, detailing the SS's relationship with Topf and Sons, and the discovery by historian Gerald Fleming of the Soviet interrogation records for Kurt Prüfer, Fritz Sander, Gustav Braun and Karl Schultze.

Jean-Claude Pressac was a French pharmacist, and a former Holocaust denier who spent years compiling an archive of sources relating to Topf and Sons. Pressac had started investigating the SS construction management files from Auschwitz in the 1970s, when he was collaborating with French revisionist Robert Faurisson who believed the Holocaust was Allied propaganda. Holocaust deniers claimed that technical information from Auschwitz proved that the gas chambers never existed and that far fewer people died there than is claimed. At first, Pressac believed this too, and set out to prove it. His own investigation, however, forced him to change his mind. His 1989 book, *Auschwitz: Technique and Operation of the Gas Chambers*, was the first to publish documents from the SS construction management office, and was used by those who sought to counter revisionist history. In 1993, Pressac published his second book in France called *Les Crématoires d'Auschwitz*.

Many historians, including those based at the Buchenwald memorial, and Annegret Schüle, had profound reservations concerning Pressac's approach, including his demands for payment before allowing other historians access to the archive material (part of which was Topf and Sons's company material he had been loaned by Udo Braun, who was by then running the renamed company) and his strange obsession with military paraphernalia.

Ronald Hirte, a key member of the team at the Buchenwald Memorial, explains:

> Pressac has always been an issue when dealing with Holocaust denial and revisionism. He wanted to become a military officer, but that didn't happen. In the '60s and '70s he started studying the feasibility of the cremations of so many people being killed in the gas chambers. He was at first what we would describe today as a 'revisionist'. This was a very strong movement in France up to the 1980s. They maintained that the Holocaust could not have taken place, because it was technically impossible to commit such a crime in Auschwitz. Pressac stood out among the revisionists, as he came to the realisation that he had been propagating false information all those years. His conscience did not allow him to continue to deny the crimes that had happened. This would be contrary to his ideology and his political actions. So he had to say 'No! These crimes happened, the mass murders and the mass cremations took place.' This made him very unusual and distinguished him from the other historical revisionists. His colleagues dropped him. So he had a very strange life – he was a right-wing, nationalist hardliner who then became a reformed autodidactic historian and author, publishing his two main books in France.[150]

Ronald Hirte and Annegret Schüle, who was about to embark on her research into Topf and Sons, travelled to Paris to meet Pressac in 2002, so that they could examine some of his documents at first hand, and also discuss access to the material. Hirte recalls:

It was a very unpleasant meeting and I didn't think that he was a very nice person. He liked to point out that he knew much more and that we were kind of ignorant in the matter. He also collected uniforms and arms, he had a huge collection, almost like a museum, and wanted us to put on the uniforms as a kind of a fancy dress and then take pictures of us. I refused. It was a really weird meeting. He was an embittered old man who felt he had not received enough recognition during his lifetime.

After Pressac's death in 2003, Hirte drove to Paris with Dr Bernhard Post, now the director of the Thuringia State Archive, to retrieve Pressac's material:

We travelled to Paris overnight. We only had hours to get the files from Jean-Claude Pressac's house before they disappeared, or any kind of argument started. The files had disappeared before and the way in which they had arrived in Paris had been illegal. So Bernhard Post and I drove off to Paris without stopping on the way, and arrived in time to meet a colleague there. We got all the material that we already knew about out of the flat and took it back to the archive in Weimar.

Regardless of whether or not Jean-Claude Pressac was a troubling and unpleasant character, he undeniably unearthed much material about Topf and Sons and played an important role in bringing it to light. Despite the flaws in his work, Hartmut Topf was armed with this new material when he heard about the Topf family claim for restitution.

Descendants of the Topf family, who were living abroad, had applied to have the company reassigned to them, but their claim was rejected in 1992 after being called an 'obscenity' by the World Jewish Congress and condemned by German Chancellor Helmut Kohl. Another claim by the Topf family, to reclaim the Topf family park, was still under consideration, however, and Ernst Wolfgang Topf's daughter-in-law Dagmar Topf, visited Erfurt, to speak on behalf of her claim. She encountered tremendous hostility. The legal ownership of the park was a matter of dispute, as it had never been formally expropriated by the East German government, however Dagmar Topf's efforts to reclaim it seemed morally indefensible to most ordinary Erfurt citizens. Hartmut Topf was made aware of her efforts by Jean-Claude Pressac.

I heard about the Topf claim from local newspaper reports and from Jean-Claude Pressac. Pressac called me because he knew that I spoke in public about Topf and Sons. He asked me if I knew Dagmar Topf and the other relatives, and I said I did not. There had already been negative articles about them, and he told me I should get in touch with her. I made an appointment with Dagmar and went to see her. I came to terms with Dagmar. She understood that I wasn't her enemy. And I understood that she had been unjustly attacked by the media and that public opinion in Erfurt was very hostile towards her. She had been portrayed as a lady from the West who wanted Topf property and was a Nazi. She had a hard time in Erfurt. She doesn't like to go back there, even today.[151]

Although Hartmut believed Dagmar Topf had been subjected to an unfair personal attack, he was equally determined that no Topf should receive any financial benefit from Topf and Sons or the Topf family park.

'I spoke out in Erfurt and said that if there is any money it should be given to victims' organisations – or it should be put into political education. Local people responded very positively to the fact there was a Topf who spoke up against the relatives.'

Dagmar Topf and the other Topf relatives lost their claim to the Topf family land in 1994, but Hartmut was emboldened by the public response to his speech and decided to bring together a society of supporters to find a suitable way to remember and reflect on the atrocities that Topf and Sons had participated in.

> The first thing I said was: we must do something to stop a general forgetting of the past. We have to mark the place. We have to leave a sign to tell people – it was here in the middle of our society. I asked the people of Erfurt to help us to preserve the memory, a memory of an average German company, an average wealthy German family, who helped the system commit this huge crime. I did not want a memorial for victims, because we have those in other places; I wanted a place of reflection and learning.

Other people joined the movement to memorialise Topf and Sons, and Hartmut began working with a diverse group that included representatives from the Green Party, the Protestant Church, the European Cultural Centre, the Heinrich Böll Foundation and trade unions. The then president of the Jewish community in Thuringia, Wolfgang Nossen, worked with Hartmut in setting up the Topf and

Sons memorial. Nossen had escaped from the Breslau ghetto, and was outraged by Dagmar Topf's claim for family restitution:

> It was the typical insolence. They were all 'innocent'. Zero morality. I would have changed my name if it had been Topf. But it is good that Hartmut kept his … Ludwig Topf showed character when he killed himself. As much as the Germans would like to, you cannot forget history. It was very difficult to establish the memorial and I was part of those who helped and encouraged it.

While the society of supporters were rallying support for a memorial, a group of left-wing, radical squatters had taken over one of the Topf and Sons buildings, where they ran their own series of social and cultural projects to remind people about the company. The occupation by the squatters lasted for eight years, until they were evicted in 2009, and became a well-known example of anti-establishment and anti-Nazi resistance in Germany.

While Hartmut Topf, and others in the society of supporters, offered encouragement to the squatters, they also continued to work towards a permanent memorial on the site – something that was actively opposed by the Mayor of Erfurt, Manfred Ruge, and some former Topf and Sons' workers.

Wolfgang Nossen remembers:

> I went to an event and there was a person who had worked for Topf and Sons who said that if Topf and Sons hadn't manufactured the ovens, someone else would have. That is a wonderful excuse. But it would be

better for Erfurt, if they hadn't done it. They were guilty to a very high degree, because they offered their own services. They invented new machinery so that even more people could be burned in a more economical way. For me, their behaviour cannot be excused. It is not only the two brothers who are guilty, but also the engineers who went to Auschwitz when the Topf brothers did not.[152]

Nossen also had a confrontation with Mayor Ruge, who had stated in a Radio F.R.E.I. interview, in December 2002, that he saw no need for a Topf and Sons memorial.

Asked if he could continue to ignore the memorial services and action groups working to draw attention to the Nazi past of the Topf and Sons site, Ruge said:

> What do you mean by 'ignore'? Then I'd ask, to put it quite plainly, where are the memorial services at the bakers and butchers who delivered their bread rolls and sausages to Buchenwald? And where are the memorial services at the dairy that provided Buchenwald with milk? Or where are the memorial services where lemonade or other drinks were produced? Or where are the memorial services in the pharmaceutical company that made the aspirin or other tablets used at the camp? This is a social question that we need to ask … But here, for this location, the question is bundled together. And I am of the view, and I've always said as much, that we should name this place, name what went on here, but that's where our responsibility ends.

The interviewer presses him further: why does the city not mention Topf and Sons's history on its homepage?

'Why should we put it on our homepage?' Ruge responds.

There are many aspects of the city's history that we don't publicise. I don't see any reason to, and I don't see anything to find fault with in Erfurt's conduct. A place is named here, this is where industrial things were manufactured for the destruction of people, questionable, abhorrent things, but many other things connected to Buchenwald were made in the surrounding area, too ... We will ultimately ensure that it isn't only named but is also documented, but nothing more is necessary.[153]

Wolfgang Nossen says: 'In the end, everything happened the way we wanted but it was a disgrace how they opposed it.' Hartmut Topf agrees: 'We had to be very stubborn to pursue our goal.' The society of supporters had to convince more and more people. 'We wanted to create a sense of responsibility, to signpost that this was the Topf company. To indicate that this was the place and cement it in the public consciousness. The authorities put up a lot of obstacles, the mayor found stupid excuses. But our small movement grew.'[154]

In 2003, the Topf and Sons site was listed as a protected historical monument by the state of Thuringia, and a memorial and education centre about Topf and Sons opened in the main administration building on Holocaust Memorial Day, 27 January 2011. Director Annegret Schüle explains why the site is a memorial rather than a museum:

The main difference between us as a memorial and other museums is that we are about the history of a crime, and there have always been victims. We are not describing history in a neutral way, and we always mention the victims. We honour their memory. We cannot just say that Topf and Sons did this and that, we always have to take into account that people suffered from the business of Topf and Sons ... There are memorials where the victims are the centre of the attention. Nobody died here, but the deaths were the object of the planning and manufacturing.

The Topf and Sons memorial is unique in being the only Holocaust memorial on the historic site of a company. 'This place has a special aura,' Schüle says.

We can show here how easy it is for a human being to ignore his responsibility towards his fellow human beings in his daily work. If I go to the memorial in Buchenwald I cannot identify myself with the SS, because I would never have become a member. But I can relate to people who harm other people by doing their normal jobs. This is happening all the time. Visitors are motivated to think about this. Processes that are completely normal within any companies have led to atrocities.[155]

A lifetime has passed since the men of Topf and Sons sat at their desks and dispassionately planned murder, but the memorial poses an eternal question: how would we act today?

CONCLUSION

'I inherited the name. I did not inherit the company, fortunately. Even so, I felt an obligation. As a child I bathed in the glory of being a Topf, and now I feel I have to tell the horrible story of their infamy. I have to make my contribution. That is my responsibility.'[156]

HARTMUT TOPF, 2017

Hartmut Topf's long involvement with the company that bore his name began more than sixty years ago – but in a surprising development it appears that he was not the only member of the family to discover the truth about Topf and Sons in a darkened cinema. In another town in Europe, a young boy was also watching the weekly newsreel when he saw the logo Topf and Sons on the oven doors of a concentration camp. This young boy had grown up believing he was the son of Ludwig Topf – and he was a child no one in the family knew existed. Florian, as he wants to be known, was born in 1936, the result of a brief encounter at a party in Munich between Ludwig and his mother, who was a young student of art history.

'I knew almost nothing at all about my father, just his name and how they'd met – and even that I didn't know at first. Other than that, my mother was totally clam-like on the subject, which put me off asking questions,' Florian says.

She'd grown up in a deeply Catholic family and giving birth out of wedlock carried a huge stigma. Because of this, she moved away from Munich before I was born and gave birth to me in Milan, where no one knew her. I had my mother's surname and I don't think she tried to get Ludwig Topf to acknowledge paternity. I don't know why she didn't, maybe because she knew he was from a renowned industrial company and didn't want to embarrass him.

Florian says he grew up desperate for a father, even as an adult he often invented names for his father when dealing with the authorities. In the aftermath of the war, life was unstable and unpredictable in Europe – Florian attended six different primary schools in the space of four years, he then went on to study at a grammar school, followed by a stint at a boarding school in Germany. It was hard to be close to his mother, he says, when she was working and he spent so little time with her. In the holidays he often lived with his grandparents: 'The absence of a father lingered over my whole childhood and spoilt it. I desperately missed having the sense of a normal home life, and I was very conscious of not knowing anything about my father.'

Then, as a teenager, he saw the name Topf and Sons on screen for the first time.

> I was watching the *Wochenschau* weekly news programme that came on before the film at the local cinema, and I saw the report on the concentration camps with the 'Topf and Sons' plaque on the cremation furnace. I can't actually remember whether I asked my mother about it at the time, but she would always fall silent at the mention of my father so I always found it very difficult to raise the subject.

Florian's maternal family were doctors, but even though his grandfather was labelled a 'Jew doctor' for treating Jewish patients after Kristallnacht, Florian is still inclined to excuse Ludwig Topf's role in the Holocaust:

> I don't think he was a Nazi; I think he acted out of necessity and pragmatism, and a sense of responsibility for the company's workers. Yes, he collaborated, but I've read both Jean-Claude Pressac's and Annegret Schüle's books and I think that the collusion was pragmatic, not from the heart. They had just wanted to be the best engineers and do the best by their business, and they hadn't really thought much beyond that. It can't have been easy for them, and when you run a company of that size, a certain amount of collaboration would have been inevitable. The work for the concentration camps only accounted for a very small percentage of the company's turnover, and was therefore commercially insignificant.

Having searched all of his life for his father, Florian now finds it hard to believe that Ludwig Topf was a bad person. Although his mother had no papers or photos relating to the Topfs, Florian has seen Ludwig's photo published in books – and thinks he looks like a nice easy-going sort of man, although, he adds, 'In order to have taken his own life, he must have been a very disappointed and disillusioned person.'

Before retiring in 2015, Florian had a long career in business and industry, working in England, Belgium and Switzerland. Very much a family man, he married in 1967 and had three children and nine grandchildren. It was his children who encouraged him to find out more about the Topf family, and he recently met Hartmut for the first time when they agreed to conduct a DNA test. Asked how his children feel about being possible descendants of the Topf family Florian says: 'They feel proud. They knew my mother came from a family of doctors, and were proud of that, but they feel that an industrial family – especially such a major one – is even better.'[157]

Florian is not the only son in this book to be seeking a missing father: Ludwig and Ernst Wolfgang Topf lived, unsuccessfully, in the shadow of theirs; Hartmut sought to redeem the family name for his 'good' father; while Udo Braun remained unreconciled with Gustav Braun to the end.

The question of family legacy is a large one. It is something that even Hartmut, who has carried out so much work on restitution and remembrance, struggles with. Visiting Erfurt in September 2017, he explains that he now believes Topf and Sons was 'partly guilty' – partly because, as Florian also states, the Topf family only made a small financial profit from their work on the Holocaust. Standing in front of the Topf and Sons' ovens at Buchenwald, and confronted with the visible evidence of the crime, he seems unsure about how to express his emotions – instead he tells a long story about the death of a family friend in Berlin. When the friend died, Hartmut's son, Till, asked him why he didn't appear to be sad. Hartmut told his son that he had known his friend's death was coming and he had grieved for a long time in his own way.

'It's a sad story,' he says about the role Topf and Sons played in the Holocaust.

> And it's a great pity that we have to deal with all those atrocities and crimes, in Europe, in our country and, of course, in our family. But this is a general grief, it's not a personal thing. I am only one of those catalysts to keep the memory alive or to ask people, at least from time to time, to reflect on that side of our history.

He adds: 'We should be decent. I am not the protagonist of this story. I always say to people I am a catalyst and I've been working on for this for so many years now, but please don't make me an angel or a hero – I'm not.'[158]

The story of Topf and Sons may be one without heroes, but Hartmut Topf is undoubtedly responsible for ensuring that the company is held accountable to history for its crimes. Through the Topf archives, and the work of historians, we can understand how one small group of men were driven by very human emotions. Ludwig and Ernst Wolfgang Topf were weak and greedy men, prepared to do anything to cement their precarious positions at the head of their father's company. They knew that in doing so they were developing technology that would enable the mass murder of millions of innocent people. This did not deter them in the least – and their collaboration in the Holocaust would be something that Ernst Wolfgang Topf would lie about for the rest of his life. They bear the ultimate responsibility for their crimes.

For the engineers themselves, Kurt Prüfer, Fritz Sander and Karl Schultze, it was a question of personal ambition, rivalry and financial gain. There they sat, on the third floor of the administration building, drawing up ever-wilder plans for the more efficient disposal of human life – all the while thousands of their victims were trapped in Buchenwald, a concentration camp that could be seen out of the window on the Ettersberg hill. And beyond the engineers were the fitters, the men on site who witnessed the horrors of the Holocaust on a day-to-day basis; more remotely the secretaries who typed the memos; the managers and paper pushers who stamped the files; and the operations director who joked that, surely, there could almost be no one left to burn.

Topf and Sons was by no means unique in serving the SS and the Third Reich; in that, they were like thousands of other technocrats, scientists, engineers, town planners, economists, doctors and business men. In making such a pact with the devil they were given permission to shed their civilised skin, and dream their wildest dreams; to make real their biggest professional ambitions without regard for human life or dignity. Even today their sheer detachment and disinterest creeps from the pages of the archive and lays its cold fingers upon anyone who reads it, yet it was the very ordinariness of their human motivations that makes them so easy to understand – and so appalling.

ACKNOWLEDGEMENTS

As an English writer and journalist living in London, completing this book required help and input from many people.

Without the research and translation work of Paula Kirby, this book could not have been tackled at all. Paula, an experienced German translator with an incredible knowledge of, and interest in, German history, devoted an enormous amount of time to translating secondary literature into English for me. She then took on the unwieldy task of sorting thousands of primary archive documents from the Thuringia State Archive, identifying relevant information and translating it. In addition, she was always happy to translate emails, work on footnotes relating to German sources – and conduct phone interviews in German, including an interview with 'Florian', who believes he is the son of Ludwig Topf.

The second person who worked extensively on the German portion of the book was Britt Pflüger, herself an author and editor. Britt proved invaluable in navigating the Thuringia State Archive, which was no easy task, and doing a preliminary sift through thousands and thousands of files to identify useful material. Britt also spent many hours reading German newspapers and magazines from the 1940s, as well as conducting and translating long interviews in Erfurt and Weimar.

The final person to help translate German material into English was Caterina Andreae, who swiftly and expertly translated a series of first person audio interviews with some of the key people mentioned in the book.

Of the many people who cooperated, helped and agreed to be interviewed, the most important, of course, was Hartmut Topf. Hartmut plays a key role in this story – his efforts played a large part in bringing the Topf and Sons memorial in Erfurt to fruition. Hartmut also spent many days being interviewed for this book, showing me his childhood scenes in Berlin and Erfurt, and introducing me to others in the story. He facilitated many interviews, and made available many photos and family documents.

I would like to thank the Thuringia State Archive in Weimar, which houses the archive for Topf and Sons, as well as the Buchenwald Memorial and the Auschwitz Memorial, for making documents and photos available to me.

For German readers interested in a detailed history of Topf and Sons, I recommend Annegret Schüle's book *Industrie und Holocaust: Topf & Söhne – Die Ofenbauer von Auschwitz*, which is a definitive text based upon the Topf and Sons archive. Annegret is also the director of the Topf and Sons memorial in Erfurt, and I appreciate the time she spent discussing this book with me, and for connecting me with Hartmut Topf.

I would also like to thank Rüdiger Bender, a trustee of the memorial in Erfurt, and the very first person to speak to me about Topf and Sons. Rüdiger was always willing to connect, and reconnect, with me over several years to discuss his project – and I have always been struck by his political passion and determination to make the story of Topf and Sons a relevant one in today's world.

This book has been a particularly difficult and time-consuming project, and so I have to thank my mother in particular for stepping in so often and helping to organise the rest of family life so that I could pursue it. I also have to thank my father and many others for believing in this book from the beginning, as well as Gaia Banks at Sheil Land, and Olivia Beattie and Bernadette Marron at Biteback Publishing for supporting with all the practical steps that turned it into a reality.

NOTES

Introduction

1   Author interview with Hartmut Topf.

Chapter One: Born and bred at J. A. Topf

2   Gerald Fleming, *Hitler and the Final Solution*, University of California Press, 1984, p. 45.

3   Ibid., p. 47.

4   Kurt Prüfer personnel file, Landesarchiv Thüringen - Hauptstaatsarchiv Weimar.

5   David Blackbourn, *History of Germany 1780–1918*, Blackwell Publishing, 1997, p. 1.

6   Annegret Schüle, *Industrie und Holocaust: Topf & Söhne – Die Ofenbauer von Auschwitz*, Wallstein Verlag, 2010, pp. 29–30.
AS footnote 69: *Mein Lebenslauf* [*My Life*] (E.W. Topf), undated (presumably early 1946). ThHStAW [PK: i.e. Thuringian State Archive, Weimar], Collection: Jean-Claude Pressac Nr. 81, sheets 1–22, this quote from sheet 1. Dieter Wettig, grandson of the Topf director, Heinrich Wettig (died 1926), was one of Ernst Wolfgang Topf's playmates. He confirmed that the family lived on company land (statement made by Dieter Wettig to the author). The baptismal register shows the address as Dreysestraße 7. Baptismal register of the Merchants' Church, Erfurt, 1903/4.

7   Blackbourn, op. cit., p. 205.

8   Ibid.

9   Schüle, op. cit., p. 64.
AS footnote 5: AS interview with Udo Braun, 31 July 2001.

Chapter Two: A deal with the devil

10   J. A. Topf commemorative brochure, Landesarchiv Thüringen – Hauptstaatsarchiv Weimar.

11   E. W. Topf justification, Power without Morals, Landesarchiv Thüringen - Hauptstaatsarchiv Weimar.

12   Willy Wiemokli letter and CV post war, Landesarchiv Thüringen - Hauptstaatsarchiv Weimar.

13   Bernhard Bredehorn's statement, Landesarchiv Thüringen - Hauptstaatsarchiv Weimar.

14   Kurt Prüfer's letter of application to Topf and Sons, Landesarchiv Thüringen - Hauptstaatsarchiv Weimar.

15   Schüle, op. cit., p. 48.
     AS footnote 154: Kurt Prüfer personnel file, ThHStAW, J.A. Topf & Söhne, no. 14, p. 398.
16   Schüle, op. cit., p. 49. Prüfer finds a way of dealing with death within ordered parameters.
17   Kurt Prüfer letter, Oct 1943, Landesarchiv Thüringen - Hauptstaatsarchiv Weimar.

Chapter Three: A beautiful name
All quotes used in this chapter have been taken from an author interview with Hartmut Topf.

Chapter Four: Buchenwald
18   Richard Alewyn quoted in Michael H. Kater, *Weimar: From Enlightenment to the Present*,
     Yale University Press, 2014, p. 263.
19   Max Mayr quoted in Gedenkstätte Buchenwald (ed.), *Buchenwald Concentration Camp
     1937–1945: A Guide to the Permanent Historical Exhibition*, Wallstein Verlag, 2004.
20   Michael H. Kater, op. cit., p. 118.
21   Ibid., p. 126.
22   Ibid., p. 134.
23   Ibid., p. 212.
24   Gedenkstätte Buchenwald (ed.), op. cit., p. 24.
25   Eugene Kogon quoted in ibid., p. 29.
26   Ibid., p. 27.
27   Ibid., p. 31.
28   Ibid., p. 19.
29   Kater, op. cit, p. 256.
30   Ibid., p. 268.
31   Gedenkstätte Buchenwald (ed.), op. cit., p. 20.
32   Kater, op. cit., p. 266.
33   Schüle, op. cit., p. 108.
     AS footnote 164: Erich Haase in *Das war Buchenwald* [*This was Buchenwald*], Leipzig, p. 79.
34   Schüle, op. cit., pp. 107–108.
     AS footnote 162: Buchenwald Memorial, *Konzentrationslager Buchenwald 1937–1945. Begleit-
     band zur ständigen historischen Ausstellung* [*Buchenwald Concentration Camp, 1937–1945: A
     Guide to the Permanent Historical Exhibition*], Göttingen, 2005, pp. 115–18.
35   Schüle, op. cit., p. 117.
     Austrian president Franz Bera's account. AS footnote 197: Report by Franz Bera, Buchen-
     wald Memorial Archive 31/455.
36   Schüle, op. cit., pp. 117–18.
     AS footnote 198: Eric Haase in *Das war Buchenwald* [*This was Buchenwald*], p. 80.
37   Author interview with Hartmut Topf.
38   Kurt Prüfer, Soviet interrogation records, Landesarchiv Thüringen - Hauptstaatsarchiv Weimar.
39   Schüle, op. cit., p. 122.
     AS footnote 212: Sworn statement by Johanna Büschleb, Gudensberg, 1/4/1946, ThHStAW,
     Collection Jean-Claude Pressac no. 81, sheets 83–90. This quote has been taken from sheet 87.
40   Schüle, op. cit., pp. 122–3. Ludwig Topf's post-war explanation concerning the epidemic at
     Buchenwald.
     AS footnote 213: Kurt Prüfer personnel file, ThHStAW, J A Topf & Söhne Erfurt no. 14,
     sheet 119.
     AS footnote 214: Minutes of Works Council meeting, 27 April 1945, ThHStAW, Collection
     Jean-Claude Pressac no. 32, sheet 230.
41   Ibid.
42   Ibid.
43   Schüle, op. cit., p. 124. Lilly Kopecky quotes about urns.

AS footnote 218: Lore Shelly (ed.), *Schreiberinnen des Todes*, Bielefeld, 1992 (first published as *Secretaries of Death*, Shengold, 1986), p. 255.

44 Schüle, op. cit., p. 151.
AS footnote 2: Report of Max Girndt, 1945, Buchenwald Memorial Archive 32/IX-63.

45 Schüle, op. cit., pp. 151–2.
AS footnote 3: 'August' presumably refers to August Brück.
AS footnote 4: Report of Hans Neupert, Buchenwald Memorial Archive 31/42.
AS footnote 5: Report of Hans Neupert, 24 July 1954, Buchenwald Memorial Archive 50-2-33.

46 Kurt Prüfer's request for a bonus, dated December 1941, Landesarchiv Thüringen - Hauptstaatsarchiv Weimar.

47 Kurt Prüfer's letter regarding a bonus, November 1942, Landesarchiv Thüringen - Hauptstaatsarchiv Weimar.

48 Kurt Prüfer' letter regarding a bonus November 1942, Landesarchiv Thüringen - Hauptstaatsarchiv Weimar.

Chapter Five: Always at your service

49 Letter to Kurt Prüfer December 1943. Landesarchiv Thüringen - Hauptstaatsarchiv Weimar.

50 Topf memo concerning Kurt Prüfer, Landesarchiv Thüringen - Hauptstaatsarchiv Weimar.

51 Prüfer's resignation, Landesarchiv Thüringen - Hauptstaatsarchiv Weimar.

52 Ibid.

53 Memo regarding a company meeting; Kurt Prüfer's comments, Landesarchiv Thüringen - Hauptstaatsarchiv Weimar.

54 Topf and Sons application for Uk status, Landesarchiv Thüringen - Hauptstaatsarchiv Weimar.

55 Letter from Prüfer to Bischoff about Ludwig Topf's army status, Landesarchiv Thüringen -Hauptstaatsarchiv Weimar.

56 Memo about E. W. Topf calling workers 'Communist pigs' 1942, Landesarchiv Thüringen - Hauptstaatsarchiv Weimar.

57 Topf and Sons memo concerning the discovery of an explosive capsule, 1942, Landesarchiv Thüringen - Hauptstaatsarchiv Weimar.

58 Fritz Meier resignation, Landesarchiv Thüringen - Hauptstaatsarchiv Weimar.

59 Memo about anonymous letter regarding Topf and Sons, Landesarchiv Thüringen - Hauptstaatsarchiv Weimar.

60 Memo about Department D being the department that complained the most, Landesarchiv Thüringen - Hauptstaatsarchiv Weimar.

Chapter Six: Auschwitz

61 Eva Schloss and Karen Bartlett, *After Auschwitz*, Hodder and Stoughton, 2013, p. 105.

62 Laurence Rees, *Auschwitz: The Nazis and the 'Final Solution'*, BBC Books, 2005, p. 48.

63 Rees, op. cit., p. 49.

64 Ibid., p. 54.

65 Ibid., p. 90.

66 Schloss and Bartlett, op. cit., p. 122.

67 Ibid.

68 Yisrael Gutman and Michael Berenbaum (eds), *Anatomy of the Auschwitz Death Camp*, Indiana University Press, 1994 , p. 262

69 Rees, op. cit., p. 171.

70 Ibid., p. 172.

71 Ibid., p. 206.

72 Ibid., p. 146.

Chapter Seven: Is there anyone left to burn?

73   Schloss and Bartlett, op. cit., p. 144.

74   Rees, op. cit., p. 327.

75   Taken from a Soviet report on the liberation of Auschwitz. Landesarchiv Thüringen - Hauptstaatsarchiv Weimar.

76   Schüle, op. cit., p. 136.

AS Footnote 252: Hilberg, Raul, Vernichtung der europäischen Jüden [*The Destruction of the European Jews*], Frankfurt am Main, 1999 (first published 1982; English edition 1961), vol. 2, p. 934.

77   Schüle, op. cit., pp. 137–8.

AS footnote 260 (on p138): Ur/T, 8.1.1941. Re: Extension to the crematorium at the Auschwitz concentration camp o/S, ThHStAW, Collection Jean-Claude Pressac Nr. 6, sheet 180; Buchenwald Memorial Archive Pressac Collection, sheet 121. [My best guess is that the 'Ur/T' will be the SS internal reference: Ur = Urbanczyk, T probably the initial of the typist.]

78   Schüle, op. cit., p. 142.

AS footnote 287: Topf and Sons to the SS Construction Management Dept, Auschwitz, 4 November 1941, Russian State Military Archive, Moscow, Special Archive Division, 502-1-313, sheets 81–3; copy in ThHStAW, Collection Jean-Claude Pressac Nr. 6, sheets 81–3; Buchenwald Memorial Archive Pressac Collection, sheets 221–3.

79   Schüle, op. cit., p. 155.

AS footnote 14: ThHStAW, Collection Jean-Claude Pressac Nr. 41, sheet 33; Buchenwald Memorial Archive, Pressac collection, sheet 314

80   Rees, op. cit., 2005, p. 215.

81   Schüle, op. cit., p. 163.

AS footnote 45: Construction Management Dept, Building expenses book, ThHStAW, Collection Jean-Claude Pressac Nr. 42, sheet 42; Buchenwald Memorial Archive, Pressac Collection, sheet 775. Construction Management Dept, Advance Payments Book, p. 2, ThHStAW, Collection Jean-Claude Pressac Nr. 42, sheet 50, and Buchenwald Memorial Archive, Pressac Collection, sheet 783.

82   Schüle, op. cit., p. 164.

AS footnote 47: Kurt Prüfer makes note of a phone call for the company directors, 8 September 1942, ThHStAW, J A Topf & Söhne Nr 95, sheet 40.

AS footnote 48: In later practice, the number of corpses cremated was significantly higher – up to 8,000 corpses per day across all the Birkenau crematoria, whereas Prüfer had assumed the number was only 3,200.

83   Braun–Prüfer head to head in Soviet Interrogation, Landesarchiv Thüringen - Hauptstaatsarchiv Weimar.

Chapter Eight: Innovators until the end

84   Fritz Sander letter to Topf and Sons regarding patent, Landesarchiv Thüringen - Hauptstaatsarchiv Weimar.

85   Ibid.

86   Ibid.

87   Fritz Sander, Soviet interrogation report, Landesarchiv Thüringen - Hauptstaatsarchiv Weimar.

88   Kurt Prüfer, Soviet Interrogation, Landesarchiv Thüringen - Hauptstaatsarchiv Weimar.

89   Schüle, op. cit., p. 201. 'SS men were forever coming and going at Topf ... not a secret.'

AS footnote 170: Hans Mommsen concludes that 'ordinary workers, especially if they had Communist leanings, recognised the reality of the Holocaust more clearly than nationalistically inclined functionaries in the government apparatus, who didn't want to believe what they were just as capable of knowing'. Hans Mommsen, 'Erfahrung, Aufarbeitung und

Erinnerung des Holocaust in Deutschland', in Hanno Loewy (ed.), *Holocaust: Die Grenzen des Verstehens*, Reinbek 1992, pp. 93–100, this quote is taken from p. 95.

AS footnote 171: Author interview with Walter Bredehorn on 5 May 2010.

AS footnote 172: It has been proven that the workers in the SS camps included Soviet forced labour, i.e. the very men with whom KPD members stayed in contact with for political reasons. Iwan Hanjutschenko, a young Ukrainian forced labourer, reported that he and a German foreman built trolleys for inserting coffins, which were used with the double- and triple-muffle furnaces in the camps, and which can be seen in the crematorium of the Buchenwald Memorial. Author interview with Iwan Hanjutschenko, 6 May 2003.

90 Schüle, op. cit., p. 196. 'The flames from the incineration were visible for miles around.'

91 Schüle, op. cit., p. 27.

AS footnote 178: Piper, *Vernichtung*, p. 286f [Bibliography lists a number of books by Piper, Franciszek, but none with *Vernichtung* [extermination or annihilation] as the key word in their title.]

92 Schüle, op. cit., p. 209 – efficiency of the crem – these are outstanding figures writes the SS.

AS footnote 193: ThHStAW, Collection Jean-Claude Pressac Nr 42, sheet 212, and Buchenwald Memorial Archive, Pressac Collection, sheet 875.

93 Schüle, op. cit., p. 209. The sentence at the start of this paragraph makes it clear that the info comes from 'the Topf fitter Heinrich Messing's timesheet for the period from 8 Monday to 14 Sunday March 1943'.

94 Karl Schultze's Soviet interrogation record, Landesarchiv Thüringen - Hauptstaatsarchiv Weimar.

95 Ibid.

96 Schüle, op. cit., pp. 212–13.

AS footnote 203: Record of the statement by Henryk Tauber, former prisoner in the Auschwitz concentration camp and member of the *Sonderkommando* [Special Unit – prisoners working in the gas chambers/crematoria], in: Piper, *Vernichtung*, p. 287f [see my note above.]

97 Ibid.

98 Karl Schultze's Soviet interrogation record, Landesarchiv Thüringen - Hauptstaatsarchiv Weimar.

99 Schüle, op. cit., p. 219.

100 Schüle, op. cit., p. 219.

AS footnote 230: ThHStAW, Collection Jean-Claude Pressac Nr. 42, sheet 452; also Buchenwald Memorial Archive, Pressac Collection, sheet 1117.

101 Ibid.

102 Schüle, op. cit., p. 230.

AS footnote 265: Topf to the SS Construction Management Dept, Auschwitz, 2 July 1943, ThHStAW, Collection Jean-Claude Pressac Nr. 42, sheet 388; also Buchenwald Memorial Archive, Pressac Collection, sheet 1053.

103 Topf and Sons sixtieth anniversary commemorative booklet, Landesarchiv Thüringen -Hauptstaatsarchiv Weimar.

104 Schloss and Bartlett, op. cit., p. 130.

105 Schüle, op. cit., pp. 192–6.

AS footnote 145: Karl/Noack, Angeklagter [PK:Accused], p. 67f.

Chapter Nine: Trials and retribution

106 Schüle, op. cit., p. 223. Special unit notices gas chambers being dismantled for use elsewhere.

AS footnote 277: *Inmitten des grauenvollen Verbrechens. Handschriften von Mitgliedern des Sonderkommandos* [*In the Midst of Heinous Crime. Handwritten notes by members of the Sonderkommando*, State Museum Auschwitz-Birkenau, Oświęcim 1996, p. 184f. This handwritten note was found next to Crematorium III in the summer of 1952. Also Ibid., p. 175.

107 Schüle, op. cit., pp. 234–5. Kurt Prüfer memo regarding rebuilding at Mauthausen.

AS footnote 280: Underlining in original. Quoted from: Terezin Memorial Archive, A 8845 Mauthausen, sheets 1–3.

108 Ernst Wolfgang Topf statement, Power without Morals, 1958, Landesarchiv Thüringen - Hauptstaatsarchiv Weimar.

109 Annegret Schüle, op. cit., pp. 240–243. Ludwig Topf's explanation of the camps to the workers.
AS footnote 10: Tuchel, Johannes: *Die Inspektion der Konzentrationslager 1938–1945. Das System des Terrors [Inspection of the Concentration Camps 1938–1945. The Terror System]*, Edition Hentrich, 1994, p. 15.
AS footnote 11: notes from the discussion, belonging to files. Works Council, 27.4.1945, ThHStAW, Collection Jean-Claude Pressac Nr 34, sheet 229f. Emphases in original.

110 Ibid.

111 Ibid., p. 243.

112 Ibid., pp. 248–9. Ludwig Topf's suicide note.
AS footnote 35: Ludwig Topf, 30/31.5.1945, sheet 6 of transcript of files, ThHStAW, Collection Jean-Claude Pressac Nr 34, sheet 211.

113 Ibid., p. 250.
Ernst Wolfgang Topf's explanation of Ludwig's suicide to workers. AS footnote 41: Notes from the meeting, 8.6.1945, ThHStAW, J. A. Topf & Söhne Nr 427, sheets 75ff; Collection Jean-Claude Pressac Nr 34, sheets 232ff.

114 Ibid., p. 248. Machemehl's account of the suicide.
AS footnote 31: Handwritten report by Machemehl (Ma), 31.5.1945, ThHStAW, J. A. Topf & Söhne Nr 427, sheets 244f; Collection Jean-Claude Pressac Nr 34, sheets 212f.

115 Ibid., pp. 254–5. Topf to resume production memo. AS footnote 64: Military Government of Germany Erfurt, 22 June 1945, ThHStAW, Collection Jean-Claude Pressac Nr 80, sheet 66.
AS footnote 65: Post list 21.6.-3.9.2945, sheet 2, ThHStAW, Collection Jean-Claude Pressac Nr 80, sheets 92–4.
AS footnote 66: A letter from Kurt Schmidt to Ernst Wolfgang Topf includes the following: 'The New Production permit relates to the Malting, Silo and Mill construction departments, excluding furnace systems. We can of course continue to carry out repairs to furnace systems.' Kurt Schmidt to E. W. Topf, 18 July 1945, ThHStAW, Collection Jean-Claude Pressac Nr 80, sheet 77.
AS footnote 67: File note, operations division, Braun, 11 October 1945, ThHStAW, Collection Jean-Claude Pressac Nr 80, sheet 117.

116 Ibid., pp. 256–7. Archive note about Major Kriwenzow.
AS footnote 76: Wiederinbetriebssetung [Resumption of production], 12.9.1945, ThHStAW, Collection Jean-Claude Pressac Nr 80, sheets 98–100.

117 Ibid., p. 258. Ernst Otto Keyser letter.
AS footnote 83: Ernst-Otto Kayser to the President of the Landeskommission für die Durchführung der Befehle 124/126 [State Commission for the Implementation of Orders 124/126], received 22.6.1946, ThHStAW, Collection Jean-Claude Pressac Nr 80, sheet 71; also ThHStAW, Collection Jean-Claude Pressac Nr 80, sheet 260.

118 Indictment against the engineers, Landesarchiv Thüringen - Hauptstaatsarchiv Weimar.

119 Charges levelled against Kurt Prüfer, Landesarchiv Thüringen - Hauptstaatsarchiv Weimar.

120 Charges levelled against Karl Schultze, Landesarchiv Thüringen - Hauptstaatsarchiv Weimar.

121 Fritz Sander interrogation report, Landesarchiv Thüringen - Hauptstaatsarchiv Weimar.

122 Karl Schultze interrogation report, Landesarchiv Thüringen - Hauptstaatsarchiv Weimar.

123 Kurt Prüfer interrogation report, Landesarchiv Thüringen - Hauptstaatsarchiv Weimar.

Chapter Ten: A change of scenery in the USSR

124 Indictment against Gustav Braun, Landesarchiv Thüringen - Hauptstaatsarchiv Weimar.

125 Author interview with Udo Braun.

126 Topf and Sons complaint against Gustav Braun 1937, Landesarchiv Thüringen - Hauptstaatsarchiv Weimar.

127 Ernst Wolfgang Topf memo complaint against Braun 1940, Landesarchiv Thüringen - Hauptstaatsarchiv Weimar.

128 E. W. Topf memo about Braun as the enemy and appalling schemer, Landesarchiv Thüringen - Hauptstaatsarchiv Weimar.

129 Soviet interrogation of Gustav Braun, Landesarchiv Thüringen - Hauptstaatsarchiv Weimar.

130 Final Soviet interrogation of Gustav Braun, Landesarchiv Thüringen - Hauptstaatsarchiv Weimar.

Chapter Eleven: Power without morals

131 E. W. Topf's response to Power without Morals, 1958. Landesarchiv Thüringen - Hauptstaatsarchiv Weimar.

132 Schüle, op. cit., p. 304. Article in Kassel newspaper *Hessische Nachrichten*.

AS footnote 95: The Major War Crimes Trial took place from 18 October 1945 to 1 October 1946 before the International Military Court of the four victorious powers: USSR, USA, Great Britain and France. See for example Helge Grabitz, 'Die Verfolgung von National Socialist-Verbrechen in der Bundesrepublik Deutschland und in der DDR' ['The pursuit of National Socialist crimes in the Federal Republic of Germany and the GDR'] in: Claudia Kuretsidis-Haider and Winfried R. (eds), Garscha, *Keine 'Abrechnung'. NS-Verbrechen, Justiz und Gesellschaft in Europa nach 1945* [*No 'Settlement'. National Socialist Crimes, Justice and Society in Europe after 1945*], Leipzig/Vienna, 1998, pp. 144–79, here pages 147ff; Annette Weinke, *Die Nürnberger Prozesse* [*The Nuremberg Trials*], Munich, 2006.

AS footnote 96: Hessische Nachrichten, Kassel, 6 March 1946, p. 6, emphases in the original.

AS footnote 97: See Philipp Kratz, Strategien der Verdrängung: Der Umgang mit dem Holocaust in Wiesbaden der 1950er Jahre [Blocking-out Strategies: How the Holocaust was Dealt With in 1950s Wiesbaden], unpublished dissertation, Wiesbaden 2007, p. 55, note 211. Kratz bases his argument on Hellmuth Merbach, 'Seife aus Judenfett' [Soap from Jewish Fat] in: Wolfgang Benz (pub), *Legenden Lügen Vorurteile, Ein Lexicon der Zeitgeschichte [Legends, Lies, Prejudices, A Lexicon of Contemporary History]*, Munich 1990, p. 172f.

133 Schüle, op. cit., p. 304.

AS footnote 98: Kurt Schmidt also wrote to the Fritzlar district commission and the district commissioner of Fritzlar-Homberg, Gudensberg, on 29 September 1946, saying that the content of the article did not correspond to reality. ThHStAW, Collection Jean-Claude Pressac Nr 80, sheet 322. In a file note Kurt Schmidt also used the abbreviation 'V-Ö' when referring to the cremation furnaces [Verbrennungsöfen]. File note on matters relating to J. Topf G.m.b.H., Gudensberg, 19 August 1946, ThHStAW, Collection Jean-Claude Pressac Nr 80, sheet 312.

134 Ibid., pp. 304–305.

AS footnote 100: Sworn statement of Ernst Wolfgang Topf, 26 March 1946, ThHStAW, Collection Jean-Claude Pressac Nr 81, sheets 71–76, here sheet 72.

135 Ibid., p. 308.

AS footnote 112: Underlining in the original. Ernst Ludwig Topf to Dr. Grünefeld 3 September 1946 (transcript), ThHStAW, Collection Jean-Claude Pressac Nr 80, sheets 339–41.

136 Ibid.

137 Ibid., p. 317.

AS footnote 144: Chief Public Prosecutor at the Hessen-South Central Appeals Chamber to the Minister of Justice of the State of Hessen, 3 March 1950, Ministry of Justice of the State of Hessen, file ref. IV-538/50, sheet 1. The details of the winding-up of the Appeals Chamber process appear first in Kratz, Strategien der Verdrängung [PK: see above], p. 58.

138 Detlef Junker, Philipp Gassert, Wilfried Mausbach, David B. Morris (eds), *The United States and Germany in the Era of the Cold War 1945–1968*, Cambridge University Press, 2004, p. 69.
139 Ibid.
140 Schüle, op. cit., pp. 320–21.
     AS footnote 153: Record of the interrogation of Max Machemehl by the Erfurt Volkspolizei [People's Police], 27 November 1950, ThHStAW, National Socialist archive of the Ministry of State Security Object 9 ZA 1492, B. 16r.
141 Schüle, op. cit., p. 324. Quote on closure of criminal case: 'it had not been possible to prove…'
     AS footnote 166: Ministry of Justice of the State of Hessen, file ref. V-90/62, sheet 17; see also the Register of Criminal Investigations at the Wiesbaden Public Prosecution office, HHStAW [Hessen State Archive, Wiesbaden], section 468, no. 1211.
142 Ibid., p. 328. Quote from the new patent application: 'process and device for the incineration of bodies…'
     AS footnote 184: German Patent Office, German patent T 1562 V/24d, 24.6.1950; see also ThHStAW, Collection Jean-Claude Pressac Nr. 25, sheets 3–11, 35f, 42f, 51–56.
143 Ibid., p. 335.
     AS footnote 206: Ernst Wolfgang Topf to the Wiesbaden municipal authorities, 14 March 1952, ThHStAW, Collection Jean-Claude Pressac Nr. 30, sheet 26.
144 Ibid., p. 331.
     AS footnote 195: The text has survived without cover sheet or covering letter. It is in two parts: A) Report on J. A. Topf & Söhne, (sheets 1–8) and B) Grounds for the request (sheets 9–10). ThHStAW, Collection Jean-Claude Pressac Nr. 30, sheets 41–57, here sheet 50. The request in question is not clear from the text; it only shows that it was about the development of Topf machine manufacturing, i.e. production of installations for the food industry.
145 E. W. Topf defence to Power without Morals, 1958, Landesarchiv Thüringen - Hauptstaatsarchiv Weimar.

Chapter Twelve: Atonement
146 Author interview with Hartmut Topf .
147 Schüle, op. cit., p. 300. 1980s company history of Topf and Sons written in GDR.
     AS footnote 89: Company timeline, p6f, ThHStAW, J. A. Topf & Söhne Erfurt Nr. 35, sheets 6f.
148 Author interview with Udo Braun.
149 Author interview with Hartmut Topf.
150 Author interview with Ronald Hirte of the education department at Buchenwald Memorial.
151 Author interview with Hartmut Topf.
152 Author interview with Wolfgang Nossen, former president of the Jewish community in Thuringia.
153 Transcript of a Radio F.R.E.I. interview in December 2002.
154 Author interview with Wolfgang Nossen.
155 Author interview with Annegret Schüle.

Conclusion
156 Author interview with Hartmut Topf.
157 Author interview with Florian.
158 Author interview with Hartmut Topf.

INDEX

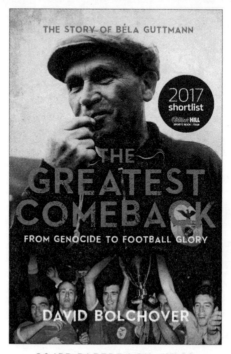

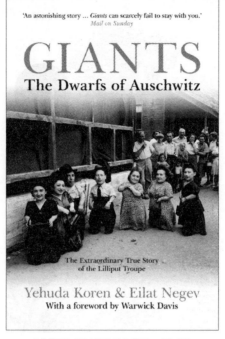

'An astonishing story ... *Giants* can scarcely fail to stay with you.'
Mail on Sunday

GIANTS
The Dwarfs of Auschwitz

The Extraordinary True Story
of the Lilliput Troupe

Yehuda Koren & Eilat Negev
With a foreword by Warwick Davis

304PP PAPERBACK, £9.99

'Through thick and thin, never separate. Stick together, guard each other, and live for one another.'

As Hitler's war intensified, the Ovitz family would have good reason to stand by their mother's mantra. Descending from the cattle train into the death camp of Auschwitz, all twelve emerged in 1945 as survivors – the largest family to survive intact.

What saved them? Ironically, the fact that they were sought out by the 'Angel of Death' himself – Dr Joseph Mengele. For seven of the Ovitzes were dwarfs – and not just any dwarfs, but a beloved and highly successful vaudeville act known as the Lilliput Troupe. Together, they were the only all-dwarf ensemble with a full show of their own in the history of entertainment.

The Ovitzes intrigued Mengele, and amongst the thousands on whom he performed his loathsome experiments, they became his prize 'patients': 'You're something special, not like the rest of them.' It was this disturbing affection that saved their lives. After being plunged into the darkest moments in modern history, this remarkable troupe emerged with spirits undimmed, and went on to light up Europe and Israel, which offered them a new home, with their unique performances. *Giants* reveals their moving and inspirational story.

— AVAILABLE FROM ALL GOOD BOOKSHOPS —